CLOSING THE IRON CAGE

CLOSING THE IRON CAGE

The Scientific Management of Work and Leisure

by Ed Andrew

BLACK ROSE BOOKS   Montréal

Black Rose Books No. K73
Hardcover—ISBN: 0-919-619-59-7
Paperback—ISBN: 0-919-619-58-9

Canadian Cataloguing in Publication Data
Andrews, Ed
  Closing the Iron Cage
ISBN:0-919619-59-7 (bound).—ISBN:0-919619-58-9 (pbk.)
1. Leisure—Social aspects.   2. Work—Social aspects.
I. Title.
HD4904.A52   306'.3   C81-090144-7

Cover Design: Gabriella Le Grazie
BLACK ROSE BOOKS
3981 boulevard St-Laurent
Montréal, H2W 1Y5, Québec

Printed and bound in Québec, Canada

CONTENTS

Acknowledgement

I would like to thank the Canada Council for providing the leisure to research this book and Margaret Grant Andrew for ensuring that the opportunity would not be wasted.

Introduction

Technological development as a means to non-economic ends or as an end in itself. Common belief that industrial labour is inherently repressive and that leisure can compensate for the vicissitudes of the job. The nature of scientific management. Its relation to leisure. A note on method and use of terms.

Max Weber's celebrated study of Protestantism and capitalism concluded that the spirit of capitalism envelops all our vocational activities like an "iron cage."[1] Weber thought that when the end of economic acquisition comes to dominate less 'worldly' aims, all endeavours come to be understood as a means to *the* economic end. All natural and social processes become the raw material or instruments of an all-pervasive calculation or 'means-end rationality'. By conceiving of all things and processes as means to capital accumulation, capitalists were able to wed the rationality of physics to financial calculation, creating a world of industrial technique. Weber wrote:

> This order is now bound to the technical and economic conditions of machine production which to-day determine the lives of all the individuals who are born into this mechanism, not only those directly concerned with economic acquisition, with irresistible force.[2]

In "this mechanism", what is considered rational is only what is serviceable to the end of capital accumulation or technological development. Technical rationality, according to Weber, requires that any heterogeneity of ends be eliminated, that procedures be standardized for the most efficient achievement of the homogeneous end, and that activities be specialized in accord with the standardized procedures. What does not accord with this system of rationality is either forbidden or else is not recognized and not rewarded in a technological civilization. This ubiquitous structure of technical rationality, Weber thought, appears as an iron cage to those who live in it.

Some of the more influential thinkers of this century, such as Martin Heidegger, Hannah Arendt, Michael

Oakeshott, Leo Strauss, Jacques Ellul, Herbert Marcuse and Jürgen Habermas, have followed Weber in expressing concern at the threat to freedom posed by technological rationality.[3] Indeed, Weber's image of an iron cage may not adequately represent the deeper formulations of this threat. For the iron cage would be the representation of our condition only if we experienced 'technological imperatives' as restrictions on our freedom. Post-Weberian critiques of technological society have suggested that Weber's view of technological imperatives as external restraints is obsolete since we have so internalized technique that we do not see it as a barrier to our freedom.[4] That is, technique is no longer a system of instruments that we may or may not employ as we choose. Rather, our choices are so conditioned by the end of technological development that we cannot conceive of alternative goals. Since no ends transcending the growth of technique are admitted which might subordinate technique to the role of a tool or instrument of people, the development of technique becomes an end in itself. Thus, the post-Weberian critique of technology asserts that technique is not an instrument we use for our purposes; rather technique uses us to the end of its maximal development.

Liberals and Marxists of the nineteenth century believed that industrial technology would overcome the scarcity of nature, would create a condition of universal abundance, and would promote the cause of an egalitarian society. However Weber's conception of technological rationality runs counter to the hopes placed in technological progress. For the methods required to bring technological abundance to fruition — subdivision of labour, separation of planning from execution in work, hierarchic co-ordination of specialized performances — create an infrastructure of domination which blocks the actualization of the egalitarian vision.

Marxist writers have criticized the post-Weberian conception of technique for its failure to distinguish between so-called technological imperatives and political requirements. C.B. Macpherson describes a "race between ontology and technology" as "fateful" and calls upon us to distinguish between technology, which in itself promotes the democratic aspiration of universal abundance and leisure, and the exploitative and undemocratic purposes to which it is put in capitalist society.[5] Of course, such a race assumes that the progressive development of our essential being (or ontology) is independent of technical change. One cannot have a race between two competitors if their legs are bound together.

10

Marcuse has written extensively on the political purposes of technique, on its uses as an instrument of exploitation and domination. Yet he believed technology is neutral with regard to the social purposes to which it is put. He wrote that "An electronic computer can serve equally a capitalist or socialist administration...."[6] However, Marcuse did not think that technique can be used to emancipate workers as workers. The precondition for automating labour is the elimination of skill, variety and judgment from manual labour (so that machines can reproduce the repetitive mechanical operations once done by hand) and the reduction of 'mental labour' to a form of calculating response to externally given orders (so that computers can 'think' for us). In short, the thrust towards automation requires the degradation of the status of skilled workers into that of dispensable tools of those who will engineer the automated society. Marcuse wrote:

> The more complete the alienation of labour, the greater the potential of freedom: total automation would be the optimum. It is the sphere outside labour which defines freedom and fulfillment...[7].

Thus, for Marcuse, technique does not emancipate workers as workers but, by the shortening of the working day, technology prepares for their emancipation as leisured citizens.

Marcuse's position is a compromise between the Marxian promise of universal abundance and freedom by means of technique and the Weberian conception of technique as a world of domination and repression. That is, contrary to Marx, Marcuse believed the realm of production to be inherently repressive and, contrary to the post-Weberians, Marcuse believed the iron cage can be restricted to the realm of necessary production. Marcuse's position is not unusual. In fact, he advocated a variant of a thesis dominant in the sociology of leisure, namely, that an expansive enjoyment of leisure will compensate for the cramped and deadening labour alleged to be inherent in an industrial civilization. The purpose of this book is to explore the dimensions and presuppositions of the leisure-as-compensation thesis found in the contemporary literature on leisure.

The title of the book links leisure to scientific management in a controversial way. Leisure, we may think, refers to a sphere of privacy, to something which cannot be organized or managed. 'Managed leisure', like 'compulsory fun', is a contradiction in terms. Therefore the terms 'scientific management'

11

and 'leisure' must be clarified in order to establish what kind of significant relation can be established between them.

Scientific management, a system of thought and practice initiated by Frederick Winslow Taylor's time-motion studies in industry at the beginning of the twentieth century, was, in effect, the second wave of industrialization. The first wave was the rapid development of machine technology known as "the industrial revolution". The second wave involved human engineering, the techniques required to adjust the mode of working and the pace of work to a level closer to the capacity of the machinery. Before the spread of scientific management, capitalists bought the labouring time of workers, but their ability to dispose of it in the most productive or profitable fashion was limited by the monopoly of industrial know-how in the hands of the skilled workers. The Taylor system broke up that monopoly and enabled capitalist management to obtain an extensive control over workers on the shop floor. If the factory clock symbolises the discipline, regimentation and synchronization of the first wave of industrial production, the stop watch symbolises the heightened time thrift, the greater intensity of production, and the dominance of external management, in the second.

The effect of the introduction of industrial micro-motion studies was to separate planning and productive execution, and thus to spur on the automation of production. Scientific management provided the means to enforce maximal intensity and pace in production, the methods of subdividing, classifying and standardizing tasks that are used in the mass production of assembly lines, and a mode of giving new recruits into industry a cheap and rapid training. The resulting increase in production served, as Taylor intended, to increase the workers' income and their time off work. Moreover, scientific management, as Taylor never tired of saying, involves an enlarged work load for management. Indeed, professional and executive strata in all industrial countries with the exception of Great Britain now work longer hours than industrial wage-labourers.[8] The militant unionists who have limited the scope of scientific management in Britain have enabled British executives to enjoy a greater amount of leisure than their peers in less 'under-managed' parts of the globe.

Thus, what is observed in contemporary studies of leisure — the shortened work week of industrial labourers and the lengthened work week of executives — may be correlated with the growth of scientific management. Some sociologists conclude that those with the greatest amount of time off work are least capable of taking advantage of that opportunity for personal growth. This so-called problem of leisure might also be correlated with scientific management. However, it is here that circumspection is required. For even if the alleged incompetence of the working class might be attributed to the degradation of skill, initiative and co-operative capabilities involved in scientifically managed enterprises, the problem-solving mentality creates "the problem" as much as what is observed as problematic. That is, "the problem of leisure" arises as much from the subjectivity of the sociologist as from his object of investigation. Thus the connections of scientific management not only with what is observed but also with the mode of observation in the sociology of leisure must be established.

Let us note some structural similarities between scientific management and the approach of some of the leading sociologists of leisure. First, sociological studies not only tend to contrast work and leisure but also to assume a relation of exclusion between them. Leisure, as we shall see in the first chapter, is conceived to be an end in itself, an activity free from any mixture of obligation and utility, whereas work is thought to be purely instrumental, necessary to obtain income and leisure. The idea of 'leisurely work' or 'puttering around', whether done inside or outside the factory or office, cannot be encompassed within this conception of leisure or work. This relation of exclusion between work and leisure echoes a favourite maxim of Frederick Taylor and Henry Ford — "work when you work and play when you play."

Secondly, sociologists conceive of leisure activities under the category of time. The unit-time approach to leisure is similar to that which Taylor applied to production; time-budgets of leisure activities correspond to Taylor's use of the stop-watch in production. Moreover, the category of leisure in sociological analysis corresponds to the division in capitalist industry between the boss's time and one's own time, working time and time free from work. Leisure comes to be understood through the practice of clocking in and out, and the time outside the factory is understood in the functional terms used inside the factory. Leisure-time is something to be used; time is spent or wasted. The tacit imperative often found in the literature on leisure is that leisure is time to be filled rather than killed, time to be employed actively rather than simply passed. In short, where Taylor explicitly wished to seize time

13

and submit it to a scientific accounting, the logic of time as money and the endeavour to master time is only implicit in the sociological understanding of leisure-time.

Third, in sociological analysis leisure is not understood as a condition of leisureliness or a state of being at leisure. Rather leisure is either conceived to be that time free from work, sleep, domestic chores and physiological necessities or else the activities occupying this time. The irrelevance, in sociological studies of leisure, of the state of being at leisure, or conversely, the condition of being harried, pressed or strained, matches Taylor's unconcern with "subjective" phenomena in his time-motion studies. For example, in one of the first sociological studies of leisure, "a most common rejoinder" of suburban housewives queried about their leisure-time activities, was to deny that they had any leisure. The investigators pointed out that the housewives had abundant leisure "according to our definition of the term."[9] Subsequent sociologists simply have not bothered to record responses which do not conform to their categories. It is of course possible that the housewives "subjective" responses illuminate the ground of contemporary women's movements as much as the valuable material garnered from time-budget studies.

Fourth, just as mental states are considered irrelevant to the sociological understanding of leisure, mental activities are also not included as leisure activities. Thinking, praying, dreaming and so forth fall outside the kinds of observable behaviour which are included as leisure activities. The "mindlessness" of mass leisure is a product of the requirements of sociological method rather than, as is sometimes thought, a direct reflection of the character of modern leisure activities. Just as Taylor insisted that thinking is not to be considered a productive activity and that the method of scientific management required a separation of thinking and doing, thinking is not deemed a wholesome recreation and the method of the sociology of leisure requires a separation between those who think about leisure and those who engage in visible recreations.

Fifth, and most importantly, the concern often voiced in contemporary literature on leisure, that workers are unable to make a productive or creative use of their leisure time, remarkably parallels the central principle of scientific management—that workers are incapable of employing their working time to maximum efficiency. If "the problem of leisure" is conceived to be due to the incapacity of workers to

14

make use of the increased amount of time they have off work, the solution to "the problem" appears to require the technicist methods Taylor applied in industry. Chapter 7 deals with the 'leisurists' who, in their organizational and educational capacities, claim to be as indispensable in managing the leisure time of the masses as the production engineers claimed to be in the employment of the working-time of incompetent labourers. The prospect of the scientific management of leisure is the source of the title.

Closing the Iron Cage.

The scientific management of leisure activities is not the only possibility advanced to resolve "the problem of leisure." However it consistently follows from the dominant thesis in the sociology of leisure, namely, that the function of leisure is to compensate for the strain and boredom of modern work. When the leisure-as-compensation thesis is wedded to the widely held view that Taylorized jobs have a deadening "spillover effect" upon leisure activities, the conclusion that leisure-time should be managed as efficiently as working-time becomes almost irresistible.

An alternative to extending scientific management into leisure is the proposal to enlarge jobs to mitigate any negative "spillover effect" of work upon leisure. Whereas the leisure-as-compensation thesis presupposes the maintenance of existing industrial relations between labour and management, job enlargement proposals counter Weberian technological imperatives with respect to the kinds and uses of machinery employed on the job and the nature of hierarchy and authority within the factory and office.

This book presents scientific management and revolutionary syndicalism as two opposing movements which grew out of the problems of industrial organization in late nineteenth century capitalist society. On the conceptual level, the syndicalist demand for self-management or workers' control of factories is the opposite of scientific management's demand for managerial control. The opposition between scientific management and syndicalism can be established on the historical level as well. Scientific management was born in an age of militant unionism. Syndicalist movements of various forms in late nineteenth and early twentieth century Europe and America aimed to overturn the structures of authority in capitalist industry and to institute self-management of mines, shipyards and workshops.[10] Scientific management developed in response to class conflict in large-scale industry with the aim of strengthening the authority of management over labour. Taylor, as we shall see, thought his innovations had a political as well as a technical or purely engineering significance; scientific management was offered as a solution to "the labour question", was heralded as an instrument of class harmony, a means to end class warfare in capitalist industry. Scientific management was vigourously resisted by workers when it was initiated and developed but, for reasons to be examined in Chapter 3, overcame that resistance during the first World War and the post-war period. The waxing of scientific management could be correlated with the waning of syndicalist movements.

The opposition between scientific management and syndicalism is presented to highlight the political dimension, the realm of conflict and alternatives, embedded in the 'technical imperatives' which scientific management represents. Since the leisure-as-compensation thesis presupposes these technological imperatives with respect to production, an examination of the syndicalist alternative to scientific management will open up questions about the relation of work and leisure.

The methods employed in this book depart from those normally used in the sociology of leisure. The chief principle of sociological studies is that of Goethe's Faust—"In the beginning was the deed." The deed is prior to the word in that "mere words" lack actuality; the act creates the actual. Logicians, poets and windbags live in the world of the possible; the social scientist scorns potentiality or any "abstraction" from actuality. Opinions or theories, unaccompanied by the facts (from *facere*, to do or make) are considered unreal. *Indeed*, not only Marxists hold practice to be more "basic" than ideology and not only behaviourists consider behaviour to be more "objective" than speech. In *fact*, the object of sociology is the factual or actual. Deeds are 'the truth' of words; that is, they are the measure of ideas, the standard by which theories may be verified or falsified. Thus, in the sociology of leisure, observable behaviour is noted in time-budget studies and concepts of leisure are formulated which are thought to capture, represent, or correspond to the observed activities. Since much of this book is derived from these empirical studies of leisure and since its findings are used to support my assertions, my method or approach will be complementary, rather than opposed, to the methods of empirical sociology. The evidence of words as well as deeds will be examined to disclose the experience of leisure.

"In the beginning was the *Logos*". *Logos*, the Greek for speech, word or reason, derives from *legein*, which means to gather, collect or pick up as well as to utter or say. The *lect*, in the English words collect and select as well as lecture and dialect, comes from *legein*. Thus speech for the Greeks was a gathering, a collection; the Logos was the One unifying the many: the word collected the phenomena observed, the things named.

This study of leisure will begin with the word 'leisure'. We will note that, at present, the uses of the word 'leisure' are dispersed; they belong to different worlds of discourse. When an empirical sociologist uses the word 'leisure', generally in adjectival relation to time or activity, it bears no relation to the economic condition of being leisured or the psychological state of leisureliness. This empirical usage of leisure has only a negative denotation; it refers to the time or activity *not* occupied in work and other necessary commitments: it lacks the positive connotation we understand when we say we are 'at leisure' or when we refer to a leisurely activity or period of time. The usage of the word 'leisure' calls for a unification of the theoretical and empirical conceptions of leisure.

The first chapter will examine what may be gathered from the many uses of the word 'leisure'. The collecting of the first chapter will be supplemented by a re-collecting in the second chapter; an historical dimension will be introduced to explain the reasons for the changing usages of the word 'leisure'. Thus the rigidity of sociological structures, and the concepts of leisure which correspond to them, will be exposed to the fluidity of the historical dimension, just as the inflexibility of 'technological imperatives' will be brought into the dimension of political possibility and conflict in subsequent chapters.

After an account of the character and development of scientific management, we shall examine the relation between scientific management and the sociological thought of Thorstein Veblen and Sidney and Beatrice Webb. Veblen's attack on leisure as culture or individual growth will be examined in conjunction with his technocratic politics. The examination of the Webbs will reinforce our model of technicist politics and explore the reasons why they felt a ruling class should eschew leisure in the full-time management of the working class. Having laid the groundwork for an examination of the presuppositions of 'technicist' sociology, we may then examine the data revealed by contemporary sociologists and the conclusions that have been drawn and might be drawn from this data.

This book will not attempt to solve the problem of leisure. Indeed, we shall see that the problem-solving mentality creates as many "problems" as it solves. Taylor's solution to the problem of production was to reduce work to labour. Those who would solve "the problem of leisure" are likely to reduce leisure into wholesome recreation. Such a reduction is essential to bring Weber's means-end rationality to bear on the "problem". Even to designate an experience as problematic is to close off certain dimensions of the experience. This closing-off, necessary to make experience amenable to problem solving, is antithetical to the aim of disclosing some facets of the contemporary experience of leisure. The aim of this book is dis-closing "the iron cage" or making the possibilities of our civilization of leisure open to us.

Chapter 1

Gathering What is Meant by Leisure

Leisure in opposition to work; freedom and necessity. Leisure as growth or culture, distinct from rest, relaxation and recreation, as general growth rather than specialized development. Leisure as distinct from consumption. Leisure as culture not necessarily wholesome or moral. The interpenetration of freedom and necessity in work and leisure; leisure excludes technical necessity. Leisure as activity; idleness and "business"; internal "activities" and observable behaviour. Leisure as time and as a condition or state of being; the "subjective" and the "objective". Gathering the uses of leisure in 'growing time'. Free time as freedom from and freedom for. The separation of leisureliness from leisure-time, a methodological expedient or a representation of contemporary reality?

The word 'leisure' has been used in various ways. However, its usage has generally been understood in opposition to work or occupation. The Greek and Roman words for business, occupation or employment (*a-scholia* and *neg-otium*) were the negative or privative forms of their words for leisure (*schole* and *otium*). That is, the Greek and Roman word for occupation literally meant lack of leisure. Although contemporary languages have no words such as 'unleisure', 'illoisir' or 'Unfreizeit', we generally understand leisure in opposition to work.

However, we tend to understand leisure in terms of work in contrast with the classics who dishonoured work by understanding it in terms of leisure. For the Greeks and Romans, work was the time or condition when one lacked leisure. For us, leisure is a time or condition when one is not working. Work involves strain, effort, exertion, pain; leisure, on the contrary, is effortless, easy, pleasurable. Work is done through compulsion or necessity; leisure is not forced upon one, nor is it necessary for subsistence. Work is thought to be a means to an end; leisure is thought to be an end in itself. Work, many think, is only an instrumental value; leisure is non-utilitarian, not productive of any good transcending the leisure activity. Work is time spent for others; leisure is "one's own time." Work is thought to be socially useful; leisure is individually enjoyable but not necessarily of service to anyone else. Work is rewarded; leisure is its own reward. Work is likely to be routine or monotonous whereas leisure is a holiday or a liberation from the everyday round, a Sabbath, a festival, a "trip". Industrial work is organized by others, scheduled, synchronized by the time-clock; in leisure, one is free of the boss, time-clocks, schedules, regimentation.

These antitheses between work and leisure have often been challenged. Some writers have pointed to a convergence of work and leisure in those fortunate enough to have interesting occupations. Others have directed our attention to various factors limiting choice, individuality or freedom in the time off work, attributing to leisure activities many of the characteristics we normally associate with working activities. Others insist that leisure exists within working time, at least in those occupations which have evaded the stop-watch of the efficiency expert.

Moreover, if work and leisure are not necessarily mutually exclusive components of our lives, they are also not exhaustive of the sum total of our time. We sleep for roughly one-third of our lives. Sleeping has not normally been considered a leisure activity, although some thoughtful observers have pointed to the leisurable components of sleep. Not only does sleep rest and repair our muscles, nerves and mind, recreate our energies and give vent to some impulses and needs that would otherwise be unexpressed but also it puts us in touch with the deeper element of ourselves, a largely unexplored sea in the world of everyday work. Nevertheless sleep is not normally considered to be a leisure activity. Sleep, like work, limits leisure time.

In addition, there is general agreement amongst contemporary observers of leisure that time spent travelling to and from work, and work related activities such as washing up, dressing, preparing for and cleaning up after work, do not constitute leisure time. Eating and other necessary bodily functions, as well as personal hygiene and cosmetic concerns, are usually deemed to fall outside leisure time. Similarly household chores and domestic obligations, such as child-rearing, cleaning the home, preparing meals, washing dishes, etc. are generally thought to further limit leisure time.

In short, anything which is not purely the product of personal inclination is not thought to be a leisure activity. The *doyen* of leisurologists, J. Dumazedier, goes so far as to state that any obligatory pursuits such as religious or civic duties, obligations to trade unions, political parties or social institutions, are not leisure activities.[1] However, as B.M. Berger and others rightly perceive, no activities are unconditioned by social constraints or moral obligations.[2] Thus Berger suggests that leisure activities should include what we are ethically obliged to do but exclude what we are expediently constrained to do.

The concept of leisure is usually characterized by two central and interrelated ideas. First, leisure refers to a realm of freedom as opposed to a realm of necessity; it refers to voluntary or chosen activities: it excludes necessary or instrumental activities. Leisure is "free-time", a liberation from onerous exertions, a strained purposiveness, taxing duties and pressing engagements. Secondly, leisure transcends the production or reproduction of biological and social existence. Leisure, as E. Barker defines it, is "growing time."[3] Or, to use the non-temporal metaphor of Lin Yutang, it is like unused space, "like room to move around."[4] With the crisp precision of the sociologist, J. Dumazedier writes that leisure affords an individual the opportunity "to enter into a realm of self-transcendence where his creative powers are set free to oppose or to reinforce the dominant values of his civilization."[5]

According to this view, leisure is developmental, a time or condition of personal growth, of expansion of powers and awareness, of cultivation*. From this standpoint, many thinkers, following Aristotle, have distinguished leisure from rest, relaxation and recreation.[6] These are seen as mere means to work and necessary existence, as a recuperation of energies for the daily task ahead. They are the recreation or reproduction of the individual at a given state of existence rather than the growth or culture of the mind and character. Rest, relaxation and recreation are necessary for leisure as for life,

---

* Cultivation of the mind is distinct from such intellectual exercises or pastimes such as bridge, chess, mathematical or crossword puzzles which sharpen the intellect or develop specialized proficiencies without enlarging the total personality.

but leisure, properly speaking, the Aristotelians argue, begins where relaxation and recreation end.

The Greek word for leisure, *schole*, from which our word 'school' is derived, suggests the Aristotelian view of leisure as "cultivation of the mind" or "culture" in the sense of growth.[7] In this conception, leisure is distinguished from such related words as play, amusement, pastime, entertainment, diversion, distraction, which seem to transcend the cycle of work and recuperation but which constitute only a pleasurable passing of time, an excitation of the senses and spirit, a diverting of the attention from serious or distressing thoughts, without a growth of mind or character. To be sure, Aristotle does not draw a hard and fast line between amusements and leisure activities. He normally distinguishes leisure, the cultivation of the soul or the entire human being, as an end in itself, from amusement which, like relaxation, aims at the cessation of pains or burdens rather than positive pleasures. Games, entertainments, diversions are restorative; leisure is expansive. Nonetheless, amusements are an essential component of the good life. One who eschews such is, for Aristotle, a boor.[8] And much of a child's play and adult entertainments is educative; in fact, culture (*paideia*) is derivative of play (*paidia*). Amusements, particularly those connected with the Muses, lighten the mind, make it more nimble and receptive, afford it the opportunity to develop. But those who are overstrained and fatigued through toil will be unlikely to experience growth or culture from the Muses; their music, games, festivals and amusements, absolutely essential to a toiling population, will be less restrained, more colourful, louder and sensational — in short, more geared to "the relaxation of which it stands in need" than to leisure or culture.[9]

If leisure in this aristocratic usage is conceptually distinct from relaxation and amusement, leisure as culture is also distinct from consumption. Leisure and consumption are both antitheses to production but whereas consumption depends on external goods, leisure does not. True leisure, for Aristotle, is the self-sufficient activity of the mind, a mind which is its own best company, one which is not dependent on external stimuli for its action. The leisured person indeed delights in the pleasures of the senses, in what pleases the sight, hearing, touch, taste and smell, and in the company of friends, but he is not dependent on them. Leisure as distinct from consumption, is "senseless" in that it is the activity of the mind which is not dependent on external sensations and in that it does not aim at a material effect.[10] Leisure, for

22

Aristotle, is the love and contemplation of what is; it is a thanking and a thinking. It is an affirmation of the world and an attempt to comprehend, not to change it. The attempt to understand the world is not easy or effortless but is graced or sustained by the profoundest and most enduring pleasures. Leisure is the end of existence, the cessation of striving.

While leisure as distinct from consumption is "senseless", Aristotle also includes as leisure activities something which might be called 'cultural consumption', that is, those sensual enjoyments which cultivate or enlarge the person. Of the senses, Aristotle ranks hearing and then sight as the senses which contribute most to the culture of the mind.[11] Although the sense of touch or feeling may be the most important sense for organic existence and for sanity, as well as being that which excites in us the most vehement of pleasures, it is not one which promotes growth or cultivation. Aristotle argues that the auditory pleasures, such as music, song, and poetry, penetrate more deeply into the mind or soul than even the visual pleasures, such as spectacles, painting and sculpture. The senses of hearing and sight thus contribute most to the mind's expansion, to leisure or culture. The senses of touch, taste and smell might be trained. But good taste, for Aristotle, is not culture.

Aristotle's dictum that the pleasures of taste, smell and touch do not contribute to culture has not gone unchallenged. In popular terms, there is the dog's philosophy — if you can't eat it, sniff it or screw it, then piss on it. Even those who have thought deeply about leisure, such as Lin Yutang, can write: "And the Chinese fails to see why a symphony of taste in the enjoyment of food is less spiritual than a symphony of sounds."[12] But, for Aristotle, it is not a question of the relative spirituality or sensuality of auditory pleasures over the pleasures of the table. Nor is it precisely a matter of the different kinds of growth involved in ingesting sounds and food. Rather it is that a musical composition is more expressive of human experience than a culinary composition. The former, for the Aristotelian, engages the human faculties more broadly and penetrates more deeply than the latter. The pleasures of the table do not disclose the range of human passions and their objects as do the pleasures derived from the Muses.

The Aristotelian conception of leisure as culture is often thought to be too lofty for a democratic age or too prescriptive for a "value-free" sociology. Consequently the distinctions between leisure and consumption and between leisure and relaxation or amusement tend to be blurred. However we see a residue of the Aristotelian understanding of leisure in the writings of "the most energetic and productive of all scholars in leisure."[13] J. Dumazedier. Leisure is defined as that which fulfills at least one of three functions; namely, rest and recuperation, entertainment, and personal development or culture.[14] Sometimes Dumazedier appears to think that these three functions are separable and thus that forms of relaxation and amusement are leisure activities regardless of whether they involve personal growth or culture. He writes that the basic task of the dawning civilization of leisure is to achieve "an optimum balance, freely chosen, from the needs for repose, for entertainment, and for participation in social and cultural life."[15] To present the claims of relaxation, amusement and culture as standing in need of balance, Dumazedier implies that social and cultural activities may not be amusing or relaxing but nevertheless they are something which ought to be done. We shall see in Chapter 7 that "the great task of leisure" is the curbing of antisocial and uncultured amusements and thus 'leisurists', those who aspire to the scientific management of leisure, must take on the burden of ensuring that citizens strive upwards from asocial amusements to culture.

However Dumazedier is not a consistent 'leisurist'. Although he sometimes presents relaxation, amusement and culture as separable and in need of harmonious balance, he also asserts that the three functions of leisure (relaxation, diversion and personality development) are rarely separable.[16] In fact, Dumazedier states, leisure is only "truly such" when it combines the restful, amusing and cultural functions.[17] Thus, to the extent that Dumazedier does not separate culture and entertainment, he does not depart from the Aristotelian understanding of leisure. Culture then is only equivalent to leisure if it is considered entertaining or fun.

It is to be noted here that culture or growth of personality does not necessarily make good citizens. In the opinion of Jeremy Bentham, music and poetry stir up dangerous passions and an arrogant exultation of the mind inimical to the requirements of work and citizenship; harmless amusements, such as push-pin or solitaire, accord more with public utility.[18] John Locke evinced an even greater hostility to poetry than Bentham.[19] Because poetry distracts one from the serious business of life, Locke would fight fire with fire and compel aspiring poets to study classical verse. The only utility of an education in the classics, Locke believed, is to suppress any inclination to poetry in young men. Contemporary Anglo-Saxons, whose sensibilities have been nurtured by Locke and Bentham, fail to understand why Plato thought it necessary to censor poetry. The Muses are considered relatively safe; they are not expected to waylay, possess and impregnate an innocent soul. Leisure activities however are seductive and not necessarily wholesome; they are amusing but not necessarily "a good thing". Leisure is growth or culture, but the growth may be malignant or benign. Agri-culture is for us "a good thing" but a bacterial culture is not necessarily so esteemed. Leisure as culture is to be understood in these terms, rather than as a "higher value" or as "wholesome recreation". The prejudice that leisure or culture is "a good thing" is manifest in virtually all the sociological studies of leisure. Unseemly activities such as sexual intercourse, "mind-expanding" drug use, streetfighting and football hooliganism, daydreaming, childbeating and thinking are conspicuously absent from the list of leisure or cultural activities.

The Greek word for leisure, *schole*, suggests that the leisured are scholars (or, to avoid the bookish connotation, students) rather than workers, learning rather than prac-tising an existing competence. However, we refer to learning activities as school-work or homework. This terminology doubtless reflects lesser emphasis on the playful components of an aristocratic education which Plato and Aristotle recom-mended, larger sizes of classes with diminished personal contact with teachers, greater scheduling and habituation to forms of industrial discipline and other such structural changes in education. But it also reflects a prevalent view, distinct from the advocates of leisure, that "growing time" refers to work as much as, or perhaps more than, leisure.

The idea that work is a means, and perhaps the primary means, of expanding human powers, developing character and exercising capabilities, has been a dominant theme in modern history. This theme, suggested in the writings of Bacon, Descartes and Locke, flowered in the writings of Kant, Hegel, Carlyle and Marx. Bentham even considered it a mark of merit that his writings were "laborious."[20] both to write and to read; such self-advertisement would have amused people in earlier centuries. But today, no leaven exists in the unre-mitting earnestness of those scholarly works whose utility is in inverse relation to their ability to compel attention. To expect wit in contemporary treatises on industrial relations is like expecting to find a string quartet on an assembly line. Thus we may conclude that the view of laboriousness as the condition of

25

all "values" and of personal merit is by no means dead. This opinion, popularly known as "the work ethic", flourishes most notably in the ruling classes who oversee our "civilization of leisure".

The claims made on behalf of the work ethic thus deserve our attention. The definition of leisure as "growing time" cannot go unchallenged when a substantial number of thoughtful people have asserted that the time spent in work is that in which most human growth is achieved. To assess the seemingly conflicting claims of leisure and work, a distinction made in Plato's *Republic*[21] would be helpful.

Plato schematized what people consider as good roughly as follows:

a) Those things which are unpleasant or painful in themselves but useful for some further good. He placed work, physical training, medical treatment, etc. in this category.

b) Those things which are good in themselves, but not good for anything else, such as harmless pleasures.

c) Those things which are good in themselves, but also useful for external ends. Plato placed health, beauty, power, virtue, etc. in this category.

This schema, I think, is more useful than a simple dichotomy between ends and means which some have used to distinguish work as a means and leisure as an end in itself. For work is not experienced as purely a utilitarian or instrumental value, as the sublime Plato to the contemporary Dumazedier have thought. Many workers, studies have shown,[22] would not retire from work even when income is not a factor, although the percentage that would continue to work, given economic security, drops sharply in those occupations requiring least skill, challenge and opportunity to express their interests. A distinction between labour and work, similar to that formulated by H. Arendt,[23] would help us distinguish occupations which are purely instrumental from those which are only partly so. The word 'work' will be used to designate those occupations which are both a means and an end, necessary to make a living but also fulfilling and affording an opportunity for growth. 'Labour' or 'production' will be used to designate those activities which are mostly or solely a means to income or consumption.

'Leisure', in our discussion, will be understood not just as a good in itself, but useless for anything else: leisure does not fall into the Platonic category of harmless pleasures. It is a good in itself, something intrinsically enjoyable, which also *may* be useful for some further end. In saying this, I do not mean to suggest that leisure is, as numerous sociologists suggest, "wholesome recreation." Leisure may be utterly unwholesome, degenerate, revolutionary or criminal. What I am suggesting is that leisure activities, while ends in themselves, may be desirable for some other purpose. Similarily, while they are the activities of freedom, they may have their roots in the realm of necessity.

On this view of leisure, there is a fluid interpenetration of, rather than a rigid demarcation between, freedom and necessity. Dumazedier refers to the large percentage of time spent on 'demi-loisirs', such as gardening, fishing, puttering around the house, do-it-yourself activities which are partly utilitarian and partly intrinsically choiceworthy.[24] And the same mixture of ends and means can be found in what some consider the leisure activity *par excellence*, philosophy. Although Kant was surely one-sided to the point of being wrong when he says that no one would engage in philosophy were it not for the status or external rewards accruing to such activity,[25] we know of few anonymous philosophic writings.

The contemporary sociology which distinguishes leisure-time from all necessary activities—work, travel, sleep, necessary bodily functions, dressing, eating, household chores, domestic obligations, etc.—implies that no leisurable components exist within the realm of necessity and no necessity exists within leisure time. Shopping for essential goods does not pertain to leisure-time but window shopping and buying luxury goods does. Eating is not a leisure activity; dining is. Dressing is a necessary activity; costume or dressing up is a leisure activity. Making love is conspicuously absent in the sociology of leisure-time. If considered part of the realm of necessity (a domestic obligation or a necessary bodily function), the absence of sexual activities in the sociology of leisure would be explicable. But since a case could be made that sexual love contains playful elements which transcend the realm of necessity, its absence is a significant omission in the literature on leisure activities. In short, the sociological distinction postulates that the realm of necessity and of leisure are mutually exclusive. For purposes of classification, our everyday activities are to be assigned to one realm rather than another.

27

Rather than opposing leisure to the realm of necessity, I should prefer to oppose it to that which is technically necessary for the fulfillment of a function. Leisurely components exist in all activities to the extent that technique has not standardized and reduced to a minimum the time necessary to perform that function. Cultural patterns, style, idiosyncrasy, ritual, personal rhythm exist universally, in the workshops, fields, marketplaces, temples, homes, etc., until "the most efficient way" supersedes these manifestations of leisure and creates additional time for other endeavours. Dining is clearly more leisurely than eating, but the time spent on eating could be considerably reduced to what is technically necessary for the continuance of life. Thus leisure will be understood to mean what is more than necessary rather than what is free from necessity. So, for example, an education partakes of leisure to the extent that it is more than a narrow technical training. But an education may be liberal or leisurely even though it serves to prepare students for an occupation.

Bertrand Russell said, "learning, in the Renaissance, was part of the *joie de vivre*, just as much as drinking or lovemaking."[26] A reading of Aubrey's *Lives* would do much to support Russell's assertion. Yet, this wanton desire for learning was not simply the spirited exuberance of a 'leisure class' unrelated to vocational considerations. Lawrence Stone attributes this thirst for learning to the break-up of the monopoly of the clergy in intellectual matters and of the aristocracy, knowledgable only in the military arts, in practical or administrative affairs. The competition for civil service posts forced the aristocracy to take on the new learning in order to conserve their position vis-à-vis the newly educated commons. But both "peers and gentry possessed an enthusiasm for pure scholarship that far outran the practical needs of an administrative elite."[27] This view accords with our understanding of leisure which may be rooted in, but also transcends, practical needs or the realm of necessity.

We have hitherto referred to leisure as an activity which is distinguished from other forms of activity. Yet the idea of an activity has certain connotations that various writers on leisure find unacceptable. Most writers on leisure, from Aristotle to the present day, in conceiving leisure as an activity, distinguish leisure from idleness, sloth or loafing. But, at the same time, some have insisted that leisure is closer to idleness than "business."[28] They assert that leisure is not doing something productive or recreational; leisure activities are passive, receptive, reflective. They are mental activities,

28

often without a behavioural manifestation. Indeed, internal "activities", such as musing, meditating, wondering, loving, wishing are usually omitted in the sociology of leisure. The psychologists, philosophers and theologians who see these activities as constitutive of the very substance of leisure rarely employ the kind of data that would supplement the sociological contribution.

If there is different emphasis placed by the various writers on the kinds of activities which constitute leisure, there is a related difficulty (which is the main bone of contention in writers on leisure) as to whether leisure should be understood in relation to a period of time (as leisure-time) or in relation to the state, attitude or condition of being at leisure. If we consider leisure to be the time away from work and other necessary tasks, then we must consider the unemployed and the inhabitants of jails and mental hospitals to be, along with the retired, the coupon-clippers and the playboys, the supremely leisured individuals of modern society. However, "compulsory leisure" is usually thought to be a contradiction in terms; the unemployed are in a condition of "enforced idleness" and not of leisure. Also, it has been stated that those who lack the means to do at least some of the activities they enjoy in their spare time lack leisure. Leisure-time usually presupposes a condition of economic security and sufficient wealth to choose amongst alternative enjoyments.[29]

More contentiously, some have claimed that leisure pertains more to a psychological than to an economic condition or state of being.[30] Leisure, it is thought, is an attitude which enables the space in the mind, unoccupied in work, to be filled and that space, occupied in work, to be cleaned, aired and refurnished. As the foremost spokesman of this point of view, J. Pieper, puts it:

> Leisure... is a mental and spiritual attitude — it is not simply the result of external factors, it is not the inevitable result of spare time, a holiday, a weekend or a vacation... (L)eisure implies... an attitude of non activity, of inward calm, of silence; it means not being 'busy', but letting things happen.[31]

In support of this view, Dr. A.R. Martin refers to the anxiety or fear people experience in their spare time; not only killing time* is common on holidays, weekends and vacations

---

* This expression is to be found in most modern languages; in French 'tuer le temps' and in German 'die Zeit totschlagen' denote this partial suicide.

but also suicides are more common than on work days.[32] As the antithesis to the suicidal killing of time, the enjoyment of leisure depends on inner resources; leisure is a condition of tranquillity, peace or calm. Restlessness, compulsive anxiety, insomnia, guilt prevent leisure, in the sense of leisureliness. Those who have to be in charge of a situation, who cannot let things be, who have not enough time, who are harried, pressed or rushed, are unleisurely despite an abundance of time off work. R. McIver depicts modern men off work as "planes with no landing gear."[33]

The antithesis of Pieper's view of leisure is expressed by the pop singer, Jim Morrison, who, shortly after making the following statement, followed Jimi Hendrix's and Janis Joplin's path to final rest.

> Everybody has to stand for something, that's what we're here for. If Spiro Agnew stands for law and order, all right, say I stand for sex. Chaos. Movement without meaning. Cop baiting. Fifty-two-week paid vacations with double overtime every year.[34]

Morrison's manifesto would be considered by few to be a demand for leisure, even though he calls for unlimited time off work. For leisure connotes, in common usage, both a period of time and a condition of being. The paradox suggested in the title of S.B. Linder's book, *The Harried Leisure Class*, plays upon both meanings of leisure. We must reject as one-sided or inadequate an understanding of leisure as units of time severed from a condition of being leisurely or at leisure. J. Dumazedier opposes the conception of leisure as a state of being because, he says, it does not accord with contemporary attitudes. Of 819 people interviewed in France in 1953, over half conceived of leisure as time, one quarter conceived of it as activity, and "none gave it the passive definition of a 'state'."[35] However, "he continues, "practically all... defined leisure by *opposition* to the cares and concerns of daily life..."[36] But since the presence or absence of such cares and concerns surely constitutes a state or condition of being, Dumazedier's own findings preclude his conclusion that leisure is no longer understood as a condition or state.

Nevertheless integrating 'leisureliness' and 'leisure-time' into a satisfactory conception of leisure is easier said than done. Not only does the empirical sociologist baulk at a conception of leisure as a state or condition but also the social theorist may disdain the unit-time approach to leisure (or sometimes even all empirical research). S. De Grazia insists that leisure as a condition of being, is not a chronological occurence and thus "has no adjectival relationship to time."[37]** But De Grazia too has made use of studies conceptualizing leisure as units of time free from necessary tasks and, in fact, has made his own empirical studies using this conception of leisure time.[38] In short, De Grazia and others have shown that one can adopt the unit time approach of empirical sociology to illuminate, and provide content to, the conception of leisure adopted by Pieper and contemporary Aristotelians. The gulf separating the conceptions of leisure as quantities of time and qualities of experience is perhaps not unbridgable.

The unification of the theoretical understanding of leisure as a condition of being with the unit time approach of empirical sociology implies bringing the "subjective" realm of meaning or significance to bear on the "objective" data of time budget studies (and the conventional variables of age, sex, occupational and income differences). That is, interpretation of what an activity means, either by the actor or observer, is necessary to designate that activity as leisurely. For the same behaviour may mean totally different things to different actors. Gardening, going to the opera, taking children to a pantomime may be a pleasure for some and a chore for others. The same activity may mean different things to different people and different activities may have the same significance to different individuals.

We do not obtain direct information on the nature of the leisure experienced on the golf course from objective data on the number of golf clubs sold, the number of people who play golf, the amount of time devoted to the sport, and so forth. Many simply enjoy the game of golf, others sell insurance, buy stocks or make business contacts on the links, others avoid their in-laws and create the justification for a few drinks at 'the nineteenth hole'. The hero of our narrative, F.W. Taylor, was compelled to play golf on doctor's orders and compared his time at the sport with visits to the dentist. Taylor, as we shall see, was incapable of experiencing leisure in his time off-work. Thus, if time off work and a condition of leisureliness are

---

** De Grazia means that the expression 'leisure time' should appear as ugly as 'love-time', 'piety hour' or 'nobility day'. However expressions such as 'a pleasant time', 'an unhurried hour', 'an easy afternoon', 'a contemplative morning', 'an unoccupied fifteen minutes' are not strained and denote the quality of experience or state of mind obtaining in a definite period of time.

gathered and unified in the word 'leisure', the significance or importance to the actor of the leisure activity must be determined.

Indeed, numerous studies have been conducted eliciting the meaning or value of individuals' leisure activities in conjunction with the enumeration of behaviour within time budgets. Such a synthesis of the realm of meaning and objective behaviour encounters a conflict between words and deeds. For example, in terms of the time occupied with it, television viewing is the most popular recreation in the West (and increasingly in Eastern Europe) but it is rarely mentioned as a favourite activity.[39] On the other hand, fishing is frequently mentioned as a favourite activity but comparatively little time is occupied with it.[40] Partly this can be explained by the ease of access to a television set relative to some fishable water. However it is apparent that people do what they say is not really worth doing. To ascertain the extent to which this represents a real dissatisfaction with leisure activities or the extent to which behaviour reflects the personal estimate of a worthy pastime while the verbal response merely expresses what the respondent considers a socially estimable pursuit, would require a closer analysis of the people involved than most students of leisure find expedient. However, interesting studies[41] integrating the "subjective" importance or significance of an activity with the "objective" data of empirical sociology indicate that the attempt to synthesize quantities of time and activities with qualities of experience are not doomed from the outset.

To conclude, our consideration of what may be gathered by the word leisure as 'growing time' unites the Aristotelian understanding of leisure as culture with the empirical definition of time away from work and necessary chores. Leisure is the time in which expansive enjoyments take place, an opportunity for non-specialized development considered under the category of time.

Leisure is synonymous with 'free time' in the sense of freedom to engage in other pursuits. Free time, as freedom for, or an opportunity to do something that working time does not permit, connotes more than rest and relaxation. In this sense, it is equivalent to leisure. However the normal connotation of "free time' derives from its opposition to the 'unfreedom' of the job. Free time, as freedom from the job, is largely just rest and relaxation.

Leisure then is not just time from, it is time for. And thus the time which constitutes leisure presupposes the capacity for more than rest, restoration of energies and nerves, distractions, diversions and pass-times. Leisure includes economic security, the means to dispose of spare time in a choiceworthy manner, and the psychic state or condition of being receptive to what engages attention or stimulates activity. That is, the adjective 'leisure' in 'leisure-time' and 'leisure-activity' denotes a positive quality by virtue of which such time and such activity partakes of the experience of leisure. 'Leisure time' and 'leisure activities' are not merely the negative or privative forms of 'working time' and 'useful activities.'

Leisure activities are those which are intrinsically choice-worthy rather than instrumental; they are the activities of freedom rather than of necessity. However, the realms of freedom and necessity are not necessarily mutually exclusive. Technical necessity excludes leisure but elements of leisure may be found in what is normally considered the realm of necessity. Leisure exists in school work, if the education provides more than a narrow technical competence, in the home or workshop, if style, rhythm, idiosyncrasy, conversation, play etc. evade the eye of the efficiency expert.

Leisure then is the time which is more than technically necessary for the achievement of an end and is that which is more than purely instrumental, although it may be rooted in the realm of necessity or utility. As such, leisure is more properly opposed to labour than to work. Indeed work is distinct from leisure in that it develops specialized capabilities of the workman whereas leisure aims at a more general development of the body, mind and character. However both work and leisure pertain to individual growth. But labour is simply a technique for maximizing consumption which is not necessarily developmental to the individual; the strain borne by the labourer may well exhaust, rather than develop, the best in him or her. The aim of scientific management was to complete the transformation of work into labour. The transformation of leisure into wholesome recreation would complete the subordination of individual ends to the requirements of the productive collectivity.

The correlation of leisure and scientific management serves to bring together the elements of time off work, opportunity for expansive enjoyment, and the condition of leisureliness which are collected in the word 'leisure'. That is, scientific management has a bearing on leisure not only insofar as it has provided industrial workers with more time off work and their managers with less time off work but also insofar as scientific management pertains to the capacity of individuals to do more than repair the stress and strain their jobs impose upon them.

Hitherto we have assumed that the quantitative approach of empirical sociology is inadequate because it fails to encompass the quality of being at leisure that is evoked by the word 'leisure'. S. De Grazia vividly expresses the objection to the purely quantitative approach in the sociology of leisure.

> A moment of awe in religion or ecstasy in love or orgasm in intercourse, a decisive blow to the enemy, relief in a sneeze, or death in a fall is treated as equal to a moment of riding in the bus, shovelling coal or eating beans.[42]

However De Grazia does not make clear whether the homogenous units of time approach to leisure is a shortcoming of empirical sociology or whether the reduction of qualities of leisure to quantities of activities done in determinate quanta of time off work is a characteristic of industrial capitalism adequately captured in the categories of empirical sociology. That is, perhaps the condition of being at leisure (which De Grazia and others take to be the essence of leisure) has been withdrawn from contemporary activities so that the unit time approach of empirical sociology adequately represents the nature of modern leisure. Perhaps time budget studies are not merely an expedient for the classification of a large amount of insignificant data (which abstracts from the real significance of leisure) but also accurately represent our contemporary condition or state of being dependent on uniform units of time, unremittingly carved out by the hands on the factory clock, distinguished mainly as the bosses' time and one's own time. In short, De Grazia does not make clear whether the unit time approach of empirical sociology is merely a thoughtless approach to leisure or whether the relative correspondence of the categories of empirical sociology to the patterns of contemporary life constitute a critique of industrial capitalism. Is leisureliness absent in our non-working activities or merely in their conceptualization in the sociology of leisure?

The subsequent chapter will try to clarify these issues as it charts the changing patterns of working and non-working activities and the resulting transformation in the conceptualization of these activities.

Chapter 2

The Factory Clock and the Stop-Watch: The Impact of Industrialization on the Conceptualization of Leisure

Traditional rhythms and clock time. The intermingling of work and play in pre-industrial societies. Dumazedier's view that leisure is the product of industrialization: exploitative idleness and compulsory holidays not leisure: ritual observance and individual choice; separation of work and play with clocking in and out. Leisure as time to be used; time as money, spending and wasting time. The stop-watch and managerial control. The effects of scientific management; the decline of "the leisure class"; time-consciousness and efficiency in leisure; passivity of scientifically managed jobs spills over onto leisure; increased leisure-time of proletarians. Leisure as compensation for scientific management; liberal and socialist variants. Job enlargement as alternative to leisure-as-compensation thesis.

Numerous thinkers have agreed with Lewis Mumford's insight that the clock is the central instrument of an industrial society and that the introduction of clock time has radically affected patterns of life and attitudes to work and leisure.[1] C. Babbage wrote a century and a half ago:

> Clocks occupy a very high place among instruments by means of which human time is economized: and their multiplication in conspicuous places in large towns is attended with many advantages.[2]

35

In contrast to the clock-bound character of industrial societies, rhythms and pace of life of agrarian societies were determined by the tasks confronting producers, by the length of the day, the climate, the seasons. The day, in northern countries, was twice as long in the summer as in the winter. The pace of life quickened in sowing and harvest time and slowed down at other times. Work was done in accordance with "an observed necessity"[3] rather than to the uniform, unremitting compulsion of a factory clock. Inclement weather might keep the peasants indoors, repairing implements, making rope, spinning wool, or might send them to the market to sell eggs or buy provisions. In winter, the rhythm of life sank to a slow dirge. Working experience was as varied and irregular as the inclinations of the workers and nature.

Moreover, work was punctuated by frequent holidays. In medieval Christendom, there were roughly 150 holidays, with somewhat more or less workless days depending on the country and region.[4] Ancient Egypt, classical Greece and Imperial Rome were not far behind in their number of holidays.[5] To put our civilization of leisure in perspective, H.L. Wilensky writes: "The skilled urban worker has now achieved the position of his 13th century counterpart, whose long workday, seasonally varied, was offset by many holidays, rest periods, and long vacations; annual hours of work now, as then, remain in the range of 1,900 to 2,500."[6] Of course, the skilled urban craftsmen were a small privileged minority of the work force. Rural labourers had considerably longer hours of work than their urban counterparts.

Work and play were much more intertwined in the less efficient pre-capitalist modes of production. E.P. Thompson describes modes of production prior to the pervasive influence of clock time:

> ...a community in which task-orientation is common appears to show least demarcation between 'work' and 'life'. Social intercourse and labour are intermingled — the working-day lengthens or contracts according to the task — and there is no great sense of conflict between labour and 'passing the time of day.[7]

Communal work and folk festivals were combined at harvests, corn-husking bees, veillées, etc. A conversation, game or drink spiced the round of intense labour and rest. Various customary observances or rituals during work relieved the stress and strain on the nerves and muscles. Siestas after a midday meal

36

were not the preserve of southern counties. Songs, chants and musical instruments frequently accompanied collective work, and festivals or dances often signalled the completion of a task.[8]

K.P. Büecher's *Arbeit und Rhythmus* suggests that much of music and poetry may have sprung from working rhythms.[9] In ancient Greece, each occupation had different kinds of song, and the airs of the flute, pipe and whistle leavened the more monotonous tasks.[10] Büecher notes that early machine technology conformed to the rhythm of muscular movements; the early planes, machine saws, sausage cutting machines, printing presses, glazing machines, etc. did not force the operator into an alien rhythm.[11] Subsequent industrial production submitted workers to the rhythm, or rather the unremitting and steady beat, of the machine.

In spite of the loss of rhythmic movement, industrial labour is usually less taxing on the muscles than pre-industrial labour. However, industrial production frequently places more stress on the nerves.[12] Unremitting attention to a task that is not intrinsically absorbing is difficult, particularly for those older workers whose attention span is less than that of younger workers. Physical labour does not demand such powers of concentration; the attention is drawn along with the rhythms and movements of the body.[13] Pre-industrial labour was onerous, particularly so when compounded by legal compulsion. But the frequently expressed view that, in pre-capitalist societies, workers toiled day in and day out, from dawn to dusk, is certainly overstated. Certainly the low level of hygiene, wealth and literacy limited the scope and enjoyment of leisure more than the allegedly constant attention to the production of subsistence.

J. Dumazedier, in defining leisure for the *International Encyclopedia of the Social Sciences*, insists that leisure is the product of an industrial civilization. He provides four reasons why leisure did not exist in pre-industrial societies. First, he claims, the dominant elites were unoccupied in any productive function and lived by the exploitation of servile labour; they were idle rather than leisured "since leisure in the modern sense presupposes work."[14] One might respond that earlier ruling classes were occupied in a different way than modern ruling classes, but they were at least sufficiently occupied to be able to exploit the subordinate classes. And, although many workers will doubtless be overjoyed to learn that the eras of exploitation have passed, the odd malcontent continues to

37

think that exploitation will end only when all contribute an equal portion of physical labour or when the division between managerial and manual labour has been abolished or when the structure of production ceases to subordinate some to others and to limit the interesting activities and rewards to the dominant elite. But, to repeat Dumazedier's first reason for insisting that leisure emerges with an industrial civilization; exploitative idleness of pre-industrial elites was not leisure.

Secondly, Dumazedier asserts that the numerous holidays and workless days of the pre-bourgeois world were not leisure time since they stemmed from religious obligations.[15] As leisure is time free from obligations, the time passed during religious festivals was not at the disposal or unrestricted choice of individuals. In fact, Dumazedier says, such enforced idleness was a burden to the peasants and artisans.[16] Were this in fact the case, one is surprised at the popular reluctance to accept the curtailment of numerous holidays that accompanied the Reformation.[17] One might note that the work in which Luther advocated the abolition of all holidays except Sunday is significantly entitled *Address to the Nobility of the German Nation*.[18] The obligation of workers to observe religious holidays is not necessarily opposed to their volition, as Dumazedier implies. That many workers today do not choose their holidays and vacations does not mean that many do not want these days off work. Similarly there is not sufficient evidence to show that most of the peasants and artisans of pre-industrial societies were involuntarily compelled to cease work during holidays. In fact, Saint Monday and Tuesday were observed well into the nineteenth century[19] and contemporary absenteeism figures suggest that the veneration of these saints is not entirely dead.

Thirdly, Dumazedier claims that leisure was absent in pre-industrial societies because workless time was governed by common ritual observances. Time off work was not leisure but a collective celebration, enjoined by church teaching or customary practice, and was not, as today, "the unfettered responsibility of the individual."[20] The time and energies of individuals off work were channelled by traditional society and were not, as today, a matter of personal inclination. A recent study of the "secularization of leisure" in Israel captures Dumazedier's sentiment in asserting that "the Jews invented leisure (in the institution of the Sabbath) and then took it back again by minutely prescribing how to spend it."[21]

Doubtless caution is required in reading the liberal dislike of celebrations into the past. The feeling that celebrations or festivals fetter the individual's will is not universal even to-day. Thus the existence of common festive practices is not necessarily restrictive of individual choice. However what Dumazedier conceives to be the difference between the activities off work of pre-industrial and industrial societies might be seen in the presence or absence of traditional garb or costume for time and space away from work. In pre-industrial societies, costume for folk dances, church, festivals, theatre was used to differentiate these activities from more mundane, work-a-day activities. Today "leisure wear" is common at work and working clothes are seen at concerts, picnics and dances. Traditional costume represented the kind of attitude and conduct expected of one away from work. Such social expectations constituted (what Dumazedier considers) limitations to individuality.

However it would be a mistake to think that all non-working activities in pre-industrial societies were enclosed within the confines of village custom or church teaching. Sermons throughout the middle ages thundered against the licentious conduct practiced during holidays. If these sermons were not in vain, it would appear that drinking, gambling, fornication, blood sports and other amusing popular pastimes were at least as prevalent as a sober or joyful observance of church teaching on holidays.[22] One might say that these amusements, as well as a pious reverence for God, were common traditional rituals, and not individually chosen, but it would seem that they are often the objects of unfettered individual choice in the modern world. Also it might be said that, since fashions exist today, the choice of contemporary leisure activities is subject to social determinants as were traditional ritual observances. To be sure, fashions do not sink into the individual personality as deeply as customary rites, and thus are not regarded as being restrictions on individuality or personal choice in the way that tradition is now conceived to be. Indeed the changing marketplace of industrial capitalism, urbanization and growth of commercial entertainments, have fostered an uprooting of traditional community practices and a certain individuation of attitudes that is of interest to students of leisure, although the individuation in choice of leisure activities is not sufficiently developed to put sociologists out of business.

The element of individual choice is central to the contemporary understanding of leisure. Modern leisure is regarded as issuing from a deliberate exercise of choice whereas customary non-productive activities, as part of a regular pattern of living, do not constitute leisure.* The so-called problem of leisure emerges with the dissolution of customary restraints on, or ceremonial supports for, non-working activities of individuals. Traditional societies may be thought to have problems of idleness but not of leisure.

Fourthly, Dumazedier asserts that leisure did not exist in pre-industrial societies because work and play were fused in "a natural rhythm" of work "punctuated by rests, songs, games and ceremonies."[23] The borderline between work and leisure was not clearly drawn. But leisure presupposes, Dumazedier says, that earning a livelihood must be clearly separable, both in theory and in practice, from free time.[24] The 9 to 5 day with regular lunch hours and coffee breaks enables us to separate the day shift from what David Riesman calls 'the night shift', vacations are clearly distinct from the rest of the working year and retirement is a clear break with working life. Just as playgrounds and recreational facilities have become spatially distinct from workaday life, leisure and work, Dumazedier claims, have become temporally distinct. Such a separation of work and leisure, a follower of Dumazedier asserts, emancipates leisure activities from a regulative association with work.

> Rather than singing along with the other field workers, one did one's job and also joined a workers' singing club; rather than drinking with the other stonemasons during a break or on Mondays, one worked steadily all day and then drank at the neighbourhood pub when and with whom one chose. In both examples the new element is choice.[25]

Of course, the solemn complement to this liberation of choice or individuality in leisure was the sense of isolation at work, the increasing repression of the possibility of singing, drinking or chatting on the job.

---

* A certain parochial chauvinism is often manifest in denying the existence of leisure in non-western or non-industrial countries. For example, E. Larrabee and R. Meyersohn write: "Where tradition rules, time empty of obligation is empty of everything else; there is literally nothing to do with it, and the peon sleeping in the sun is the perfect image of the man with free time but no leisure. And in the Orient, where men have always made a virtue of transcending the human lot through inactivity, there least of all does leisure in our sense exist..." (*Mass Leisure*, ix.)

Dumazedier's definition of leisure, based on the separation of labour and free time, accords with a model of proletarian existence in which all leisurely components have been removed from work and all work-related interests do not occupy free time. However a difficulty with such a conception of leisure is that it does not apply to all people in modern society. The self-employed, the housewives, the students, etc. have "a pre-industrial rhythm" to their lives; they allot their time to their necessary tasks and to their relaxations and amusements. Their pace of work is not as regular as a proletarian's. Nor is the beginning and cessation of work completely regulated by the clock. But, more importantly, the non-proletarian strata within industry — the executives, professionals, sales-personnel, etc. — frequently integrate their work and play in such a manner that Dumazedier's definition is inapplicable. The businessman's luncheon with clients, the expense account living, the paintings and decorative furnishings in the offices, the "morale-lifting" pinch on the posteriors of secretaries, the fraternal associations and clubs, the business chats over drinks, the reading of newspapers, business and professional journals, the dinner invitations to the boss, colleagues and clients, the preparation of work at home or on the commuter trains, the travel, the out-of-town conferences, the sales competitions and collegial contests and games, etc. suggest that the line of demarcation between leisure and work is difficult to draw. For Dumazedier's definition of leisure as time completely separable from work to be universally applicable, the efficiency experts or time-motion men would have to get busy on the non-proletarian strata to remove the leisure from their work, to determine the extent to which the above-mentioned activities are necessary for maximal productivity. Moreover, the separation of work and play does not exist wherever wage-labourers have resisted time motion study; for example, a recent British study revealed "in shipbuilding leisure activities most definitely take place in work time..."[25 a]

Thus, it can be seen that Dumazedier has overstated the difference between pre-industrial and industrial leisure patterns. However, the changes in productive practices from pre-industrial to industrial societies, the industrial discipline and regimentation, the subdivision of tasks, the supervision, scheduling and synchronization of production, which can be symbolized in the dominance of the factory clock, has affected our understanding of time, of working time and leisure time. That opposition between work and leisure which is part of the modern understanding is a product of industrial time. As E.P. Thompson has stated, there is no problem of leisure in pre-industrial societies (as life is passed in undifferentiated rhythms of productive and playful activities) and until the problem is resolved in industrial societies, we might well be cautious in recommending the dominant forms of modernization to agrarian countries.[26]

This so-called problem of leisure, expressed frequently in general form (as distinct from specific "problems" of adjusting to retirement, of juvenile delinquency, of school curricula, of day-care centres, etc.), usually refers to a fear that free-time will be dissipated in unprofitable ways. That is, leisure, seen as units of time derived from the industrial practice of clocking in and out, is not just to be enjoyed, but is itself to be made productive. Thus the concept of leisure invoked in "the problem of leisure" depends in form and content on our beliefs and practices regarding work. As T.F. Green has written:

> ...leisure is defined through categories of work. The notion that time should be used profitably, productively, or efficiently clearly obtains its meaning from the notion of work. Indeed, the idea that time can be used is a peculiar one; the more one reflects upon it, the more difficult it is to see how that idea can have any meaning at all, except within a pattern of thought dominated by categories of work. The idea is that free-time, unlike work-time, is empty time, yet like work-time it must be filled by "productive occupation." Thus the concept of leisure, like the concept of free-time, is a derivative one; it derives its meaning from the idea of work.[27]

The notion that our time is not just lived, passed, endured or enjoyed but is spent or thrown away, used or wasted, employed or left idle emerges in Protestant thought and flowers with the development of capitalist society. For capitalism is based on the sale and employment of labour-time. A merchant, as Marx put it, buys products; a capitalist buys labour-time and in that purchase commands the disposition of that labour-time. The capitalist must see that time is employed to a good purpose, that the productive power contained within that time is not wasted. Time becomes a commodity. Or, in the words of that shrewd old Yankee, Benjamin Franklin, "time is money."[28] It might be thought that

42

Franklin's maxim reflects an economy of self-employed farmers and artisans as such "petty-bourgeois" elements predominated in an economy with some manufacturing enterprises and a number of slave-based plantations. But that usurer of time also said, "The Eye of a Master, will do more Work than his Hand."[29], which illustrates the applicability of time as money to capitalist and slave-owning enterprises.

If the major difference between the wages system and a system of slavery is that wage-labourers are masters of their time off work, it is not difficult to understand why leisure time would be valued in distinction to working time. Leisure is one's own time whereas the capitalist owns one's working time.

In spite of the relatively small amount of the workers' own time, "the problem of leisure" appeared quite obvious in the early days of industrial capitalism. Not only were the working hours approximately twice as long as is the norm today but also the public facilities in which to occupy one's leisure, such as parks, libraries, museums, etc. were often inaccessible to the working class and the crowded and noisy home environment did not provide an atmosphere conducive to repose and leisure.[30] Moral appeals against the "misspense of time" and for the frugal and sober recreation of working energies were cheaper and thus more prevalent than the provision of urban facilities for healthy and educative entertainments.[31] Although the working classes attempted to fill this need by bringing the pastimes of the open fields into the urban setting, from the onset of industrialism in England, various campaigns were waged against working class amusements, such as drinking, gambling and blood sports in an attempt to "methodise" workers, to habituate them to the more regular and disciplined patterns of industrial capitalism.[32] The charitable concern to prevent dissipation of health and moral fibre corresponded to the industrial need to have everyone as "regular as clock work." Absenteeism or lateness, perhaps generated by last night's carousing or a cock fight, undermined the synchronization necessary for industrial productivity. Leisure time, no longer bound by collective celebrations and customary rituals and no longer connected to individual working rhythms and patterns, became a problem. But for whom?

The industrial revolution was then a radical alteration in social interaction and attitudes; it generated enormous changes in social and work relationships, in the rhythms of life and patterns of work. The transformation from agriculture and cottage industry where individuals determined their methods and pace of work to an industrial regimen determined by the factory clock, and enforced by overseers armed with various penalties to ensure industrial discipline, was momentous. The close connection of the early factories with prisons and workhouses, the rigorous methods of factory discipline, the use of the more docile elements of the population — women and children — meant that a large number of workers were unwilling to sell their time and their independence to the manufacturers.

Industrialism eventually triumphed over the working class, but the triumph was not complete, as workers fought back against the disruption of their working and non-working patterns. They formed unions, friendly societies, clubs, workingmen's libraries, associations for the production of Shakesperian plays, saloon entertainments, anti-sabbatarian movements and other political organizations. Self-help on and off the job preceded scientific management and "mass culture."

The ignorance of capitalists limited the scope of their management of workers. Manufacturers, as a rule, did not know enough about the various kinds of tasks to have a uniform, synchronized control over workers. Writers such as Charles Babbage and Andrew Ure preached theories and techniques of management. But the actual management of most enterprises was divided or subcontracted to overseers or foremen who wielded the stick more than the carrot over the workers to maximize productivity. Manufacturers were dependent upon these taskmasters to get the work done, and as the strength and unionization of the working class grew, manufacturers also became dependent upon the skills and know-how of a united working population. Capitalists bought the labouring time of workers, but their ability to dispose of it in the most productive or profitable fashion was limited by the monopoly of industrial know-how in the hands of the skilled workers. As F.W. Taylor's biographer, F.B. Copley writes of pre-scientific management:

> What the manager bought or thought he was buying was the worker's time. At the best he had only a hazy notion that time is but the package in which effort, the real goods, is wrapped.[33]

However, the conservation of customary standards of working inevitably conflicted with improvements in machinery and technique and the traditional claim of renumeration as "a fair day's work for a fair day's pay" ran counter to the market calculation of the capitalists who wanted to get the most from the time they were paying for. The customary standards of doing a job well while not over-pacing oneself, or working too fast to keep others out of work, in part lasted within a working culture until F.W. Taylor's stop watch "scientifically" classified jobs, and the minimum time required to do them. Taylorism, while it arose from the logic of wage-labour and of time as money, depended for its genesis and ubiquitous acceptance on a complexity of factors which we shall analyse in the subsequent chapter. Let us just note here: first, the factory clock distinguishes that part of a worker's day belonging to the capitalist and that belonging to the worker; second, the stop watch becomes a necessary adjunct to the factory clock, given that the working day belongs to the capitalist.

It is worth noting that Adam Smith could see no utility in watches. Smith stated that love of such timepieces was born of a desire for mechanical perfection and was quite independent of any useful purpose they might serve.[34] After reviewing the life's work of F.W. Taylor, one might conclude that Smith was both remarkably short-sighted and extremely perceptive.

The goal of scientific management or Taylorism was efficient production. Its application aimed at the most intensive utilization of labour, a "speed-up" of production corresponding to the higher speed machine technologies introduced in the latter third of the nineteenth century. Scientific management was directed against leisurely work practices, against the restriction of output or "soldiering" as Taylor called it. He wished to "increase the pace of work to a rate closer to that of which the physical equipment was capable."[35] The mastery of nature was to be effected, in the second wave of the industrial revolution, by the systematic control over those instrumental in that transformation.

One can hardly overemphasize the impact of Taylorism on the structure of industrial relations in this century. However our primary purpose is not to assess Taylor's role in the development of technique towards the automation of production and in contemporary managerial practices and industrial organization. Our primary concern is to assess the relationship between scientific management and current patterns of leisure activities.

The first pertinent factor is that "the leisure class" described by Veblen, a contemporary of Taylor and an exponent of the ideas of scientific management, no longer exists. Empirical studies reveal that the ruling classes of capitalist and socialist countries work longer hours and are more committed to their work than are production or clerical workers.[36] The ruling classes, since the advent of scientific management, have taken more of the world's work on their shoulders and believe that the assumption of these responsibilities is essential for human progress. As P. Drucker, a leading contemporary exponent of management science, claims: "It can be said without too much oversimplication that there are no 'underdeveloped countries'. There are only 'undermanaged' ones."[37] Moreover, the ruling classes justify their dominance in terms of the work they do. Mrs. Gromyko admirably captured the ideology of ruling hierarchies in her remark: "Oh, Andrei does work hard, yet not as hard as Mr. Vishensky, and even that is not so hard as Mr. Molotov works."[38] It may be thought to be just that the ruling class pays for its power through hard work, on the assumption that such work is more of a toilsome duty than an opportunity for a challenging and interesting occupation, the satisfaction of ambition and the material and status rewards attendant on such responsible work. But it remains to be shown that societies are better governed by elites that do not enjoy, or lack the time for, leisure and whose vocational preparation has not flowed over the rim of technical competence.

The second effect of scientific management is an enhanced time-awareness and an increased concern for efficiency in our time off work. What S. Parker means by 'time-famine'[39] and S.B. Linder means by 'harried leisure'[40] might well be associated with scientific management. Although each generation for the past few centuries has tended to characterize itself as more rushed and restless than in "the good old days", the high wages and high intensity consumption derivative of 'rationalized' industry would seem to have exacerbated a sense of time thrift. An economist, G.S. Becker, argues that Americans are more wasteful of things and more economical of time than other people because time has a higher price in America than elsewhere and things are cheaper.[41] In short, it costs more to do nothing in a high-wage economy than in a low wage economy. Increasing affluence and time off work may make people less prodigal and more careful of how they "spend" their time. Time-consuming practices such as prolonged courtship, S.B. Linder assures us,

46

do not accord with high intensity production and consumption.[42] For this reason, S. Parker and G. Godbey claim, the practice of taking a mistress has been replaced by the 'one-nighter'.[43]

Moreover, productivity in the less-capital intensive service and recreation industries has not kept pace with that in the production of goods. An orientation towards consumption rather than leisure is economically sound, the most efficient purchase of other's time with one's own. Goods are "a better buy" than services. According to G.S. Becker, there is a tendency to assess the cost and productivity of the services and entertainments in the leisure industry in terms of the value of one's labouring time; in short, to determine whether or not an hour's labour will purchase an hour's service or an hour's entertainment.[44] That is, a desire to go out to the theatre may be counterbalanced not only by the costs of the tickets, transportation and babysitting but also by the price of one's time in not doing some moonlighting or doing something useful around the house. The most efficient way to "spend" time may prove to be painting the bathroom and then relaxing with a pint or two in front of the television.

The efficiency mentality is not conducive to a sense of timelessness or to the condition of being carefree or tranquil. As C. Greenberg has said, "no one is ever efficient enough."[45] A cost-benefit analysis of the employment of time, the sense of time thrift obliging us to employ our time productively or efficiently, leaves many contemporaries hurried and harried, pinched with the thought of a more productive use of one's time and worried with a sense of not having enough time to do the things one really wants to do.

Efficiency is a virtue when it is a means to economize on the time engaged in disagreeable activities in order to enlarge the time for some end or unconditional interest. But the concern with efficiency has tended to make all interests conditional on getting the best market price for one's time. Efficiency, or the productive employment of time, becomes an end, not a means. This imperative to spend time productively, not to waste it or throw it away, did not begin with scientific management or the efficiency movement, but was certainly accentuated by it.

Nor are these unleisurely attitudes associated with understanding time as a commodity peculiar to capitalism. G.A. Prudenski writes:

The old bourgeois proverb, "time is money", is foreign to the socialist society. However, the price of time in our country is exceptionally high, since in the economising of time lie the conditions for a colossal increase in the productive forces of our country and the spiritual culture of the Soviet citizen in his advance towards communism.[46]

If the above libation to the shade of B. Franklin had not passed through the kidneys of Mr. Prudenski, the ghost of that old Yankee might arise, clench his fist, and exclaim, "Comrade."

Since Lenin's first major speeches in power called for the introduction of Taylorism into the Soviet Union, numerous "Time Leagues" and All-Russian Scientific Management Conferences were established.[47] In the 1930s, Taylorism was "Russified" into Stakhanovism.[48] And the recent studies of leisure time in the USSR suggest that the application of time-motion studies "for reducing individual kinds of irrational non-labour time use" is in advance of the capitalist countries.[49] As Prudenski notes, "The steady increase and rational utilization of the workers' free time represent a great task for communism."[50] It is not clear whether the workers, as well as the scientific managers of soviet society, will shoulder this "great task" of leisure. However, it is clear that scientific management has penetrated the thoughts and actions of the socialist as well as capitalist world; the ubiquity of the stop watch, the concern for efficiency in time off work, the "problem" of a productive use of leisure time, has affected, to a greater or lesser degree, contemporary industrial civilizations.

The third result of scientific management relates to the increasing amount of time off work made possible by the various applications of the Taylor system. While scientific management has increased the amount of time off work for the working class, even for those who are regularly employed, it has not created a working environment which prepares workers for self-directed enjoyments in their time off work. The severance of planning from the execution of work, inherent in the structure of scientifically managed industry, has deprived the working class of initiative in the organization of their working lives. Since most writers on leisure have asserted that there is an interrelationship between the kind of work people do and the kind of leisure they enjoy, we might hypothesize that the lack of initiative experienced by

48

scientifically managed workers will be carried over into their experience of leisure-time-activities.

However the theory of the interrelationship between work and leisure is far from satisfactory. The most searching theories of leisure, such as those of J. Pieper and S. De Grazia, have nothing useful to say about the possibility of an industrial working environment which might facilitate an appreciation of leisure.* The theories of the interrelationship of work and leisure that have been put forward are usually variations of themes set forth by Engels in *The Condition of the Working Class in England*; namely, that leisure activities are a compensation for muscular and mental activities not utilized during work or that there is a spillover from the passive, monotonous working experience to an inactive and dulled leisure time.[51] That it is work that is generally perceived to have an effect on leisure, rather than vice versa, is explained by I. Howe as follows:

> Whatever its manifest content, mass culture must therefore not subvert the basic patterns of industrial life. Leisure time must be organized as to bear a factitious relationship to working time: apparently different, actually the same. It must provide relief from work monotony without making the return to work too unbearable... .[52]

However, even if we accept as cogent the reasons for thinking that the character of leisure activities are decisively shaped by the nature of work, we have no generally accepted theory which would explain the manner in which a determinate working experience would condition specific modes of leisure activities. There is considerable data, which we shall analyse in subsequent chapters, to suggest some correlation between the passive execution of scientifically managed jobs and "passive" or unreflecting pastimes off work, between the managerial revolution and declining participation of the

---

* Pieper asserts that the "deproletarianizing" of the population is one of the most important issues of our day. This aim is to be effected, he says, "by giving the wage-earner the opportunity to save and acquire property, by limiting the power of state, and by overcoming the inner impoverishment of the individual." (*Leisure, The Basis of Culture*, p. 54) De Grazia does not think that the deep enjoyment of leisure is possible within the schedules and demands of an industrial civilization.

working class in social or political organizations and activities. Yet it would be presumptuous to present a causal theory explaining the patterns of leisure-time activities by the character of the jobs required in scientifically managed industry, especially when we have yet to establish prevalent patterns of leisure activities and the dominant characteristics of Taylorised production. However, the proposition that the structure of scientifically managed industry does not prepare the working class for enterprising, reflective and co-operative leisure-time activities makes no such explanatory presumptions.

The characteristics of the jobs inaugurated by Taylor's reforms might be summarized here, before being amplified in **Chapter 4. H. Dubreuil**, an admirer of Taylor and an engineer conversant with the application of Taylor's principles, wrote that the subdivision of labour introduced by scientific management did not merely result in a limitation to the variety of movement.

> Its most important consequence is probably the isolation of the individual, his separation from every human tie, his lack of practice in collaboration and mutual aid. He no longer has to adapt his activities to those of others, for all this labour of adjustment is provided for mechanically and, so to speak, outside of him. The *planning department, methods of organization*, all the minute preparatory work that is the mark of modern production have absorbed, exhausted, centralized that spiritual activity which used to be the complement of the workers' purely physical exertions.[53]

Co-operative skills tend to atrophy when the labour force is divided and reintegrated from above, when the organization of standard methods and working relations are determined and enforced by technical experts outside the working class, when the task to be done is presented to the worker by the planning department. The instruction card not only symbolises Dubreuil's perception of the isolation of mass production but also signifies Taylor's view that workers are not expected to think about their work. As Taylor frequently stated, (and to his honour he often said it directly to workers), time spent in thinking about work is unproductive; workers are not paid to think.[54] The primary characteristics demanded of industrial workers by scientific management are promptness, diligence, and a willingness to follow directions. These characteristics do not prepare workers for initiative, responsibility and "inner-directedness" in their time off work.

An opportunity for exercising leadership at work has become rare for workers; those with capacity in this regard often move to union positions far from the shop floor or are moved to posts in lower management: initiatives from the shop floor conflict with Taylor's principles. Moreover little choice in the disposition of one's working time — for a smoke, a chat, the repair of one's machine or whatever — is available to workers once their jobs have been classified and standardized by management. The possibilities for experimentation, innovation or learning from fellow workers are now extremely limited. The lengthy apprenticeship that Taylor had in most facets of machine shop operations was also experienced by the illiterate Henry Ford who spent his youth as a machinist wandering around the shop floor, watching others and learning about the operations of machines other than his own. Needless to say, no such "shop culture" or leisurely work is possible in any 'Taylorised' or 'Fordised' plant. A lengthy apprenticeship or vocational training to learn a variety of skills is not common in industry.*

Thus while the working class has increased leisure time, its education for work, income and working experience are not conducive to self-directed, expressive or reflective activities off work. A number of workers do enjoy a rich and rewarding leisure but it is a triumph of character over circumstance. H. Wilensky concludes, after an intelligent observation of the leisure activities of 1354 men, that:

For students of American culture who look for-

---

* Sociologists frequently refer to the upgrading of skills that has occurred in the last century, particularly, the transformation of unskilled to semi-skilled labour. However, the category of semi-skilled labour is rather amorphous; it refers to any job which is powered or paced by a machine, whether it requires less than a week's training or a few months training. Also as most non-mechanized and agricultural labour is classed as unskilled, much of the alleged upgrading of skills is just the transformation from agricultural to mechanical or clerical jobs. It is perhaps to be noted that the earliest writers on the division of labour in manufacturers, Ferguson and Smith, concluded that industrial work required only a fraction of the capacities of the agricultural worker and emphasized education as the means to prevent one-sidedness in the working population. Whatever one thinks of Ferguson's and Smith's conclusions, they are to be praised for at least weighing the relevant considerations.

51

ward to the leisure-oriented society, in which we retreat from work to the more diversified joys of ever shorter hours, the moral is that those who have the most leisure have least resources for its creative use.[55]

We have indicated above that scientific management destroys "shop culture" in order to exemplify an aspect of working experience which might have a "spillover effect" upon leisure activities. Contemporaneous with the decline of "shop culture", "mass culture" progressively eroded and incorporated forms of working class culture, except that conserved within ethnic groups, pubs and workingmen's clubs. Thus the absence of resources that Wilensky believes to be a limit to "the creative use" of leisure time might be interpreted to mean the absence of working class facilities for expressive entertainments in "the mass age" as well as the absence of working class abilities to make "creative use" of the mass media.

Mass culture is that "culture" fabricated by an elite in the entertainment industry, critically assessed by ad-men and commercial magnates, and disseminated by the mass media.[56] The mass media are not, properly speaking, "communications", any more than the instruction card the worker receives is a "communication" with management; they are transmissions. The producers of mass culture are separated by a wide gulf from the undifferentiated mass of consumers. The "creative" consumption of culture is difficult when its producers have a range of experience different from one's own.

The dominant theme in the sociology of leisure is that leisure serves to compensate for the vicissitudes of industrial labour. However some leisure-as-compensation theorists, frequently concerned at the trivial and perhaps socially undesirable entertainments put upon the market, assume the impossibility of reawakening popular avenues of cultural expression and look to the state, particularly in its educational role, to rectify the perceived inadequacies of mass culture.[57] Corresponding to Dumazedier's distinction between entertaining and cultural functions of leisure, liberal leisure-as-compensation theorists imply that commerce is to handle the fun and the state is to manage the edifying functions of the leisure industry.

A variant of the leisure-as-compensation thesis is evident in socialist thinkers, such as Marcuse, who insist that leisure cannot compensate for the cost of alien toil in capitalist society, but will compensate for the cost of alien toil in a socialist society. All industrial labour is held to be inherently repressive and demeaning but redemption for the consequences of "original sin" are at hand in automatic machinery. Rather than foreseeing a restructuring of industry to emancipate workers as workers, automation will liberate workers, not as workers, but as leisured citizens.[58] As with the liberal leisure-as-compensation thesis, the socialist variant looks to the state for a leisure-centered education. Moreover, it assumes that workers would be content to be servile automatons for a working day of two to four hours, and joyous, superabundant players for the rest of the day. This split personality of the worker-player would be intensified since the precondition of total automation is the elimination of skill, judgment, intelligence and independence in work. But, even if this goal of a drastic reduction of working time to avoid the spillover of the repressiveness of work upon leisure is desirable or psychologically possible, it is a long way off. The "post-industrial" society seems to be generating a large service sector (which is less susceptible to the replacement of labour by automatic machinery than the productive sector), and thus hours of work are unlikely to plummet as quickly as some have anticipated.[59]

The main alternative to the leisure-as-compensation thesis is derivative of the Marxian view that industrial work is not inherently oppressive and does not necessarily have a debilitating effect upon leisure activities. Rather it is the capitalist form or organization of production that transforms work into toil and leisure into recreation or reproduction of energies. A socialist economy would integrate work and leisure to promote the highest development of individual capabilities:

> It goes without saying, by the way, that direct labour time itself cannot remain in the abstract antithesis to free time in which it appears from the perspective of bourgeois economy... Free time — which is both idle time and time for higher activity — has naturally transformed its possessor into a different subject, and he thus enters into the direct production process as this different subject.[60]

The transcendance of the bourgeois perspective which opposes free time to work time, one's own time and the boss's time, depends upon a radical alteration of the kinds and uses of machinery and of the organizational forms or relationships by

53

which workers produce. The future integration of work and leisure is not seen as a means to subordinate individual wants and abilities to social requirements and optimal productivity. Rather it reflects Marx's anticipation of a life of work and leisure where individual activities are not incompatible with social welfare, where individual growth or culture is encouraged not because of, or in spite of, social needs.

However, the practice of Marxism has diverged from the theory. For Marx, socialism was to be a 'de-proletarianization' of the working class, an emancipation from the productive collectivity of capitalism. But in practice, Marxism has been introduced into primarily agrarian regions where the state, in fulfilling the role of the bourgeoisie in Western countries, has proletarianized the population. It is within this context that we are to understand Lenin's and Trotsky's enthusiasm for the application of Taylorism in the Soviet Union.

Lenin's aim to transform Russian society into one large factory[61] reveals his often expressed view that socialism does not involve new kinds and uses of technology or new forms of organization of work. The elimination of private profiteering and the centralization of ownership and control of the means of production does not abolish the productive infrastructure of capitalism; the machine, Lenin asserted, now will serve the proletariat. The application of Lenin's ideas has meant that the type of work done by the Russian proletariat is not materially different from that of the western proletariat, although it may have a different meaning to the workers involved. The kinds and uses of machinery in the U.S.S.R., the levels of skill involved, the subdivision and reintegration of the labour force from above, the managerial authority and systems of supervision and control, have been and continue to be similar to the methods used in capitalist countries.

While the Soviet Union has placed a great deal more emphasis on forms of industrial recreation and vocational training in leisure-time activities than capitalist countries do, it has not overcome "the perspective of bourgeois economy" which opposes work and leisure. The integration of work and leisure that Marx advocated has proved, in its Soviet application, to be the subordination of leisure or individual activities to the requirements of the productive collectivity.[62] In short, socialist practice does not actualize the clear alternative to the leisure-as-compensation thesis offered by Marxist theory. Rather, it conforms more to the technicist perspective of western 'leisurists'.

However, prior to an analysis of the effects of scientific management and an exploration of proposals to extend the application of scientific management into leisure activities or to check the negative effects of the system in our lives off work, we must begin at the beginning and examine the life-work of Frederick Winslow Taylor.

Chapter 3

The Birth of Scientific Management: The Rough Beast of Bethlehem

The historical roots of scientific management. Syndicalism and a solution to 'the labour question'. Correspondence of needs of monopoly capitalism and Taylor's personal pathology. Taylor and 'the leisure class'. Worldly asceticism and leisure; Reduction of play to competition. Taylor's views on education. Rising from the ranks; development of the Taylor system. The pacific mission of overcoming unionism. The redemption of 'Schmidt' by Taylor. The speed-up. The opposition between scientific management and financiers. The spread of Taylorism at his death; its export during World War I and the immediate post-war period; its adoption in the Soviet Union.

The word 'manage' derives from the Italian *maneggio*, the training of a horse, and more distantly from *manus*, the Latin for hand. Etymologically then, management is the hand-ling of animals. As we shall see, Taylor repeatedly referred to workers as horses, oxen or gorillas, and frequently drew parallels between scientific management's selection and training of them and the selection of the right kind of horse for the right kind of job and the training of animals for specific functions. His understanding of management thus accords with the etymology of the word, which situates the class of beings to be managed, those incapable of self-direction in the function desired by the manager.

Moreover the usage of the word 'manage' reveals a crucial tension at the heart of scientific management. To manage connotes both omni-competence and impotence, and thus captures the ambiguous relationship between scientific management and its capitalist environment. If one says "He managed to do something", this could be construed as a fortunate accident or as the virtue which overcomes fortune. Either one somehow managed to muddle through in spite of one's deficiency of character or intellect or one's qualities of intellect and character were such as to overcome adverse circumstances. Whether a fortunate bumbler or a masterful hero, the manager stands in a relation to fortune or to external circumstance which one has not chosen or initiated and to which one must adapt oneself. The manager is not an autonomous actor but is rather a reactor to circumstances beyond control who nevertheless strives, Sisyphus-like, for mastery. Scientific management could not rise above the historical circumstances which gave rise to it nor transcend its subordinate position to the capitalist class. Taylor, who came to prominence by quadrupling the productivity of those sectors of Bethlehem Steel under his management, was fired by its owners who, for reasons we shall analyse, opposed his innovations. The ultimate success of scientific management was due more to historical factors external to Taylor's system of management than to the innate excellence of his system.

Scientific management arose in response to the needs of large-scale capitalist production in iron and steel at the end of the nineteenth century. Large trusts, cartels and oligopolies dominated smaller competitive capitalist enterprises, particularly in the United States and Germany. Competition within the nation was exported along with capital; competition of an economic and military character became increasingly international in character. Scientific management answered to this sharpened emphasis on efficiency and productivity in a period of imperial rivalries[1].

The growth of large-scale joint stock companies enhanced the need for professional managers. Capitalists could no longer participate in the management and control of all the enterprises in which they held stocks. Scientific management moved into the place made vacant by non-managing owners. In addition, the rapid growth of industry drew large numbers of new recruits into industry. Scientific management offered a useful technique for preparing a formerly agrarian population for proletarian labour.

Further, as previously stated, scientific management was born in a period of militant unionism or class conflict throughout the industrial world. Taylor presented his system as a means to prevent class warfare in industry. Taylor's biographer and friend F.B. Copley asserted that "all his work in developing a system of scientific management was the direct outcome of his purpose to find a remedy for the labour problem...."[2] A contemporary assessment is that "...Taylor... found the way out of the apparently hopeless impasse of nineteenth century 'class war' between the 'capitalist exploitation' of the labouring man and the 'proletarian dictatorship.'"[3] Indeed, it is this factor that explains the enthusiastic reception given Taylor's *The Principles of Scientific Management*. Within two years of its publication in 1911, Taylor's book was translated into French, German, Dutch, Swedish, Russian, Lettish, Chinese, Hindi, Italian, Spanish and Japanese.[4]

The above considerations do not explain why scientific management arose in the United States and why Taylor was the person to spearhead the movement. Although unionism was growing in the United States, it was less advanced than in some European countries. The pioneering experiments of scientific management were conducted near Philadelphia with a largely non-unionized and ethnically heterogeneous labour force. The absence of united and organized workers in any of the plants in which Taylor introduced scientific management helps to explain why Taylorism was not aborted at the outset.[5]

In addition, relative to Europe, a condition of high wages and labour scarcity prevailed in America. This factor provided a greater motivation to those with Yankee know-how and financial grasp for the intensive exploitation of human capital.

Taylor was the leading light of the managerial movement because of a unique combination of class background, remarkable engineering talent and technological imagination, and a markedly pathological personality. First, Taylor was a member of the capitalist class who rebelled against his background and worked in industry, getting a broader experience in various aspects of machine shop operations than workers ordinarily obtain. He then used that experience to turn on his fellow workers and initiate a system of reforms that could not have been implemented without Taylor's class background.

Secondly, Taylor studied to become an engineer while working as a machinist. His purely engineering achievements, as we shall see, were outstanding, earning him a significant place in the history of engineering. His ability in this area cannot be disassociated from our primary concern, the political dimension of Taylor's innovation. To the extent that Marx's dictum that "the hand mill gives you society with the feudal lord; the steam mill, society with the industrial capitalist." is true, engineers are the real creators of history, of the politics and culture of an age. And to the extent that engineers are not aware of the political or cultural implications of their "purely engineering" innovations, history proceeds independently of the will and consciousness of men. Taylor was an engineer whose ignorance of politics and culture did not prevent him from decisively shaping this century, a man who embodied the drives and conflicts of emerging capitalism and who was in a position to rechannel those conflicting forces.

Thirdly, Taylor, if not quite a certifiable lunatic, was certainly an obsessed and driven man. The compulsiveness, which led to various nervous breakdowns and a relatively early grave, should not be seen as limiting his achievements. Nor should it be seen simply as complementary to his genius, as something which provided the stubborn determination to implement his theories. Rather his madness was his genius, his ability to reduce life experience to problems and to solve the problems he set to himself. It was precisely Taylor's obsessions which placed his technical imagination beyond other efficiency engineers, which made him stand out and lead the scientific management movement.

The following biographical account of Taylor will demonstrate how personal, pathological drives could converge with the needs of industrial expansion in a climate of conflict to produce the dominant pattern of contemporary industrial relations. We shall dwell on Taylor's views on education and leisure because they help to illuminate the principles of scientific management which will be examined in the subsequent chapter. Taylor's "solution" to his own problem of leisure is pertinent insofar as it graphically illustrates his approach to problem-solving and, in particular, his widely acclaimed solution to the "problem of labour."

Frederick Winslow Taylor was born in 1856 at the beginning of the industrial expansion of the United States. The grandson of a wealthy merchant, Taylor was born into what Veblen called "the leisure class". His father was a lawyer who occupied his time in civic affairs, social gatherings, charitable good works, travel, theatre, concerts and literature more than in the practice of the law. Taylor fought against "the leisure class" which his father embodied. He "scorned all his father's qualities and the things his father loved: classical education, scholarly tastes, tact, good-breeding, remoteness from practical affairs, and a fondness for abstract ideas."[6]

Taylor thought his father's gentleness of character bordered on effeminacy. Frederick took after his mother who did not possess this failing. Incorporating her tough-minded puritanism, Taylor became a walking archetype of "worldly asceticism".

Taylor's inner life, which throughout his life he either ignored or sought to control by "mechanistic means, by activity and attention to external detail."[7] bothered him from his youth. Beset by nightmares at the age of twelve, Taylor tried sleeping on corn husks, on a hard floor, on tufted haircloth pillows. Finally, he constructed himself a harness which kept him from sleeping on his back. However, Taylor was an insomniac all his life; he could only sleep when propped up vertically by drawers and pillows. Throughout his life, Taylor had a horror of illness and death. Taylor disliked religious and theoretical speculation as something he could not get a grip or a hold on. Poetry was also anathema to Taylor; he read, and counselled his adopted children to read, only adventure stories. "No introspective literature. No morbid stuff of any kind."[8] Taylor did not value anything which he could not grasp or control. Nor could he trust others to shoulder the burdens he assumed until "the time came when he appealed to his physician to help him stop thinking, to help him cast off the thoughts that were oppressing him."[9] He and his wife both suffered a few nervous breakdowns. Since chemical techniques to oil troubled waters were then not very advanced, Taylor had to accept various home remedies for the cure of anxiety. On the receipt of one such pamphlet, Taylor replied to a friend:

> I have really never before given any thought as to the real cause and essence of worry. It seems to me that your short treatise on the subject ought to be a great help to a lot of us who spend a very large part of our lives in foolish worries.[10]

But his chief cure for inner turbulence was work. As he wrote just before he died, "I look upon work as the greatest blessing which we have, and almost every day of my life thank my stars that, in spite of Lou's (his wife's) illness, I have enough work to occupy my spare time."[11] The principle that governed his activity, derived from Carlyle and the Methodist hymnal, was "Work, for the night is coming."[12]

From his youth, Taylor exteriorized his inner chaos into methodical, disciplined and routinized behaviour. He irritated his friends by his scrupulous adherence to the rules of games and his scientific investigation of the most efficacious way to "play" such games as croquet. "Before going to a dance he used to list, as systematically as he could, the attractive girls on the one hand and the "wallflowers" on the other hand, with the object of dividing his time equally between them."[13] On a tiresome youthful trip to European art galleries, museums, and historical sites, Taylor compiled a list of all the stations the train passed through, with the arrival and departure times. He studied his gait to determine the greatest length of stride with the least expenditure of energy. His personal relations were rarely spontaneous. "There was calculation in his friendliness as there was in his frightfulness. He had figured out its effectiveness."[14] The fear of impulsive instinctual activity led Taylor to calculate, plan and control his inner life and to regulate his behaviour by schedules, routines and mechanically contrived standards. A curious anomaly is that Taylor constantly lacked the punctuality he insisted upon for others, although he levied the same fines for lateness on himself as he exacted from those he managed.[15]

There is a parallel between Taylor's attempt to separate thinking and doing in production, and in his personal life. His desire to transform all work into a mechanical and automatic execution of the orders of the planning department reflects his externalization of inner disorder, his attempt at self-command through the subjugation of his instincts in work and regimented behaviour. Taylor attempted to escape oppressive thoughts and pressing desires by creating, as it were, out of his life a scientifically managed factory where all motions are subject to the planning department and all thoughts are occupied in the efficient regulation of productive behaviour.[16] The irony is that, whereas his personal life was pathological, the effect of Taylor's compulsive drives, which met the technical needs of large-scale capitalist industry and sought to allay industrial conflict, shaped in no small part the character of twentieth century society.

Taylor received the education of a member of "the leisure class". In his youth, Taylor travelled widely throughout Europe, was educated in Paris and Berlin, spoke French and German fluently. At the age of sixteen, he entered the prestigious Phillips Exeter Academy. He led his class in Greek and Latin and passed his entrance examination to Harvard University with honours. His intention to follow his father's career in law was halted at this stage when he developed his father's illness of eyestrain and headaches.[17] Taylor complained of failing eyesight after passing his entrance examination to Harvard and as a result, after a period of restlessness at home, joined the Enterprise Hydraulic Works as an apprentice pattern-maker and machinist. Because the Taylor family knew the owners of the firm, Taylor had the opportunity to learn various kinds of shop operations.

Taylor was a strong proponent of an education on the shop floor. One year in a shop was worth, he felt, twenty years in school. "Taylor believed that technical education was important but not so much as shop culture. Ironically, he did as much as anyone to help destroy it."[18]

In addition to his machine shop experience, Taylor later studied for an engineering degree at night. The reading of complicated mechanical drawings by day and engineering text-books by night led to the disappearance of the eyestrain and headaches which had barred his entry into "the leisure class".

Taylor believed travel and classical education were not only a waste of time but positively unhealthy for youth. He recommended that healthy outdoor sports should be primary for a young boy "with education a long way back, second." And even at university, Taylor felt, football and athletic training was "one of the most useful elements in a college course."[19] Organized sports breed the spirit of competition and co-operation, both of which are necessary for modern production. They motivate young men to give their "all" for the college team. Sport calls forth the most intense exertion, rouses the spirit to overcome opposition, disagreeable obstacles and the desire for ease; it prepares the player for the great game of life. Taylor, who attempted to take all leisure out of work, attempted to impart the spirit of a contest or athletic competition in the time trials and speed records of production. However few workers considered time study men to be disinterested time-recorders and coaches of athletic prowess.

Indeed, one reason why play cannot be equated with leisure is that a major component of play, as J. Huizinga's *Homo Ludens* and R. Caillois' *Man, Play and Games* observe, is the unleisurely element of contest or competition (in Greek, *agôn)*. The agony of contests and competitions, while it promotes maximal physical efficiency and may restore muscular harmony, distorted in mechanical toil, is not conducive to repose or leisure.

Taylor conceived of all play as contests; he was unable to experience leisure. His friend Copley remarks: "Even when he sought relaxation in sport, that same terribly earnest spirit took possession of him and sport became for him almost as nerve-draining as work."[20] As we have seen with regard to "playing" croquet and walking, Taylor saw all activities as an expenditure of energy for some purpose, and devoted his time to the efficient achievement of that purpose.

Whereas others have regarded sports as involving components of fun, sociability, physical recreation and so forth, Taylor viewed games one-sidedly as contests or competitions. For most people, there is no one end or purpose of games. But for Taylor there was. In the mental reduction of games to contests, the plurality of ends is eliminated; the one purpose of a contest is victory. Having established that the sole aim of games is winning, his technical imagination was emancipated to eliminate any obstacles to victory.

While captain of his school's baseball team, he was the first person to pitch overhand; it got results.[21] He "played" tennis, but his backhand was poor. So he fashioned himself a racquet, shaped like a spoon, which sufficiently improved his backhand to enable him to win, with his friend Clark, the U.S. men's doubles tennis championship in 1881.[22] On doctor's orders, he was forced to "play" golf in his middle age. He went about it in the same problem-solving or workmanlike way. He abandoned traditional golfing costume for a more efficient attire, put a file on his irons to impart more backspin, lengthened the woods to allow greater force to his drives (but, alas, with prejudice to his accuracy), and introduced a putter which he strapped on to his arms and legs and then used, croquet fashion, with such scientific accuracy that it was banned by the U.S. Golf Association.[23] Other innovations of his in tennis and golf are still with us — the winch for tightening tennis nets, the double netting, new kinds of turfs for putting greens, etc. But the element of games that was lost by this master problem solver was the component of fun. Taylor said that he would rather go to the dentist than play golf. In losing the element of fun or relaxation in sports, Taylor could not prevent his strained nerves from breaking. His nervous breakdowns, sententious biographers note, resulted from an inefficient use of leisure time.[24]

63

Taylor sought to bring the spirit of contests to the workplace in the form of time records and competitions for maximal performance, while trying to remove all elements of play from work. The application of "science" removed playful components from work as it did for Taylor's play, although the spirit of athletic contests promoted, rather than conflicted with, the one purpose of production. As the reduction of play to contests was the precondition for problem-solving in his leisure time or for discovering the means to eliminate obstacles to victory, the preconditions for applying his technical innovations to industry was a reduction of work to production, the sole end of which is maximal productivity. The problem of work was simply the task of eliminating any obstacles to increased output. But this reduction of work to production also eliminated many of the components of work that workers had valued. The nature and significance of this reduction of work to production will be examined in the subsequent chapter.

So we have seen how Taylor's obsessiveness was an integral part of his engineering approach and inventive genius. His reduction of life experience to problems was the precondition of applying science or technique to the "problems" perceived. His problem-posing and "solutions" to the problems of leisure and work involved the transformation of leisure into contest and work into labour. In this transformation all aims other than victory or maximal productivity are eliminated. Once *the* end has been established, the means or the techniques can be determined by dogged experimentation.

Thus a major aspect of Taylor's emphasis on sports pertained to the stimulating effects of the spirit of a contest and its potentially productive uses. In addition to rousing the competitiveness needed in industry, team sports habituate players to patterns of industrial discipline.

> The boy who joins the football squad is given no sixty cuts a season, nor is he allowed to choose what he will do. He does just what someone else tells him to do, and does it at the time and in the manner he is told, and one or two lapses from training rules are sufficient cause for expulsion from the team or crew.[25]

The importance of athletics in a college curriculum, Taylor believed, was proportional to the failure of the liberal arts to prepare men adequately for work in industry. The humanities are of doubtful social utility and the elective system in a liberal arts programme lacks the restraint and direction men are to have in their working lives. Taylor recommended that the elective system and the lamentably lax discipline in university life, "both of which are better suited to medieval times when each man worked for himself than to the present day when the road to success lies through true co-operation."[26] be replaced by a prescribed course of studies and forms of discipline modelled on industrial methods. It is wrong to think "that the child and young man should be free to develop naturally, like a beautiful plant or flower" as the bent and spontaneous inclination of most students is to pursue the easiest and most agreeable courses. For most of the world's work is disagreeable, tiresome, monotonous. Without industrial methods of discipline and punishment to secure appropriate standards in studies and moral conduct, university graduates will lack the character to succeed in their vocation. Taylor advocated the introduction of a corps of student supervisors who are to be entrusted with the task of spying on their fellows and reporting cases of disorderly or immoral conduct to the university authorities.[26 a]

In Taylor's view then, universities allow an unrealistic degree of freedom to students. Their programme of studies is too individualistic. Students have more options and less structure and discipline than they will ever have again. They are masters of their time like pre-industrial workers; they have no schedules and supervision and thus are prone to sloth and then overwork; they are subject to no restraint but meeting the standards of the examiner. How much better preparation for industrial life is the training for the football team; regimentation, co-operation, supervision and discipline, a division of labour between a coach who thinks and a synchronized corps of bodies who execute the orders of the coach, and so forth.

Taylor's break with the liberal education his father wished him to have led to a completed apprenticeship as a machinist and pattern maker in 1878. As a result of an industrial recession, Taylor was forced to start work as an unskilled labourer in the Midvale Steel Company. His boss was a family friend, William Sellers, whom Taylor referred to as "uncle" but who became, a biographer perceived, his chosen father, a "real man", a captain of industry who could "growl like a lion, kick like a steer, and bawl like a bull."[27]Sellers was a harsh disciplinarian but, unlike most of the other executives and professionals at Midvale, did not consider Taylor demented and in fact encouraged him in his experimentation. Six years after entering Midvale, Taylor rose from the ranks of labour through the positions of gang boss and shop foreman to the position of the works' chief engineer. In his promotion from labour to "management's side of the fence", Taylor earned the enmity of his former friends amongst the workers who reacted strongly to Taylor's innovations and attempts to speed up the pace of production. The strain of fighting with the workmen to speed up production made the youthful Taylor feel "like an old man."[28] Despite threats to his life and industrial sabotage by the workers,[29] Taylor steadfastly embarked on his investigations into the scientific management of the working class and was supported in this perilous adventure by Sellers.

Taylor was forthright in asserting that, had he been born into the working class, he would have been unable to initiate his reforms.[30] Social pressure, in the form of threats, criticism and ostracism, might well have sapped his bulldog determination to speed up production if he had been a fellow member of the class putting such pressures upon him. Moreover, without his social position, management would not have supported him when workers complained that Taylor's methods led to costly machine breaking and work stoppage. But a person of Taylor's class background, without his broad experience in various forms of machine shop operation, would have lacked the know-how to implement his system. Thus the genesis of scientific management depended upon the unusual combination of a capitalist class background and working class experience. More precisely, scientific management began when a member of the ruling class penetrated and learned the "mysteries" of the working class.

Although he clearly used his knowledge in the service of the capitalist class, Taylor consistently maintained that it did not matter whether efficiency experts were employed by labour or management;[31] they did not create the laws of production, but rather discovered, declared and enforced them.[32] Taylor declared that he was non-partisan in the class struggles inherent in capitalist industry, a friend to both labour and capital.[33] Taylor stated that the perspective of scientific management is that of the consumer (a point which will be elaborated on in Chapter 6). He wrote that if we look at production from the partisan point of view of the employer or employee, "we overlook the third great party, the whole people — the consumers... The rights of the people are therefore greater than those of employer or employee."[34] Taylor saw himself to be a mediator of seemingly divergent class interests, a man who sought to end class warfare by focusing workers' attention onto the benefits of increased productivity and away from a concern over the division of the product.[35]

In contrast to the pacific mission of scientific management, unions functioned, Taylor felt, as organs of class warfare; they fought to restrict output and maximize the workers' share of the restricted produce.[36] Taylor employed no union men in any enterprise in which he was involved. Unions, he believed, were an essential means of defence for the workmen in predatory days before science had been brought to capitalist management but they had become functionally unnecessary in an age of disinterested, scientific management.[37] As Taylor's Boswell, F.B. Copley noted, "As a manager he was his own labour leader."[38] The former function of the unions in collective bargaining had become superfluous; Taylor maintained, "As reasonably might we insist on bargaining about the time and place of the rising and setting of the sun."[39] But unions had not simply become redundant with the advent of scientific management, they had become a wholly negative force, blocking technical progress and social harmony. They represented, Taylor thought, the mentality of divisiveness and the convervatism of traditional know-how.[40] In fact, Taylor's life work was the attempt, in the words of Lenin decribing his different revolutionary endeavours, to overcome the trade-union mentality.

Taylor's career at Midvale, which lasted until 1890, not only initiated micro-motion time studies, standardization and classification of jobs, an extended division of labour, and a new premium system of payment (all of which shall be analyzed in the subsequent chapter), but also was notable for his purely engineering innovations in cutting, grinding and tool-feeding mechanisms. He also designed a faster and more durable steam hammer than any of those in operation at the time.

During the 1890s, Taylor worked, with uneven success, as a consulting engineer and a manager in various firms and also wrote a few articles which earned him a limited reputation. Then, in 1898, he was employed in the Bethlehem Steel Company where he achieved world-wide prominence in raising the productivity of unskilled labourers. "To such men, at that Bethlehem which is not in Judea but in Pennsylvania, at length, appeared a Fred Taylor."[41] The coming of Taylor redeemed the working class through their obedience to the laws of the planning department. Taylor's view of the redeemed was less charitable than befits a redeemer*; workers, such as 'Schmidt', immortalized in *The Principles of Scientific Management* and other revered texts, were portrayed by Taylor as having more of the characteristics of oxen or gorillas than of intelligent beings. One might ask, with apologies to Yeats,

> "And what rough beast, its hour come round at last/Slouches towards Bethlehem to be born?"

At Bethlehem, Taylor, together with J. Maunsel White, discovered a new method for making steel which enabled steel tools to cut metal at twice the speed of which they were formerly capable, thus doubling the efficacy of the machine shops in Bethlehem and eventually around the world.[42] But what gained "Speedy" (as the workers called him) wider attention were his micro-motion studies, his use of the stop watch to ascertain standard times for jobs, to subdivide jobs into simpler, less varied tasks, and to co-ordinate these subdivided and more rapid operations under the control of a more complex system of supervision. The extraordinary rise in productivity under Taylor's "speed-up" system was, however, not considered to be an unmixed blessing by the directors of the Bethlehem works. Taylor was fired in 1901—though not

---

* Copley's comparison (Vol. 1, p. 171) of Taylor to Orpheus "who moved stones and charmed brutes" reveals the Taylorites view of the redeemed as much as of the redeemer. A more frequently made comparison was between Taylor and Jesus. Taylor's efforts at overcoming class warfare in capitalist industry and at dislodging the pharisaical "labour aristocrats" or unionized workers from their privileged position earned him a messianic reputation amongst his disciples. To call The Taylor Society's *Frederick Winslow Taylor: A Memorial* a hagiography would be an understatement. Taylor's repeated insistence that scientific management involves a "great mental revolution" on the part of labour and management suggested a religious dimension in Taylorism to his disciples. Copley writes (Vol. 1, p. 124-5): "Yet it actually was the fact that men to follow after him had to undergo a mental revolution singularly like that of a religious conversion. To the undeveloped soul, liberty of self-expression means liberty to follow one's individual ways. That it is hard to give up these ways, no one can deny. It is a giving up of one's self. And life knows no fiercer battle than the struggle of a soul with its self-will. To give up one's self is to find one's self. The individual, having sacrificed his individuality, becomes a greater individual." Increased productivity and profits are secondary to the redemption of ignorant workers.

as a result of pressures from the workmen who were non-unionized. As Taylor said:

> I got into a big row with the owners of the company on that labour question. They did not wish me, as they said, to depopulate South Bethlehem. They owned all the houses in South Bethlehem and the company stores, and when they saw we were cutting the labour force down to about one-fourth, they did not want it.[43]

However his dismissal was not due just to the fact that the rise in productivity meant fewer tenants and customers in this company town. Management also baulked at Taylor's desire to raise the salaries of those subject to the speed up. In addition, Taylorism involved a revolution in managerial procedures in the accounting, inventory, planning, analysis and control of production. The functions of planning, routing, maintenance of materials and tools, job training, preparing future work on job cards, supervising, analysing the work done and alloting the requisite premiums become proportionately more complex as manual labour is simplified. As Taylor never tired of saying, scientific management places a great burden upon management. The work load, transferred from labour to management during the implementation of the Taylor system, was not deemed to be a challenging responsibility by the management of the Bethlehem works. Moreover, the directors of the steel company believed non-production workers to be non-productive and Taylorism necessarily increases the ratio of non-production to production workers. Finally, Taylor's pugnacious and tactless manner in introducing his managerial revolution created many opponents within management and the board of directors. For these reasons, the man who doubled, and in some areas, quadrupled, the productivity of the Bethlehem works was unceremoniously given the sack.[44]

Upon leaving Bethlehem, Taylor said that henceforth he could not afford to work for money.[45] Taylor, who believed it was sentimentality to view labour other than as a commodity, understood his own work to be a moral act and an opportunity to express his abilities. He cited Thomas Carlyle on the advisability of giving oneself away, not selling oneself.[46] That is, the conditions under which the proletariat laboured and which Taylor did so much to exacerbate were markedly uncongenial to the father of scientific management.

69

There was another reason why Taylor could not afford to work for money. Refusing "to work for money" meant that he was free of those financiers who knew nothing of production and had thwarted his work. The opposition between finance capital and scientific management partly explains why such reformers, progressives and socialists as Louis Brandeis, Walter Lippmann and Herbert Croly of *The New Republic* championed Taylorism in the U.S. and why the Webbs spearheaded the anti-syndicalist left in a British endorsement of scientific management.[47] The apex of the hostility of scientific management to finance capital occurred after the Bolshevik revolution and Lenin's avowal of Taylorism, in the call by Veblen, the opponent of the leisure class and a critic of Marxism, for "a soviet of engineers" to rule America. Veblen contacted followers of Taylor in the American Society of Mechanical Engineers in pursuit of this end. Like Veblen and Ford, Taylor considered financiers to be obstacles to technical progress, although none of them thought very clearly about alternatives to capitalist methods of incentive, investment, accounting and control. The three men thought that the captains of industry should rule production unencumbered by financial gnomes; the problems of distribution, they thought, are secondary to those of production and would, in the main, take care of themselves.

Whatever the reasons for Taylor's un-American disinclination to work for money, his new amateur status, made possible by revenue from his patents and from investments, provided him with the opportunity to propagate his principles. Taylor wasted no time in his retirement from paid work. He gathered a large coterie of admirers around him, was consulted frequently on the theory and practice of scientific management and wrote numerous papers and speeches. In 1903, *Shop Management* was the first systematic articulation of his principles. In 1905, he wrote *On the Art of Cutting Metals* and accepted the presidency of the American Society of Mechanical Engineers. His reforms of the Society were such that "there were grave fears that he would Taylorize the whole society."

Taylor than set about the elimination of 'soldiering' in the Armed Forces as well as in private enterprise. However the application of scientific management to government arsenals and shipyards was opposed by the workers affected. In 1911, the year of the publication of *The Principles of Scientific Management*, scientific management was brought to public notice by a strike of workers at Watertown Arsenal against time-motion studies and Taylor's premium system of payment (as well as by Louis Brandeis' championing Taylorism as the means of lowering freight rates).[48] Although it was not the first strike against the introduction of scientific management, the strike at Watertown Arsenal led to the first public scrutiny of Taylor's principles.

In August 1911, the U.S. House of Representatives appointed a committee headed by W.B. Wilson, later to be Secretary of Labour in Woodrow Wilson's administration, to investigate scientific management. Based upon the conclusions of this report, both Houses of Congress considered legislation to outlaw Taylorism in public employment but compromised on a proviso, passed in both Houses in 1914 and 1915, stipulating that appropriations for the army, navy and post-office be withheld if Taylor's system were to be introduced[49]. In 1914-15, a committee, employed by the Federal Commission on Industrial Relations and headed by R.F. Hoxie, produced a balanced report entitled *Scientific Management and Labor*. Despite the publicity for his system of management, Taylor found attendance at these committee meetings sorely exhausting and disheartening. In the face of labour's opposition to scientific management, Tayor's nerves collapsed at the hearings — "a magnificent stag worried and brought low by a pack of wolves."[50] The strain on his constitution prevented him from seeing his principles adopted in his country and in the entire industrial world during the First World War and the immediate post-war period.

In 1915, five years after his father had died at the age of eighty-eight, Taylor went into hospital with pneumonia. While he was in hospital, no one appeared unduly concerned about the gravity of Taylor's illness. "Every morning he wound his watch — systematically. It was a great joke between him and the doctor, this watch-winding of his."[51] His ninth day in hospital was his fifty-ninth birthday. "About half past four the next morning he was heard to wind his watch. It was an unusual hour, but nothing was thought of it. Not until half an hour later did the nurse enter the room, to find he had died there alone."[52] Overwound, his ticker had stopped.*

---

* Readers of Agatha Christie might like to mull over the following facts. Taylor and his followers were attempting to introduce scientific management into hospitals. Taylor hated to waste his time and quite possibly was unable to do nothing productive while in hospital. Although the Mayo Brothers clinic and some other hospitals had applied some of Taylor's principles to the practice of

To be sure, in the last few years of Taylor's life, scientific management spread, despite working class opposition. From 1911 numerous efficiency societies mushroomed, although Taylor considered many members of these societies to be fashionable charlatans.[53] By 1913, *The Principles of Scientific Management* had been translated into the language of every industrial nation. Yet not until the World War, when restriction of output and class warfare were considered treasonable, when numerous efficiency experts flocked from private enterprise to government service and the provisos on government appropriations were overlooked, when hitherto untrained women who lacked the know-how and solidarity required to resist the speed-up methods were trained by Taylorites, did scientific management get widely practiced.

For example, a not uncharacteristic leader in the prominent British vocational journal *The Engineer* (19 May 1911) referred to Taylorism as follows:

> But there are fair ways and unfair ways of diminishing labour costs... We do not hesitate to say that Taylorism is inhuman. As far as possible it dehumanizes the man, for it endeavours to remove the only distinction that makes him better than a machine — his intelligence.

However, the inhumanity of the Taylor system — the thoughtless execution of the orders of superiors — appeared less alien and abnormal to those who experienced the first World War. New sensibilities emerged in wartime. The aspiration of Tory imperialists and Fabian socialists to counter German industrial and military power by the introduction of scientific management into British industry and munitions was actualized during the war.[54]

America's allies in the war sent experts to the U.S. to learn the methods of scientific management, as did Germany and Austria after the war.[55] The French Michelin Company promoted and sent young engineers to the U.S. to learn the new management methods.[56] G. Clemenceau, as French Minister of War, directed a circular to all heads of military

---

medicine, doctors and patients resented micro-motion studies to establish the most efficient procedures. The threats of murder that had been voiced by those subjects to micro-motion studies could be made good more easily by medical personnel than other workers. But of course Taylor's constant attention to his watch might just have been taken as "a great joke".

establishments advocating the introduction of Taylorism.[57] In 1918, the Harvard School of Business Administration adopted the Taylor system as a central feature of its curriculum.[58]

The European working classes, faced with the exigencies of warfare, the shortage of labour, the need to employ unskilled workers and the development of mass production in armaments industries, were unable to mount as concerted an opposition to Taylorism as they had done before the war; "as was only natural in what was practically a state of seige, the workers' organizations tended to abandon any resistance they might have offered to the introduction and spread of American methods...."[59] The rationalization of industry in Europe following the first World War reveals "the direct influence of Taylor's principles, even when the word Taylorism is not uttered, and even, and above all, when care is taken never to speak of systematic scientific management."[60]

Moreover, that most notable product of the war, the Russian revolution, weakened working class opposition to scientific management. The Red Scare, following the war, meant that any form of class conflict in industry was thought to be communist inspired and thus was frequently suppressed. In 1918, over one hundred leaders of the Industrial Workers of the World were tried and convicted of subversion of the American war effort. From 1919 to 1924, 21 states passed Criminal Syndicalist legislation and 31 states passed Red Flag laws.[60 a] In California, over 500 individuals were indicted under Criminal Syndicalist laws.[60 b] In this hostile environment, the I.W.W. was mortally crippled and in general unionism was weakened.[61] The number of workers in the U.S. organized in unions dropped from five million in 1920 to three and a half million in 1921 and remained at this reduced figure for the rest of the decade.[62] An even more marked reduction in trade union membership occurred in Britain at this time.[62 a] Before the World War, every American union was opposed to scientific management.[63] But "both organized labor and the heirs of the Taylor system learned much from the enforced cooperation of the war years. The unions, in their post war zeal for productivity demonstrated their new awareness that, in a hostile climate of opinion, organized labor could not safely allow itself to be depicted as a massive deterrent to material progress."[64]

Moreover the prestige of the Bolshevik achievements amongst the European and North American working class led to a split in the left between the formerly powerful syndicalist movement and the Leninists who stressed political over industrial militancy.[65] Lenin shared the Webbs' and other social democratic leaders' distaste for syndicalism or their desire to manage the working class movement. Lenin denounced syndicalism as "childish", "petty-bourgeois" and "anarchistic" and subordinated trade-unionism to the hegemony of the communist party. In fact, Lenin in *The Immediate Tasks of the Soviet Government*, written a few months after the revolution, said:

> We must raise the question of piece-work and apply and test it in practice; we must raise the question of applying much of what is scientific and progressive in the Taylor system.... The task that the Soviet government must set the people in all its scope is—learn to work. The Taylor system, the last word of capitalism in this respect, like all capitalist progress, is a combination of the most refined brutality of bourgeois exploitation and a number of the greatest scientific achievements in the field of analyzing mechanical motions during work, the elimination of superfluous and awkward motions, the elaboration of the correct methods of work, the introduction of the best system of accounting and control, etc... We must organize in Russia the study and teaching of the Taylor system and systematically try it out and adapt it to our own ends.[66]

And in May 1918, in *"Left-Wing" Childishness and the Petty-Bourgeois Mentality*, Lenin invoked a soviet counterpart to the Red Scare against those who objected to the use of capitalist methods of industry. He wrote that "it would be extremely useful indeed for the workers to think over the reason why *such lackeys of the bourgeoisie* should incite the workers to resist the Taylor system...."[67]

The effect of the Soviet adoption of Taylorism on the world Marxist movement was that "the technology of capitalism, which Marx had treated with cautious reserve and the organization and administration of labor which he had treated with passionate hostility, became relatively acceptable."[68] Thus the workers' movements were split over the opposition to scientific management. The post-war years saw the waning of revolutionary syndicalism in France, the shop stewards movements in Britain and Germany, the Industrial Workers of the World in North American and the waxing of scientific management in these countries.[69] The idea of a managed economy replaced that of workers' self-help as the structural innovations Taylor pioneered became established. The focus of class struggles changed from the question of who should run the mines, shipyards, factories, etc. to the question of in whose interest should the economy be managed.

Scientific management developed after Taylor's death, in part because of the emergence of industrial psychology. Industrial psychology probably owes its birth to Taylorism. Hugo Müensterberg's *Psychology and Industrial Efficiency*, published in 1913, acknowledges this debt at the inception of this discipline. Although Taylor did not explore human motivations very deeply, the study of the means to induce people to work follows from the principles of his system as psychological testing follows from a major principle of Taylorism, namely the scientific selection of workmen. Given the end of maximal productive efficiency and the means to police it (which Taylor provided), the attempt to accomodate workers' attitudes (or morale) to the new structure of industry is a large footnote to scientific management.

However psychological testing in personnel departments, the discovery by the human relations school of "the human element" in production, etc., have been thought to be a modification of Taylorism.[70] Nevertheless, jobs remain Taylorized in spite of the elaboration of new forms of inducement to perform unattractive work.[71] Taylor was doubtless old-fashioned in thinking that inducements to work besides wages "were demeaning and unmanly."[72] But industrial psychologists have not altered the structure of Taylor's managerial revolution; like camp followers and missionaries that follow a conquest, they have attempted to legitimize the new order, foster its acceptance and raise morale. Only rarely, but increasingly in recent decades, do industrial psychologists criticize the kind of work produced by Taylor's reforms or correlate job attitudes to Taylorized jobs. As H. Braverman writes: "Taylorism dominates the world of production; the practitioners of 'human relations' and 'industrial psychology' are the maintenance crew for the human machinery."[73]

A more important development in scientific management is the participation of unions in establishing standards of work and wage-rates. But this departure from Taylor's system has not blocked the penetration of management into what was formerly the enclaves of workers and rarely has led to union encroachment into the prerogatives or responsibilities Taylor

75

established for management (the nature of which will be established in the next chapter).

G. Friedmann writes of the eventual acceptance of scientific management:

> What the facts do show is that, among the working classes, the lure of consumer goods is stronger, in many individuals and families... than their aversion to fatigue and regimentation in work.[74]

The facts however are not as straightforward as Friedmann suggests, since workers almost invariably opposed the introduction of scientific management while aware of the increased income and shorter hours of work made possible under the new system, until the first World War. The initiative to adopt Taylorism during the war did not come from the workers and their powers of resistance were weakened during the war and in the post-war period.

A. Thomas, the director of the International Labour Organization, wrote, in the decade after the first World War, that scientific management had established itself as a given fact about which workers can do nothing. What Friedmann sees as the working class preference for income and leisure, Thomas interpreted as a compensation for what workers were forced to accept — namely, the heightened pace, the strain and the diminished autonomy of Taylorized production. Thomas' preface to the I.L.O. study, *Scientific Management in Europe*, concluded:

> If the work to be done becomes more trying or more exacting, compensation must be found in the increased leisure and in the shorter working hours which the new methods make possible.[75]

Thus the leisure-as-compensation thesis comes to have a prominent place in the literature of social science with the birth of scientific management. Having located the genesis of Taylorism historically, we shall now examine in detail the principles of scientific management.

Chapter 4

Taylor and Schmidt: The Natural Laws of Democratic Elitism

The principles of scientific management. The separation of planning and productive execution. The stop-watch and job redefinition. Overcoming the trade union mentality. The science of production beyond the grasp of workmen; the untenability of Taylor's assumption. Coercion of workers for their own interests. Separation of play and work. Limits to Taylor's aspiration of universal application of scientific management on and off the job. Results of scientific management: higher wages and shorter hours for wage-labourers; increased stress and 'killing time'; atrophy of initiative and cooperative skills; the "problem of leisure"; increased work load for executives and professionals; class cultures and mass culture. "The outside agitator"—irrationalism within technocratic rationality.

The biographical sketch of the father of scientific management, contained in the last chapter, did not include a close analysis of the character of Taylor's innovations. We shall now examine the nature of Taylor's revolution and its underlying assumptions.

Scientific management, Taylor declared, in *The Principles of Scientific Management* and in his testimony before the Special Committee of the House of Representatives, is based on four main principles. The first is "the deliberate gathering in on the part of those on the management's side of all of the great mass of traditional knowledge, which in the past has been in the heads of the workmen, and in the physical skill and the knack of the workmen, which he (sic) has acquired through years of experience. The duty of gathering in of all

77

this great mass of traditional knowledge and then recording it, tabulating it, and, in many cases, finally reducing it to laws, rules, and even to mathematical formulae, is voluntarily assumed by the scientific managers."[1] The second principle of scientific management is to "scientifically select and then train, teach and develop the workman, whereas in the past he chose his own work and trained himself as best he could."[2] The third principle is the establishement of a system of supervision and control "so as to insure all of the work being done in accordance with the principles of the science which has been developed."[3] The fourth principle is to institute "an almost equal division of the work and the responsibility between the management and the workmen. The management take over all work for which they are better fitted than the workmen, while in the past almost all of the work and the greater part of the responsibility were thrown upon the men."[4] That is, management is better fitted to plan, prepare and determine the methods and pace of work. The other half of the work, to which labour is best suited, is the execution of the orders of management.

Taylor makes it quite clear that scientific management does not involve the creation of more work and thus, a greater outlay of wages, except for the task of micro-motion time study. Rather it involves a radical division of labour between thinking and doing and a transfer of the functions of planning production from labour to management.

> It must be borne in mind, however, that, with the exception of the study of unit times, there is hardly a single item of work done in the planning department which is not already being done in the shop. Establishing a planning department merely concentrates the planning and much other brainwork in a few men especially fitted for their task and trained in their especial lines, instead of having it done, as heretofore, in most cases by high priced mechanics, well fitted to work at their trades, but poorly trained for work more or less clerical in its nature.[5]

As a follower of Taylor put it, "The imposing of duties upon the planning department, therefore, consists... in relieving the grimy hands of the machinists of certain clerical routine...."[6] To be sure, the amount of clerical work grew with the Taylorite division of planning and execution. Instead of general instructions from management on the quantity, the form and the date of delivery of produce, scientific management introduced particular instructions on the methods of work, the materials and tools to be used, the standard procedures to be followed, etc. Instead of personal contact and oral communication, the instruction card written in the planning department was sent to the worker. Taylor's standardization of operating procedures involved, as we shall see, supplying the worker with the appropriate tools for a particular task which workers had formerly owned. This change stimulated stockroom and inventory jobs. Instead of letting workers organize their own work teams and establish their own working routines, the scientific managers created managerial jobs in the scheduling, routing and preparation of production. In replacing the apprenticeship system or the vocational training organized by the workers themselves, scientific management instituted new non-production positions. Moreover, the system of supervision required to enforce scientific efficiency opened up additional lower managerial posts. In short, scientific management accelerated the growth of white collar jobs.[7] With the advent of scientific management, Taylor said, "the clerk becomes one of the most valuable agents of the company."[8] In a small factory in which Taylor was completely responsible for its re-organization, the ratio of management to production workers was increased more than five fold. Prior to scientific management 5 persons were employed in the office of the Tabor Manufacturing Works and 105 were employed in shop work; after Taylor's reforms, 20 were employed in the office and 75 in production.[9] Taylor repeatedly insisted on the efficiencies of a high proportion of non-production to production employees.*

However, the sole new function Taylor introduced into production (from which all the other changes arise) was time-motion study. This study consists of breaking a job down into

---

* No such figures are available in the large enterprises, for which Taylor worked, such as Midvale or Bethlehem. He was not responsible for the organization of the entirety of these large enterprises. Thus, pertinent data are difficult to obtain. Certainly he reduced the number of production workers within his sphere of all the firms in which he was employed. But he said the redundant workers were usually employed in other areas of an enterprise in which they worked. The extent to which workers were in part employed as he said is difficult to measure, as is his repeated boast that many formerly production workers were elevated to managerial positions under scientific management.

its simplest component motions and recording the unit times with a stop watch of these motions. By comparing the times taken by various workers in similar motions and by eliminating wasteful movements, the time in which a complete job could be done, barring unforeseen accidents and delays, could be determined by adding up the total of the quickest times of the component motions. This analytic-synthetic method provided Taylor with what he thought was an objective measure of the time in which work could be done and hence should be done. Taylor did not consider the strain involved in imposing upon workmen a motion pattern alien to their individual rhythms. J.J. Gillespie insists, contrary to Taylor, that

> the shortest and fastest motion is not necessarily the best motion, that the structure of the whole pattern of a motion cycle is more than the sum of its atomised parts, and that any motion pattern will be conditioned by the larger physical, emotional and mental pattern of the human organism and the environment.[10]

Moreover, as the Federal Commission on Industrial Relations reported, subjectivity invariably pervades time study and task setting.[11] Wide variations in time studies were common. The divergencies arose from the selection of the workers to be timed, the determination of normal times, the number of readings, the percentage to be added for unavoidable delay, and other factors which were subject to the decision of the time-keepers, many of whom knew little about the character of the jobs they were timing. But even if it were possible to establish accurately the amount of time in which a job *could* be done, this objective measure would not ascertain the amount of time in which a job *should* be done. The workers at the Hoxie Commission insisted that the setting of time standards, without taking into account long-term fatigue, the stress of following non-habitual motions and routines, the monotony or lack of variety, initiative, and skill involved in Taylorised production and other effects of scientific management, was far from a determination of norms for efficient performance.[12] The basis of the unionists' objections to Taylorism was that the job, recomposed of efficient micro-motions, was not the same as the job prior to the time study.[13] Not only did "scientific" analysis lead to an intensification of production but also it tended to eliminate various motions, subdivide jobs amongst various operatives, and constrict the range of skillful application required by the job.

Time study, for Taylor, necessarily involves the transfer from labour to management of the initiative in determining methods of work. Management must take over the responsibility for organizing the methods of production for two basic reasons. The first in that labour, Taylor thought, is prone to restrict output below the optimal level. The second is that labourers, Taylor claimed, are unable to comprehend the scientific laws inherent in their jobs and hence, cannot apply science to raising productivity.

Restriction of output arises from the natural tendency to take it easy or to "soldier". Except when people are playing sports, and straining every nerve for victory, they are inclined to operate at less than maximum efficiency. This natural propensity to "soldier" is exacerbated, especially when workers are organized into trade unions, by "systematic soldiering" or a deliberate policy of restricting output.[14] Taylor insisted that such deliberate withholding of maximum efficiency is misguided since greater productivity in a trade will lower costs, expand the market and ultimately increase the employment in that trade, despite temporary layoffs.[15] He had little sympathy with the workers' view that unemployment arose from overproduction relative to consumers' purchasing power and that such disequilibria of supply and demand, manifest in trade crises, are inherent in the capitalist or market form of production and distribution.[16] Given the absence of planning, Taylor's "speed-up" would, workers thought, aggravate the problem of unemployment. But Taylor believed that the world's ills arose from problems of production and not from problems of distribution. Therefore the restriction of output should really be considered a crime against the world's poor. Taylor thought that since labour believes that it is in its interest to spread out employment by "soldiering", management must take upon itself the responsibility of overcoming the natural inclination to loaf and the deliberate policy of withholding productive efficiency. Thus, he concluded, even if the workers were able to replace their rule of thumb methods with "the one best way" of science, they would find it in their interest to reject the standards of scientific efficiency.

Taylor's view that labourers cannot understand the science of work and apply it in their working lives is more complex.[17] This claim is premised on various assumptions; namely, that workers are likely to have less intelligence and education than those in management, that they lack the time and money to make a systematic study of work and that they lack the interest and inclination to apply science to their

81

working experience. Systematic investigation and application of scientific principles then must have its source from outside the working class.

In order to assess this claim, we must understand what Taylor meant by a science of work. First of all, Taylor's science of work has nothing to do with the principle of physics that work is the product of force and distance or that labour-power is to be measured in units of horse-power, determined by the ratio of the foot-pounds performed by the time taken.[18] Taylor's science was not the application of the theoretical principles of mechanics or dynamics but rather was the systematization and classification of practical know-how. The science of work was not deduced from general theoretical principles but was induced from the observation, comparison and measurement of numerous ways of doing things. Comparative measurement of existing proficiencies established the most efficient methods of the many observed. When Taylor said that scientific management replaces empirical, traditional, tried-and-true, or rule of thumb methods, he did not mean that theoretical science had transcended practical wisdom but rather that a new and more systematic form of empirical practice has replaced the old, less systematic empiricism. Thus, when Taylor asserted that workers cannot comprehend and apply science in their working lives, he was not claiming that it was the workers' ignorance of the principles of thermodynamics that prevented the achievement of an optimal level of walking, of shovelling coal, of operating a lathe or whatever. Rather, he thought, the workers lack the opportunity and relentless determination to observe and compare differing techniques of getting a job done and, as different methods of work cannot be equally efficient, to conclude what is the one best technique and to apply such a standard in production.

Although Taylor stated that his science is beyond the mental grasp of the worker, he also suggested that lack of motivation might account for the failure of workers to analyse and apply the science of efficient production. Earlier forms of capitalist management, according to Taylor, failed to provide incentives for efficient performance (since piece rates were lowered when productivity was raised and thus workers were rarely rewarded for improved performance). Taylor insisted however that scientific management rewards workers for productive innovations and efficient performance. The practice of scientific management only partly substantiated Taylor's claim that workers were no longer inadequately rewarded for their contributions to increased productivity. In one scientifically managed shop, the Hoxie commission reported, a worker invented a machine that did the work of several workers. His pay was increased from 17 to 22 cents per hour.[19] Clearly the inducements to apply science in production are less powerful for workers than employers or management after the introduction of the Taylor system as they were before its implementation. But, since Taylor tended to discount the factor of motivation, he left the misleading impression that the application of science to work must be the task of management because of deficient intelligence in the working class.

This impression is manifested in the examples Taylor cited to illustrate his contention that there is a science of working hitherto undiscovered in all forms of productive activities. The first of these is Taylor's demonstration (which he publicized to exemplify his claim that science is involved in even the most elementary work) of "the one best way" to carry pig iron and load it on to boxcars. Prior to Taylor's time study at the Bethlehem Steel Works, labourers handled 12 ½ tons of pig iron per day. As a result of the study of the science of handling pig iron, labourers loaded 47 ½ tons per day. Such an impressive increase in productivity might be thought to substantiate Taylor's view that "the workman who is best suited to handling pig iron is unable to understand the real science of doing this class of work."[20]

How then did Taylor establish the scientific method of handling pig iron?[21] First of all, he selected one of seventy five pig iron handlers, a 130 pound Pennsylvania German whom Taylor called Schmidt. Schmidt was chosen for his ability at this form of work and for his "character, habits, and ambition". Also the fact that he ran to and from work (since he was building a house for his family in his hours off work) indicated to Taylor that there were untapped energies in Schmidt which might be employed in the service of science. Since Schmidt had the reputation of being fond of money, Taylor approached him with an offer of a sixty percent increase in salary if he would obey orders, without backtalk, about when to pick up pig iron and walk and when to sit down and rest. Taylor's experimentation determined that when pig iron weighing 92 pounds is handled, the optimal level for a first class pig handler is to be under load 43 percent of the day and free from load 57 percent of the day. "If Schmidt had been allowed to attack the pile of 47 tons of pig iron without the guidance or direction of a man who understood the art, or science, of handling pig iron, in his desire to earn high wages he would probably have tired himself out by 11 or 12 o'clock in the day."[22]

Clearly Taylor's conclusion is conjectural. He did not scientifically verify this hypothesis by letting Schmidt determine his pace of work. Taylor's unwillingness to use scientific methods of verification appears to be determined by his attitude towards Schmidt. He assumed that Schmidt was of subhuman intelligence:

> He merely happened to be a man of the type of the ox, —no rare specimen of humanity, difficult to find and therefore, very highly prized. On the contrary, he was a man so stupid that he was unfitted to do most kinds of labouring work, even. [23]

Despite the fact that Schmidt built his own house, Taylor assumed that he was too stupid to do anything but carry pig iron under the direction of management. Taylor's assumption that Schmidt was merely an ox or a gorilla[24] and thus lacking the mental equipment to comprehend the science involved in his work precluded scientific testing of the hypothesis that Schmidt would have worn himself out by noon without the guidance of scientific management. Since Taylor's "science" was based upon speculation, conjecture is necessary if one were to consider the amount of pig iron Schmidt could have handled if left to his own devices.

Clearly it would not be the standard of 12 ½ tons which obtained before Taylor's rationalization, as Schmidt was one of the best men at the job. Seven-eights of the men were laid off by Taylor as they could not handle 47 ½ tons per day, once Schmidt had set the new pace.[25] We do not know how many tons Schmidt was in fact handling per day in a pre-scientific manner, although we can safely assume it was above the average of 12 ½ tons per day. And we do not know how much Schmidt could have handled by himself, given the incentive of a sixty percent raise in wages. It is not impossible that Schmidt's muscles might have told him to rest somewhat more than half of the working day and that he might have loaded the 47 ½ tons without the direction of the scientific managers.

These considerations are not intended to belittle Taylor's achievement in raising the productivity of the pig iron handlers. It is just to note that Taylor has not proven that the science of efficient pig iron handling is necessarily beyond the grasp of the worker. What is demonstrated is that Taylor developed a method whereby management could set standards of efficiency and enforce them in the absence of strong union opposition. Taylor did not demonstrate that time-motion study uncovered laws of motion beyond the grasp of workers; he did demonstrate an effective means to police those "laws".

Another frequently cited example of bringing science to the workers is the science of shovelling coal and iron ore.[26] Taylor managed to raise the productivity of shovellers at the Bethlehem Steel Company from 16 to 59 tons per day, and, in doing so, reduced the number of yard labourers from about 500 to 140. Taylor believed that prior to scientific experimentation, workers were using the same shovel to handle rice coal. with a load of 3 ½ pounds, and iron ore, with a load of 38 pounds. When the optimal load had been scientifically determined to be 21 pounds, the most efficient procedures could be established and maximum output from workers could be obtained. The introduction of "science" to shovelling is predicated on Taylor's assumption that shovellers are too ignorant to vary their shovel size in accordance with the nature of the material to be shovelled.

However, the untenability of Taylor's belief in the ignorance of workers was exposed in his testimony to the Special House Committee. Responding to Taylor's assertion that workers, without the guidance of scientific management, would not be inclined to take a large shovel for light material and a small shovel for heavy material, the chairman of the committee, W.B. Wilson asked, "Is it not the case for hundreds of years that men have used different sized shovels for different weights of materials... so as to get nearer the proper weight a man can handle?" Taylor responded: "I have not the slightest doubt that different size shovels and implements for handling dirt have been in existence for hundreds of years. I do not know it, but I have not the slightest doubt of it."[27] But, despite not having the slightest doubt on this point, Taylor thought that the science of shovelling was beyond the grasp of workers and thus they have nothing to contribute, besides their bodily strength, to the science of shovelling.

Prior to Taylor's rationalization, the workers preferred to own their own shovels.[28] But since a load of 21 pounds was established as optimal, Taylor could not allow the workers to select and own their own implements. Numerous different kinds of shovels were kept in a storeroom and the appropriate one was issued to the workers to ensure an average load of 21 pounds with whatever material was to handled. Taylor then oke down large work teams into individuals or small groups that the output of individuals could be measured and controlled. The implementation of the science of shovelling produced a marked transformation in the relationship between labour and management, a more rigorous system of control over individual workers.

> Dealing with every workman as a separate individual in this way involved the building of a labour office for the superintendent and clerks who were in charge of this section of the work. In this office every laborer's work was planned out well in advance, and the workmen were all moved from place to place by the clerks with elaborate diagrams or maps of the yard before them, very much as chessmen are moved on a chessboard, a telephone and messenger system having been installed for this purpose.[29]

Taylor repeated the metaphor of chess to describe the new science of shovelling in his testimony before the House of Representatives: "It was practically like playing a game of chess in which four to six hundred men were moved to be in the right place at the right time."[30] Establishing the right relation between the men, the tools and the materials was a matter of great pride to Taylor: "Now, that meant mechanism, human mechanism."[31] The metaphor of chess in planning what the ignorant workers are to do is significant not only in the role as objects workers are assigned by the planners but also that efficient performance or mechanical perfection was conceived to be at least partly a game. The idea of human mechanism is a delight in itself, independently of the utilities Taylor expected from such efficient mechanism. When the chairman of the investigating committee repeatedly asked Taylor for the reason for the urgency of a more intensive extraction of labour-power, Taylor was completely without an answer.[32] Efficiency or technique was, for Taylor, an end in itself, as in the playing of chess. W.B. Wilson's questions about the utility of his innovations must have struck Taylor as singularly obtuse, although, on other occasions, Taylor sold efficiency as a means to health, wealth, happiness and culture.

The application of scientific management resulted in an almost fourfold increase in productivity, a corresponding reduction of the work force to almost one quarter of what it had been, a sixty percent rise in the wages of the remaining workers, and a lowering of the unit cost of shovelling material by more than a half. Taylor argued that it is not unjust to increase wages 60 percent for an increase of 369 percent in productivity.[33] For it must be remembered that there are increasing numbers of non-production workers whose wages must be subtracted from the wages of the production workers; the time-study men, supervisors (or teachers as Taylor preferred to call them), accountants establishing new piece rates, clerks writing out instruction cards, messengers bringing directions to the chessmen, and the chess-players in the planning department must also be paid from the profits made possible by the heightened intensity of production. Nevertheless the Bethlehem Steel Company even after paying wages of production and non-production workers and the increased costs of stocking the toolroom, building new facilities for planning and communication, etc., had a 218 percent lower per unit cost.[33 a] If one were to think that the workers deserve a higher increase from these savings, Taylor pointed out that the initiative for the speed-up did not come from the workers.[34] Moreover Taylor indicated that the amount of wage raises was determined scientifically; that is, through experimentation, one can determine the just wage, namely, the lowest wage that will overcome opposition to the new, faster methods.[35] Although Taylor insisted that scientific management does not entail more work from the workers, he was adamant that it is necessary to increase wages to induce workers to go along with it.[36] Taylor did in fact raise wages substantially in many of the enterprises which he re-organized, but he frequently counselled that an excessive raise may lead to loose living and more moderate raises would stimulate proper ambition and an orderly family life.[37] In short, the economic results of scientific management were to increase wages as a fraction of the increase in productivity and to increase profits by lowering labour costs.

The non-economic results of Taylorism are more difficult to quantify but might nevertheless be mentioned. First of all, "Taylor's standardization of tools wiped out the last vestiges of an almost emotional relationship that had existed between the worker and his tools...."[38] Taylor's experience with the Bethlehem shovellers was not unique; in the machine shops as well as the yards, Taylor sought to remove the markings of craftsmanship—the ownership and maintenance of one's tools—that remained in modern industry.[39] Secondly, scientific management strove to reduce working class solidarity through a piece rate and premium system of payment instead of a standardized day rate.[40] Thirdly, Taylorism aimed to eliminate the opportunity for workers to organize their working lives, to choose their work teams and production procedures and to exercise leadership during work. Those workers manifesting leadership or organizational capacities were to be co-opted into management; the players were not to be left with the chess pieces. The planning department relieved the workers of the necessity of adapting their activities to those of others, of establishing work relationships or forms of cooperation amongst themselves.[41]

Another example Taylor cited of bringing science to the workers is derived from the experience of one of his epigones, F.B. Gilbreth.[42] Gilbreth trebled the rate of bricklaying by means of raising the bricks by a scaffold to the level of the workers, subdividing the labour by having one man prepare the bricks and mortar while another lays them, reducing the number of motions in laying a brick from 18 to 5, bringing both hands into operations simultaneously, etc. Since these developments were not directly his own work, Taylor readily asserts that Gilbreth's science was in no sense beyond the grasp of workers. Whether in an uncharitable appraisal of Gilbreth's work or as a more objective judgement of the capacities of workers, Taylor testified:

> Now, I have not the slightest doubt that during the last 4,000 years all the methods that Mr. Gilbreth developed have many, many times suggested themselves to the minds of bricklayers. I do not believe Mr. Gilbreth was the first man to invent those methods, and yet if any man or men had invented Gilbreth's improvements and methods prior to the time that the principles of scientific management were understood and accepted, no useful results could have come from them, because the adoption of Gilbreth's methods demands a degree of cooperation, coupled with a kind of leadership on management's side, which is entirely impossible with the independent individualism which characterizes the old type of management. Under the old system a resourceful man might persuade some, or even most of your bricklayers to adopt the new and scientific methods, but one stubborn man, by refusing to join with the rest, could prevent a realization of any great increase in output. It, therefore, requires in the development of those methods that the management shall assume the responsibility

for seeing that each workman either learns an entirely new method of doing his work or else gets off the job. This is something which no management ever thought of doing in the past.[43]

Thus, scientific management is not so much bringing science, which is above the grasp of workers, to the workers as it is of bringing the science of policing workers to management.* Taylor writes of Gilbreth's results:

It is only through *enforced* standardization of methods, *enforced* adoption of the best implements and working conditions, and *enforced* cooperation that this faster work can be assured. And the duty of enforcing the adoption of standards and of enforcing this cooperation rests with the *management* alone.[44]

The examples Taylor cited of the application of scientific management to loading weight, shovelling and bricklaying do not decisively support his claim that the science brought to the work place is beyond the grasp of the workers. However the case of Taylor's transformation of a machinist's job is more problematic, as Taylor undoubtedly did bring new knowledge to the process of production and did provide standards of performance above those established by the machinists themselves.

Taylor's innovations in this sphere were the result of the combination of the talents of an outstanding engineer and inventor and the qualities of a dedicated sergeant-major. These latter qualities were displayed at his first job at Midvale. Although he was himself apprenticed as a machinist, Taylor broke the apprenticeship system by providing a machinist's training to some unskilled labourers when the other machinists would not follow his orders to speed up production. After training his own machinists, and drastically cutting their wages when they too opposed the speed up, Taylor was able to get the workers to follow directions.[45]

Over the years, Taylor experimented with new alloys of cutting steel, higher speeds of cutting, new angles of feeds, etc.

---

* Aristotle's dictum that there is nothing great or sublime about the science of management, that the manager must just know how to command what the labourers are to do, was transformed both by the growing prestige of science in the modern world and by the democratic ethos that there is no nobler end than maximizing productivity to relieve the estate of people.

He discovered new techniques for cutting and turning metal that doubled the capacity of machine shops around the world. Together with Carl Barth, Taylor devised a slide rule to determine the appropriate speed and feed for different metals.[46]

While his engineering achievements in raising the capacity of machine shop operation were notable, the use to which he put his inventions in order to actualize this increased capacity was not less worthy of note. Taylor did not provide his slide rule to the machinists so that they could determine the standard adjustments to their machine. He thought the machinists would likely bang the slide rule around or else dirty it with their greasy hands.[47] Rather the desired speeds and feeds were determined in the planning room and sent to the machinists on an instruction card. Scientific management eliminated the waste of workers thinking about work. As Taylor insisted, "The time during which the man stops to think is part of the time which is not productive."[48] Thus, although Taylor brought new knowledge to the process of machine shop production, he did not bring science to the producers. It was not that the technique of cutting metals efficiently was beyond the grasp of machinists but that the efficient control of the machine process required a monopoly of science in the hands of management.

In fact, the discovery and application of the science of work led to a depreciation of skill in many kinds of work. Prior to Taylor, the machinist was like a carpenter working in metal. The skilled artisan who had oiled and repaired his machine, tightened its belting, adjusted the speed and cutting angle of his machine and ground his own tools became, after Taylor's innovations, a semi-skilled machine operative mechanically executing the directions of the planning department.[49] Machines were oiled, adjusted and repaired for workers in order to keep the machines in steady operation; tools were provided by the stockroom and ground by a specialist in order to maintain standards of efficient performance. Thus the varied work of skilled machinists who made their own tools and were attached to the machine whose operations they determined was transformed into a standardized function of a replaceable unit within the machine shop. That Taylor was able to do this can only be accounted for by the fact that he never employed unionized men in any shop he managed. Or perhaps, as Taylor commented on the necessary unfolding of history and the limitations to the freedom of the human species, it is that "any device which results in an

90

increased output is bound to come in spite of all opposition; whether we want it or not, it comes automatically."[50]

A question we might consider, upon reflection of this example of applying science to production, is whether efficient machine production inevitably involves repetitive and mechanical toil or whether the kind of jobs Taylor created were predicated on his unverified assumption that a science of work is beyond the grasp of the workers.

A final example of the effects of scientific management is Taylor's experience in raising the productivity of women employed in the inspection of bicycle ball bearings in the Symonds Rolling Machine Company.[51] 120 women were employed 10 ½ hours per day inspecting the ball bearings for defects. Taylor decided, after a time-motion study, that, because the working day was too long, a good part of it was spent in idleness and gossip. He proposed a shortening of the working day to the women.

> The writer had not been especially noted for his tact so he decided that it would be wise for him to display a little more of this quality by having the girls vote on the new proposition. This decision was hardly justified, however, for when the vote was taken the girls were unanimous that 10½ hours was good enough for them and they wanted no innovations of any kind.

> This settled the matter for the time being. A few months later tact was thrown to the winds and the working hours were arbitrarily shortened in successive steps to 10 hours, 9½, 9, and 8½ (the pay per day remaining the same); and with each shortening of the working day the output increased instead of diminishing.[52]

The pace of work was heightened and the chairs of the women were moved far enough apart to prevent talking while at work. The analysis of work revealed that concentration lapsed after an hour and a half of work. Thus, four ten-minute recesses interspersed the working day in which the women "were obliged to stop work and were encouraged to leave their seats and get a complete change of occupation by walking around and talking, etc."[53] These measures allowed the intensity of working time to be heightened so that eventually 35 women did the work that formerly 120 did. "And unfortunately this involved laying off many of the most intelligent, hardest working, and most trustworthy girls merely because they did not possess the quality of quick perception followed by quick action."[54]* The secret of this heightened productivity is "to plan working hours so that the workers can really 'work while they work' and 'play while they play', and not mix the two."[55]

This example of the discovery of the science of efficient work illustrates two central propositions of scientific management. The first is that workers do not know what is best for them. The women had to be forced to accept the shorter hours, the compulsory recesses as well as the more intensive and isolated production. As R. Bendix has written:

> While it has been assumed from the days of Adam Smith to the present that the masses of men were motivated by economic self-interest, Taylor made it clear that workers did not really know enough to maximize their prosperity. ... Hence, they had to be taught and guided by management to achieve their maximum efficiency.[56]

Thus the principles of scientific management conflict with classical liberalism on the assumption of the rationality of the working class. To be sure, capitalist theoreticians and practitioners before Taylor had assumed that workers were deficient in rationality and required external management of their working and leisure lives. However, the point is that a tension exists between classical liberalism and the managerial movement which emerged from that liberalism. We shall see in the next two chapters that advocates of Taylorism are often opponents of liberalism or individualism, paternalistic socialists who share Taylor's assumption of the differential rationality of mankind. The concluding chapters will show that Taylor's view that workers do not know what is best for them has a parallel in the perspective of the leisurist who sees the necessity for the rational management of the leisure activities of the people.

The second proposition is that the application of "science" to production in effect eliminates any elements of play from the experience of work. Taylorism completed the process begun with industrial capitalism of untangling playful components from production. The historians and sociol-

---

* Unfortunately the remaining girls were unemployed the subsequent year when the Symonds plant was closed because of a general over-production of bicycle ball bearings. (Copley, 1969 Vol. 1, p. 466)

ogists of leisure who assert that modern leisure is characterized by its radical opposition to work mirror the maxim of
Taylor that work and play should not be mixed.

We have set forth the principles of scientific management and have attempted to elucidate in the examples Taylor
cited, the assumptions underlying the application of science to
work. Indeed Taylor insisted that scientific management
could be applied to any kind of work, and in part applied it to
clerical as well as manual labour.[57]* He in fact asserted that
time studies could be made on mental operations, and cited his
mathematics teacher at Exeter Academy, "Bull" Wentworth,
who studied the average time students took to solve math
problems.[58] Taylor recommended that his colleague, M.L.
Cooke, study the administration of universities and the efficiency of imparting knowledge in various university departments;[59] Cooke's study *Academic and Industrial Efficiency*
was published in 1910. Taylor and Gilbreth were concerned to
apply time-motion studies to the practice of medicine and the
latter even conducted micro-motion studies on the vocal cords
of opera singers in order to produce a high standard of vocal
quality.[60] In fact, Taylor's friends spoke of "his dreams of the
ultimate applicability of Scientific Management principles
and ideas, not only to every industrial activity but to every
conceivable human activity."[61] Taylor's introduction to *The
Principles of Scientific Management* announces that he intended "to show that the fundamental principles of scientific
management are applicable to all kinds of human activities,
from our simplest individual acts to the work of our great
corporations...."[62] Taylor predicted:

> The determination of the best method of per-
> forming all of our daily acts will, in the future, be
> the work of experts who first analyse and then
> accurately time with a watch the various ways of
> doing each piece of work and who finally know
> from exact knowledge — and not from anyone's

---

* The application of Taylorism to office work was underway towards
the end of Taylor's life but it was not until a few years after his
death that the pioneering works, W.H. Leffingwell's *Scientific
Office Management* and L. Galloway's *Office Management: Its
Principles and Practice*, were published. In 1919, inspired by
Taylor's ideas, the National Association of Office Managers was
formed. The application of scientific management and the resulting
proletarianization of clerical workers is ably presented in H.
Braverman's *Labor and Monopoly Capital*.

opinion — which method will accomplish the result with the least effort and in the quickest time. The exact facts have in this way been developed and they will constitute a series of laws which are destined to control the vast multitude of our daily personal acts which, at present, are the subjects of individual opinion.[63]

Although Taylor thought that efficiency experts could bring scientific standards of excellence to any kind of activity, he was unable to claim any great successes other than with the jobs of the proletariat. It was Taylor's ignorance of the politics of industry that led him to hope that the principles of scientific management could be extended to the professions and the boardrooms of capitalist enterprises.

Despite Taylor's aim of extending the scope of scientific management to include activities off the job, Taylor did not advance very far into the management of workers' leisure time. Taylor's abstinence from alcohol, tea, tobacco etc. were "based on economic considerations as applied to himself personally; were the result of a truly scientific analysis of ways to conserve one's forces."[64] Taylor's charity however led him to universalize his scientific study of personal efficiency. He not only prohibited smoking and drinking at work, fired those with liquor on their breath and prevented his workmen at Midvale from going home for lunch but also worked with church temperance societies and advocated total prohibition of liquor.[65]

As Taylor believed that a steady drinker cannot keep up the pace of scientifically managed production, one might think that the scientific management of labour would render unnecessary the rational regulation of leisure. However scientific curiosity prompted "a careful inquiry" into the domestic lives of his workers.[66] Even those who did not work for Taylor were subject to his views on "proper and sane amusements"; Taylor often interrupted and lectured to courting lovers.[67]

Despite holding strong views about the profitable employment of leisure time, Taylor was not in a position, as Henry Ford was, to incorporate a "sociology department" within his works to prohibit drinking and other unhealthy habits in the private lives of workers. Ford hired an Episcopal minister to head "the sociology department" which was entrusted to spy upon the private lives of Ford employees and root out any disorderly characteristics.[68] If Taylor had the resources of Ford behind him, his most famous workman might not have taken to drink. The Taylor Collection reveals that Schmidt's wife left him four years after he was introduced to the Taylor system because, she said, her husband drank too much.

Contemporary sociology departments which investigate the private lives of individuals are not in the direct employment of large industrialists and thus are unable to prohibit unwholesome leisure-time activities. But the dean of the sociologists of leisure, J. Dumazedier, exhibits the same zeal to suppress drunkedness as Taylor, with the same lack of analysis into the reaons for drinking.[69] Play when you play, but not in a manner which interferes with the kind of work that maximizes play time and makes it harmless. The Russian Time League in 1923 exactly represented Taylor's sentiments on the separation and inseparability of work and leisure.

> Divide your time correctly, time for work and time for leisure. Utilize your leisure so as to work better afterwards.[70]

Despite Taylor's attempt to extend scientific management directly into the sphere of leisure, the impact of scientific management on our behaviour in, and attitudes to, time off work was largely an indirect result of the structural changes in scientifically managed industry. The higher wages and shorter working hours of the industrial working class, which are in part due to the efficiencies of scientific management, have created increased time off work and greater means to afford chosen spare time activities.

However, increased leisure time also arises from the longer life expectancy in the twentieth century. This triumph of medical science appears to have come about in spite of Taylorism. Stress appears to be a major cause of "physical" and "mental" illness. A recent report of a special task force to the U.S. Secretary of Health, Education and Welfare, entitled *Work in America*, concludes that stress and job dissatisfaction, which are attributed to the ubiquity of Taylorism, shorten the life span.[71]

In addition, empirical studies have established a connection between the stress and anxiety engendered by repetitive tasks lacking initiative or skill and the habit of "killing time" off work or occupying one's spare time in a passive, unrewarding and guilt-ridden manner.[72] We have said that Taylorized work does not prepare workers for expansive enjoyments in the increasing spare time that efficient production makes possible. The possibility of thinking about and organizing one's working life, choosing one's routines and methods, adapting them to those of others, cooperating in the organization of work teams, exercising leadership or organizational abilities, learning from one's fellow workers—all of which would better dispose workers to exercise initiative off work as well as on—have been eliminated by the assumption of these functions by the planning departments of management. Cooperative skills become superfluous when the labour force is divided and re-integrated from above, when working methods and relationships are organized by technical experts outside the working class.

The separation of thinking and doing, inherent in the scientific management of work, has a curious parallel in the literature on leisure. Thinking is not included in any of the hundreds of sociological studies on leisure that I have read.[73] Such an omission should not necessarily be taken to be an indication that thinking off the job is as unproductive as Taylor thought it to be on the job. Yet the allegedly mindless activities of citizens are thought to require expert planning and organization by those concerned with "the problem of leisure". Taylor's unverified assumption, at the basis of the separation of planning and productive execution, that the 'Schmidts' need the 'Taylors' is extended into a managerial perspective on leisure. As the authors of *The Social Organization of Leisure in Human Society* assert:

> There are behavioural tendencies associated with certain positions in the social hierarchy; however, the upper/strata are more consistent in their behaviour, while the lower strata do not always follow their own "best" interest.[74]

The ruling classes of modern societies are not the objects of humane and moralistic concern expressed in the so-called problem of leisure. Some concern is expressed by psychologists and theologians about the inability of executives and professionals to relax, to throw off the harness, to retire from the burden of shouldering the world's problems.[75] The addiction of such people to work is thought to be a false religion which prevents an openness to deeper levels of being than is possible when one is striving to be in control of a situation. However such fears are outside the mainstream of "the problem" in the sociology of leisure.

There are two interrelated reasons why the leisure of the ruling classes is not considered problematic in the sociology of leisure. First, since the managerial revolution, the ruling class has less free time to waste than the working class. Second, sociological studies reveal that professional and executive strata participate in more social and cultural activities and have a more varied and active life of leisure than do members of the working class.[76] T.F. Green concludes:

the leisure that many see just around the corner is not likely to be available to the managerial, executive and professional population... Leisure... will probably be available in fullest measure to those who are likely to be least able to understand and appreciate it in its classical sense.[77]

The marginally richer leisure life of the ruling class does not serve, in the sociology of leisure, as a model of productive ease and enjoyment, of culture and contemplation. In fact, the frequently expressed claim that ruling class culture is generally of a lower standard than a century ago or that "high culture" has been debased into "mass culture" has not been vigorously opposed, even by sociologists like J. Dumazedier, N. Anderson and M. Kaplan who insist that the average level of culture has risen in the last century. As stated, the leisure of the ruling class is not a problem for sociology; the alleged decline of cultural standards is not part of "the problem of leisure".

To be sure, members of the ruling class do not see their responsibility to consist in providing object lessons to the workers in the "preferred" use of leisure-time. Its responsibilities consist in the time-consuming function of seeing that the world is not under-managed. A study of 17,000 American executives indicated that, although many said they wanted more leisure time, few availed themselves of the opportunity to take it.[78] As H.L. Wilensky writes:

It seems likely that we are headed toward an organization of work in which a small group of executives, merchants, professional experts, and politicians labour hard and long to control and service the masses, who in turn are going to 'take it easy' on a progressively shorter work week, in jobs which de-emphasize brawn and native shrewdness and play up discipline, reliability and trained intelligence.[79]

While members of the ruling class would perhaps not accept Taylor's characterization of them as "servants of the workmen,"[80] the Taylorite principle that management is to assume much of the work load which previously burdened

97

workers would appear to be widely accepted. The education necessary to obtain dominance over the working class may not be the kind of technical specialization that Taylor desired but it is certainly not the liberal education advocated by Cardinal Newman and lampooned in Veblen's *The Theory of the Leisure Class*. Contemporary ruling classes then have established a hegemonic position by relegating leisure activities to the periphery of life interests.

Before concluding our chapter on scientific management, it is perhaps fitting to discuss the contribution made by the best-known of the practitioners of scientific management, Henry Ford. Ford's mass production techniques are simply an extension of Taylor's subdivision of tasks, standardization of tools, parts and operating procedures, separation of planning and execution of production, concentration of the organization and routing of production in the planning department, etc. Doubtless Ford's development of the assembly line further raised productivity, lowered costs of produce, and separated workers from the products of their toil and an understanding of what in effect they were doing. Also the high wages Ford paid, prompted by the desire to reduce the high turnover rate of mechanics doing repetitive and unskilled work,* and by the aim of eliminating the influence of "Wobbly" agitation outside Ford plants, brought workers increased buying power and enlarged the market for produce. Of course, this is simply an application of Taylor's principle that high wages are necessary to induce workers to accept the direction of scientific management.

Ford's creative contribution to scientific management is the development of the theory of "the outside agitator". The idea was suggested to Taylor during the walk-outs and strikes against scientific management after 1910. Taylor simply could not believe that there was spontaneous opposition by the workers to his reforms on their behalf and so was forced to the conclusion that some labour agitators from outside the yards and plant where scientific management was introduced had

---

* The turnover rate for 1913, when Ford brought in assembly line innovations and later introduced his five dollar per day wage, was 380 percent. In order to add 100 men to factory personnel, it was necessary to hire 963. High wages, Ford said, were one of his chief cost-saving devices. Labour turnover and absenteeism dropped drastically; Ford could "skim the cream" from the labour market and could greatly reduce the costs of training new workers. See Burlingame, 1957, p. 76; Sward, 1948. p. 48-56.

gulled the workers into action against their own best interests.[81] However, a fully developed theory of the outside
agitator required the creative genius of Henry Ford. Ford
wrote:

> There is in this country a sinister element that
> desires to creep in between the men who work with
> their hands and the men who think and plan for the
> men who work with their hands. The same influ-
> ence that drove the brains, experience, and ability
> out of Russia is busily engaged in raising pre-
> judice here. We must not suffer the stranger, the
> destroyer, the hater of happy humanity, to divide
> our people. In unity is American strength — and
> freedom.[82]

Ford's great contribution was to unite Taylor's exe-
cration of financiers and labour agitators into one race of
outsiders. Ford's identification of the sinister element which
subverts the work of the men who think and plan for brainless
labourers earned him the highest award of the Third Reich,
The Grand Cross of the German Eagle.[83]

Since the theory of the outside agitator has had a
significant history in this century, it might be worthwhile to
analyse the components of the theory and locate its centrality
in the principles of scientific management. The outside
agitator is mentioned in C. Babbage's *On the Economy of
Machinery and Manufacturers*, published in 1832. Babbage
presented a cardinal component of this theory by insisting that
the long term interests of capitalists and workers are identical.[84] However, he admitted that short-run unemployment
from technological innovation and trade depressions makes
the interests of the two classes appear to be opposed. This
appearance of diverging class interests prompts union agitation and requires the education of workers for them to see
the reality of a harmony of class interests.[85] But Babbage's
view lacked the modern perspective on the outside agitator, as
capitalists were not viewed as the disinterested servants of
humanity and workers were seen to have at least apparent
sources of grievance.

The outside agitator appears in *Hard Times* in the
person of Slackbridge and Dickens adds the essential ingre-
dient in the person of Stephen Blackpool, an honest, industrious patriotic worker, possessing every excellence but that of
intelligence, who is employed as a power-loom weaver in the
factory of Mr. Josiah Bounderby. Although the industrial

unrest at Bounderby's factory appears to be due to Slack-bridge's agitation — certainly the Stephen Blackpools of this world are too loyal and too dumb to rebel — Dickens makes it clear that even if all the Slackbridges in the world were drowned, the sources of industrial unrest would remain.[86]

It is when the Stephen Blackpools are coupled with a humanitarian materialism, directed by an elite armed with science, that the theory of the outside agitator gains momentum. For there can be no legitimate arguments against science, that impartial but warm-hearted judge of the aspirations of humanity. Taylor's Schmidt is a Stephen Blackpool who is managed not by Bounderby but by science. The natural fit between the solid, honest, hard-working and stupid Schmidt and a management that uses science for Schmidt's interests can only be severed by a malevolent outside agitator who is able to lead Schmidt astray.

Ford developed this theme. He insisted that the division of labour and mechanical pacing of work required by his methods accord with the inclinations and capacities of most people who like unskilled repetitive routines about which they are not compelled to think.[87] The division of production into the thinkers and the doers is not just a fact of modern production but a requirement of human nature.[88] The sound judgement of the unthinking masses would recognize the authoritiy of the thinkers were it not for that selfish Orientalism which does not understand the cult of service of the planners and which worms its way between the natural interdependence of the brains and the hands, leading to class warfare.[89] The natural virtue of the solid average American working man, who needs others to do his thinking for him, would never oppose the capitalists who serve him. Outside agitators are necessary to activate class conflict. The fact that Ford tapered off his anti-Semitism when Ford sales slumped should not offset his contribution to the theory of scientific management.[90]

A non-capitalist parallel of the marriage of science and the average working man can be found in Lenin's portrait of the proletariat in *One Step Forward, Two Steps Back*. Lenin portrays the proletariat as serious, honest, industrious, resolute but lacking the intelligence to go it alone;[91] science must be injected into the workers' movement or else they will fall prey to labour aristocrats who will misdirect the movement for their own particular ends. Needless to say, the outside agitator has played a significant role in socialist as well as capitalist scientific management.

The designation of opposition to scientific management as outside agitation introduces the politics of irrationality into twentieth century industrial societies. 'The outside agitator' can be used as an instrument of state by a technical elite. When J. Habermas asserts that "there is no administrative production of meaning,"[92] he overlooks the possibilities contained in 'the outside agitator' for orienting those subject to administration. On the other hand, J. Ellul's prognosis that a narrow calculating rationality will increasingly permeate industrial states, reducing politics to a cost-benefit analysis of technical experts,[93] does not take into account the hysterical irrationality engendered by any opposition to technocracy. The image of the loyal, patriotic and industrious American, German or Russian who needs leaders and whose naturally sound judgment can be corrupted by un-American, un-German or un-Russian agitators can generate paranoia even within the scientific leadership.

Establishment fears about the commitment of workers to parliamentary democracy have recently been raised in connection with scientific management. For example, the defection of a number of workers from the Democratic Party to George Wallace's Independent Party prompted a special task force of the Federal Department of Health, Education and Welfare, as well as some unofficial concerned citizens, to call for a reversal of the effects of scientific management.[94] Industrial workers, increasingly uprooted from a sense of community and unattached to work, are thought to be, as it were, floating without ballast and apt to be swept away by whatever demagogic winds play upon their resentments.

However Taylorism is only a threat to liberal democracy to the extent that industrial authoritarianism and political democracy cannot co-exist. Indeed one might even say that liberal democracy is based on the paradox that workers may not exercise judgment within the areas of their special competence but may safely exercise judgment outside their sphere of expertise. That is, although workers are expected to judge policies and candidates for government, they are not allowed to exercise judgment within their working experience, even to the extent of electing their managers. In fact, industrial self-government might well be incompatible with the kind of capitalist economy in which liberal democracy flourishes. Capitalists, as well as Marxists and syndicalists, are inclined to think that the maintenance of industrial authority is more essential than the character or constituency of political representatives. Scientific management, along

101

with syndicalism, rests on the postulate that the roots of authority and subordination live in industry, rather than in political parties, parliament and other state institutions. Thus, while political democracy does not entail industrial democracy, Taylorism highlights the tension in liberal democracy between industrial authoritarianism and political democracy.

The paradox that workers are subject to unquestioned authority within the sphere of what they know best while they are free of authority outside their area of competence may even be taken as a contradiction, that is, as something wrong, unsupportable, in need of a decisive resolution: The manner in which Thorstein Veblen resolved this contradiction is the subject of the next chapter.

Chapter 5

The Supersession of Leisure by Technocratic Socialism

Veblen's view of "the instinct of workmanship" passing from industrial workers to production engineers. His advocacy of a soviet of engineers; opposition to trade unionism; socialism from above. Efficiency and leisure as "the non-productive consumption of time". Liberal education as "a conspicuous waste of time" and "idle curiosity". Utility of social science. Organization and routinization of entertainments — a problem of efficiency.

Taylor's contemporary and admirer, Thorstein Veblen, was the first sociologist of leisure and the theoretical progenitor of the political movement of the 1930s known as technocracy.[1] The following analysis of Veblen's thought will reveal the intimate association between his understanding of leisure and his advocacy of scientific management in an overtly political form.

Veblen's best known works, *The Theory of the Leisure Class* and *The Theory of Business Enterprise*, were published in 1899 and 1904, before scientific management came to public prominence. In these books, Veblen supported working class opposition to capitalism, and attacked the mode of life and cultural pretensions of the financiers, politicians, warriors, athletes, priests and other such gentlemen and gentlewomen that comprised what he called the leisure class. What Veblen detested most about capitalism was not so much the extraction of profit from producers or the oppression workers experience in the process of production as it was the waste and restricted output inherent in the chaos and class divisions of a competitive mode of life.[2] The leisure class impeded productive efficiency; it blocked, Veblen alleged, "the instinct of workmanship" residing in the working class, preventing the public from having the optimum benefit of those technical skills essential to industrial society.[3]

In *The Theory of Business Enterprise*, Veblen particularly champions the Nordic strain of the working class as "more socialistic" than other progressive elements of the population.[4] He writes that "...the dolicho-blond stock*... is perceptibly more efficient in the machine industries, more readily inclined to think in materialistic terms, more given to radical innovation, less bound by convention and prescription...."[5] However, in *The Instinct of Workmanship*, published in 1914 when scientific management had come into public prominence, Veblen considered this "instinct" to have its most vital embodiment in the efficiency engineers.[6] The technical skills and drive essential to a technological civilization had passed, with the emergence of scientific management, from labour to management, or more precisely, to the production engineers. With his espousal of scientific management, Veblen not only ceased to think that 'dolicho-blond' workers were the chief bearers of advancing machine technology but also came to believe that the "the population of Christendom as it stands" cannot tolerate "that unmitigated materialism and unremitting mechanical routine" required by machine technology.[7] Thus Veblen advocated the creation of a hybrid race with instincts of workmanship more compatible with the requirements of modern industry than those of workers of European stock.[8]

No eugenic infusion of workmanship was necessary for the capitalist class however. Veblen wrote, in *The Instinct of Workmanship*, that "no class of men have ever bent more unremittingly to their work than the modern business community. Within the business community, there is properly speaking no leisure class, or at least no idle class."[9] Yet the inefficiencies of capitalist production are such that Veblen looked forward to the day when the efficiency engineers would govern society at large.[10]

Veblen contacted members of the Taylor Society and attempted to influence the American Society of Mechanical Engineers in the direction of social concern and political organization.[11] But it was not until the United States participated in what Veblen held to be a capitalist world war[12] and

---

* The dolicho-blonds are those long-faced lugubrious types found in Scandinanvian movies or in portraits of Veblen.

the Bolshevik revolution provided a practical example of a non-capitalist form of industrial and political organization that Veblen wrote a series of articles calling for "a soviet of engineers" to take power in America and destroy the pecuniary interests of finance capital and organized labour which inhibited maximum productive efficiency. These articles, later published as *The Engineers and the Price System* and favourably reviewed in *The Bulletin of the Taylor Society*, argued that trade unions were one of the vested interests concerned with salesmanship, or the endeavour to make as much as one can from the market for as little as one can, than with workmanship, or efficient service to the common good.[13] The engineers, on the other hand, were amply endowed with the instinct of workmanship. Moreover, they had greater power than the working class since they could cripple American industry with a general strike and, subsequent to a revolutionary crisis, could re-organize and administer the national economy.[14] Veblen wrote:

> The material welfare of the community is unreservedly bound up with the due working of this industrial system, and therefore with its unreserved control by the engineers, who alone are competent to manage it. To do their work as it should be done these men of the industrial general staff must have a free hand.... [15]

Veblen continued to advocate the creation of a technical general staff of engineers and to castigate the unions and other pecuniary interests for sabotaging an efficient economy in *The Vested Interests and the Common Man*, and *Absentee Ownership*, both published in 1924. Veblen called the American Federation of Labour a monopoly or vested interest "which unbidden assumes to speak for the common man."[16] Since Veblen identified "the consumer" with "the common man",[16a] union elections are not considered a mandate from the common man. The self-selecting general staff of technicians, which Veblen recommended, represent consumer interests and thus, although "unbidden", "speak for the common man". The common man is thus best served by the unhindered direction of the economy by the efficiency engineers. It was a few years after Veblen died, during the ill-fated presidency of the engineer Herbert Hoover, that Howard Scott used Veblen's prestige to found the Technocracy movement.

Veblen's earlier commitment to the industrial working class as the source and motive force of a new, non-pecuniary industrial civilization was transformed into a desire to impose socialism from above, from outside the working class. Despite this change in politics, Veblen's basic ideas remained unchanged and recurred constantly throughout his writings.

These ideas derived from the evolutionism and Social Darwinism of Herbert Spencer and William Graham Sumner.[17] Historical evolution, according to Veblen, was a struggle for existence, conditioned by the manner in which people produce their means of subsistence, beginning with a predatory hunting type of society, through a pastoral nomadic type, a settled agrarian mode of hierarchical estates, a commercial contractual society of independent artisans and farmers, and culminating in an industrial collectivity. These types of societies are rarely found in a pure form as the legacy of past modes of the struggle for existence pervade more advanced forms; the activities and attitudes of pre-commercial status societies continue into market societies, the individualist and commercial thoughts and practices appropriate to a contractual society of farmers and artisans pervade (inappropriately, Veblen believed) an industrial society. Thus although historical evolution is powered by technical developments which shape the manner in which the struggle for existence manifests itself, cumulative archaic residues constitute a drag on the drive for technical mastery and for an efficient organization of society which promotes material betterment.[18]

Although Veblen conceived of human societies historically, he believed that various constant needs or drives actuate historical evolution. Besides material needs, Veblen postulated three basic innate drives; the instinct of workmanship, the desire for disinterested knowledge or idle curiosity, and the need for pre-eminence or status.[19] Human cultures are largely variations compounded of differing proportions of these components of human nature.

The instinct of workmanship which Veblen says "might well be called the engineer's conscience"[20] has existed throughout the ages but only has come to the fore in late nineteenth century America.[21] Man, Veblen asserts, "is possessed of a taste for effective work, and a distaste for futile effort. He has a sense of the merit of serviceability or efficiency and of the demerit of futility, waste or incapacity."[22] Hitherto futility has often been preferred to utility because of the opprobrium attached to labour, to the low status of the labourer. The invidious comparisons people make with one another leads to a degradation or a contamination of the instinct of workmanship.[23]

In all societies, various occupations are considered worthy and others unworthy; the former are those requiring prowess, challenge, a sense of exploit or adventure; the latter involve diligence, constancy, industriousness, drudgery. In primitive societies, the division between worthy and un-worthy occupations followed sexual lines.[24] The men killed the animals, the women dragged them home. Hercules could once clean the Augean stables but repetitive domestic chores were unworthy of a man. More advanced societies, based on slave or serf labour, gave rise to a conception of work as base and non-work as noble.[25] Leisure or "the non-productive consumption of time"[26]acquired a value. The source of the utility of leisure is not so much material satisfaction as it is the mark of social status; leisure activities are primarily means to flaunt social superiority and to obtain the respect of others. The greatest honour accrues to the least visibly useful activity or to the most futile or luxurious display. Thus the desire for status has submerged the instinct of workmanship and has elevated conspicuous consumption, leisure and waste. The activities of leisure are born of a desire for status; they are not intrinsically choiceworthy but are chosen to flaunt one's power, to display that one does not have to labour.[27]

Veblen failed to see the utility that Taylor saw in sports; they were just a waste of time for him, futile except for the purpose of displaying one's leisured status.[28] Similarily, cour-tesy or good manners not only displays that much time has been spent in acquiring these skills but also is a symbolic recreation of the mastery and subservience of a hierarchical age, manifesting a desire to conciliate or show goodwill. Such a ceremonial code is unnecessary in a vigorous industrial age but its futile continuance indicates the prevalence of the desire for status.[29] Furthermore, with modern contrivances, domes-tic servants have no utility, Veblen asserted, but the futile activities of servants conspicuously add prestige to their employers.[30] An education in the classics or the humanities is not only a "conspicuous waste of time and labour"[31] but its concern with "values" rather than facts and causes reflects a honorific rather than a scientific viewpoint, a pre-industrial rather than an industrial standpoint.[32] The higher learning of the leisured class enables it to make invidious comparisons or judgments of value but contributes nothing to "civic and industrial efficiency."[33]

Reversing the customarily accepted causal relation between science and industry, Veblen asserted that the industrial age fathered modern science. Science or factual knowledge, according to Veblen, emerged not only from the recognition of causal sequence in phenomena but also from the desire to control and systematize man's environment and to eliminate chance and subjectivity from human experience. The empirical, materialist outlook of modern science arose from the mechanical efficacy, the prosaic cause and effect, the statistical computations, the planning to avoid chance and individuality, and the methodical and disciplined character of modern industry.[34]

Industrialism fosters a depreciation of waste and futility[35] as well as the materialist perspective of modern science. The development of industry then provides increasing outlet for the instinct of workmanship and leads to a devaluation of status-seeking or leisure activities, thus diminishing the emphasis on the humanities and other non-scientific components of what was formerly a liberal education. By emancipating the sense of workmanship or securing its dominance over the desire for status, industrialism also liberates idle curiosity, or the desire for knowledge "apart from any ulterior use of the knowledge so gained."[36] The object of idle curiosity is science or factual knowledge (as distinct from the cultural attainments of the leisure class which serve ulterior purposes of display and honorific judgment). Such factual knowledge is potentially useful. Veblen asserted that the knowledge gained through idle curiosity will later be put to effect through the instinct of workmanship.[37]

The education of the leisure class is not an expression of idle curiosity since it serves the purpose of display and of making invidious comparisons or judgments of value. Thus a liberal education, by Veblen's dialectical twist, becomes servile; it serves the base purpose of enhancing, demonstrating and enforcing one's social status: it does not enlarge the store of human knowledge or power.[38] No one was more fully Baconian than Veblen, with regard to the proper use of education, or ascribed more completely to the following dictum of the great progenitor of utilitarianism:

> For men have entered into a desire of learning and knowledge, sometimes upon a natural curiosity and inquisitive appetite; sometimes to entertain their minds with variety and delight; sometimes for ornament and reputation; and sometimes to

enable them to victory of wit and contradiction; and most times for lucre and profession; and seldom sincerely to give a true account of their gift of reason, to the benefit and use of men; as if there were sought in knowledge a couch whereupon to rest a scarching and restless spirit; or a terrace for a wandering and variable mind to walk up and down with a fair prospect; or a tower of state for a proud mind to raise itself upon; or a fort or commanding ground of strife and contention; or a shop for profit on sale; and not a rich store-house for the glory of the creator and the relief of man's estate. But this is that which will indeed dignify and exalt knowledge, if contemplation and action may be more readily and straightly conjoined and united together than they have been... that knowledge may not be as a courtesan for pleasure and vanity only or as a bondwoman, to acquire and gain to her master's use; but as a spouse, for generation, fruit and comfort.[39]

Veblen's *The Higher Learning in America*, which lobbied for the vested interests of scholarship and science, for their independence from business, commercial and professional interests, appears to conflict with Veblen's thorough utilitarianism and his view that an industrial system must be fully integrated. Since he believed that an industrial society is an integrated network of activities the efficiency of which depends on the coordination of its component parts,[40] his view that a university should be independent of its surrounding environment, an oasis for the gratification of idle curiosity,[41] appears to be inconsistent.

To be sure he favoured the expansion of technical and professional colleges and institutes, but these are to be kept quite distinct from universities. Universities are not to provide vocational training and are not to be subject to the pressures of commercial and professional life. Whereas time-motion and cost-efficiency studies are appropriate to technical and professional colleges, they are inappropriate, Veblen felt, for a university.[42] Earlier universities, from the Middle Ages to the present, Veblen asserted, were largely professional schools but a modern university should transcend utilitarian concerns.[43]

Universities are a unique part of an industrial system in that they do not directly serve the machine. But since Veblen believed that the discipline and mechanical character of modern production imposes itself on, or governs, the habits of thought of scholars,[44] there will be a correspondence between the factual, causal rather than honorific, non-animistic or non-teleological, statistical, quantifiable, impersonal research and the needs of the industrial system. That is, although universities are not part of the industrial machine, they produce raw material or facts that will later be put to use by the social engineers.[45] A higher utility dictates that the function of universities is not geared to immediate utility so that there will be progress in the knowledge which will be building materials of the new civilization.

An education of the tastes and sensibilities, a development of the character and of general culture has no place in Veblen's scheme of things; the factual knowledge of "subjectless" science eschews these decorative displays which inhabit productive serviceability. The character type, or form of personality, produced by a liberal education is not an interchangeable, replaceable and useful cog in the industrial machine.[46] But the idle curiosity of the scientific researcher, formed, by the workmanlife performance of the industrial system and unencumbered in his education by any cultural accoutrements, is of great service to the development of the race. Thus there is no incompatibility between Veblen's demand for independent universities where curiosity may be idle and his advocacy of greater practicality in all forms of education, once one considers his view that the form of the quest for knowledge is governed by a habituation to current working practices. Freeing the university from outside influences will emancipate it from the interests of the leisure class; left to itself, the university will increasingly emphasize the natural and social sciences at the expense of the liberal arts.

Veblen stated that he was not dishonouring the humanities in calling them "a conspicuous waste of time and labour"; he was only concerned with pertinent facts.

> ...however substantial may be the merits of the contention that the classic lore is worthier and results in a more truly human culture and character, it does not concern the question in hand. The question in hand is as to how far these branches of learning, and the point of view for which they stand in the educational system, help or hinder an efficient collective life under modern industrial

circumstances, — how far they further a more facile adaptation to the economic situation of the day.[47]

A liberal education, like other leisure pursuits, does not further an efficient collective life. Leisure activities are residues of a pre-industrial system and must be transformed, made less individual and irregular, scheduled and synchronized to make optimal use of time off work. Veblen wrote:

> ...amusements and diversions, much of the current amenities of life, are organized into a more or less sweeping process to which those who would benefit by the advantages offered must adapt their schedule of wants and the disposition of their time and effort. The frequency, duration, intensity, grade, and sequence are not, in the main, matters for the free discretion of the individuals who participate.[48]

Modern leisure is then to accord with the instinct of workmanship or "the engineer's conscience" whereas the leisure activities Veblen attacked, the play and display born of competitive status-seeking, conflict with such an instinct. Efficiency or workmanship demands that superabundant expression, play, or activity with no productive purpose, be suppressed or at least integrated with a form of collective life that maximizes productivity.

> To take effectual advantage of what is offered as the wheels of routine go round, in the way of work and play, livelihood and recreation, he must know by facile habituation what is going on and how and in what quantities and at what price and where and when, and for the best effect he must adapt his movements with skilled exactitude and a cool mechanical insight to the nicely balanced moving equilibrium of the mechanical processes engaged.[49]

The leisure activities of industrial societies require scheduling, synchronization and coordination as do productive activities. Leisure, or the non-productive consumption of time, must be harmonized with its productive consumption. Veblen did not discuss the manner in which leisure activities will be managed by the soviet of engineers who are to oversee industrial society and plan the most efficient way to integrate productive and non-productive activities. Doubtless Veblen wished to leave "the problem of leisure" to that problem-solving race of engineers. Engineers, after all, have least pretension, of all professional groups, to that culture Veblen despised.[50] They could reasonably be entrusted with the task of eliminating leisure as traditionally understood, as Veblen impishly characterized it in *The Theory of the Leisure Class.*

However much one may sympathize with Veblen's acute debunking of the cultural pretensions of the American rich — and Veblen possessed considerable perceptiveness and a magnificient prose style to support his acuity — it is essential to realize that Veblen's thought is an attack on culture in general. Veblen's critique failed to account for the expressive, the playful, the outpouring, the artistic, the erotic, the religious, the reflective and the meditative components of culture;[51] he reduced culture to a struggle between the agonistic and the utilitarian elements of human life. Veblen's pose as a detached observer of human affairs, a sociologist beyond good and evil, has fooled none of his commentators.[52] Rather one should visualize Veblen as a dolicho-blond beast with battle axe raised to lay low a culture he cannot understand.

Chapter 6

The Management of the "Average Sensual Man"

The Webbs' relation to communism and opposition to syndicalism. The perspective of the consumer rather than the producer. The dictatorship of the proletariat seen as the dictatorship of consumers' representatives. Reasons for opposition to syndicalism and syndicalist opposition to 'Sidney-webbicalism'. Overcoming sensuality in the name of the consumer. The work ethic as the religion of the new ruling class. Conservatism and leisurely practices in the working class. Why the 'average sensual man' needs scientific management and why the Webbs needed to manage the 'average sensual man'; industrial relations as psychological conflict writ large.

In order to illuminate more fully the politics of scientific management, we shall explore the thought of two dominant members of the Fabian Society, Sidney and Beatrice Webb. Although the connection of the Webbs to Taylorism is limited to an endorsement of scientific management[1], the structure of their industrial sociology closely parallelled the thought of Taylor and Veblen. S. Webb's definition, "Civilization, so far as it is real, is everywhere at war with waste"[2] might well have been enunciated by Taylor and Veblen as their guiding principle. While the Webbs' advocacy of the scientific management of the working class arose from somewhat different sources than the American thinkers, their independent articulation of the principles of scientific management reveals some socio-political aspects of the efficiency movement that were only implicit in the writings of Taylor and Veblen.

H.G. Wells' *The Time Machine* portrays a society divided into a beautiful leisure class playing in the sun and a troglodyte working class which supports the beautiful players in order to eat them. Wells' friends, Sidney and Beatrice Webb, although they never expressed this fear of the working class so vividly, may very well have shared this upper class apprehension. The Webbs sometimes fantasized that, when their life's work was done, they would both be shot dead by an anarchist on their fiftieth wedding anniversary.[3] No one, even in fantasy, could consider the Webbs succulent, or even edible.

Beatrice Potter, like F.W. Taylor, was born into Veblen's leisure class; she inherited a yearly income of a thousand pounds which, invested in her working partnership with Sidney Webb, yielded an enormous literary output. The indefatigable Webbs proved by their labours, most of which decried unearned income, to have forsaken the leisure class but they were never comfortable with the working class movement unless it were guided by non-working class leaders, the "intellectual proletariat" or "brain-workers".

Throughout their long lives, the Webbs displayed remarkable consistency in spite of the fact that their championship of Soviet communism in the 1930s appeared to be a departure from the non-revolutionary, democratic socialist creed which they had earlier espoused. Yet Fabianism and Bolshevism have a common denominator in their fierce rejection of syndicalism or working class self-emancipation.[4] Lenin, shortly after translating the Webbs' *Industrial Democracy* into Russian, enunciated a central principle of the Webbs in *What is to be Done* which serves as the basis of communist party organization; namely, that trade-unionism will not inevitably develop into socialism and that the success of socialism thus depends on leadership, from outside the working class, transforming its trade union mentality.[5]

The translator of *Industrial Democracy* into German was E. Bernstein whose work, *Evolutionary Socialism*, published a year after the Webbs' work, was the first radical revision of Marxism from within the Marxian tradition. *Evolutionary Socialism* advocates what is perhaps the central idea of the Webbs; that is, industry is to be reorganized in accordance with the interests of consumers rather than of producers (workmen or capitalist).[6] Socialist production is to be controlled by the consumer or representatives of consumers rather than by the producers themselves.

Marx rejected the utilitarian perspective (which the Webbs later adopted) of work as merely a means to income and

114

leisure. Marx's "work ethic" (as distinct from the production ethos of the Webbs and of the scientific management or efficiency movement) stipulated that work is not only a means to obtain income and leisure but is also the activity of developing and expressing human capacities.[7] Work, for Marx, may not be just an instrumental value, as it is for wage-labourers, but may be an end in itself, "life's prime want."[8] Thus Marx could not advocate a society, no matter how benevolently managed, which maximizes productive output, and hence workers' income and leisure, by subordinating the needs and autonomy of workers to a "Papacy of production" which determines consumer requirements and working methods and conditions.[9] In contrast, the Webbs' utilitarianism lacked the perspective of the producer; they did not wish to transcend the proletarian condition, as Marx and the syndicalists did, but to universalize it.

Thus the Webbs consistently opposed the syndicalist movement within the workers' movement just as the syndicalists opposed 'Sidney Webbicalism'. Before and during World War I, when Sidney Webb advocated the introduction of Taylorism into Britain, the Webbs were adamantly opposed to the syndicalist, guild socialist and the shop stewards movement.[10] Their rejection of the idea that workers should control the working conditions and methods used in the mines, shipyards, factories, etc. earned the Webbs a reputation in working class circles as bureaucratic collectivists.[11] At that time, the English working class, and particularly the revolutionary element of it, did not share the Webbs' view that nationalization of industry, efficiently run in the interests of consumers, would fundamentally change or improve their working lives. Even when the Webbs and the workers were on the same side, such as on the Coal Industry Commission of 1919, which was widely held to be a trial of capitalism, a marked divergence is manifest between the views of Sidney Webb, a government appointed member of the Commission, and the miners' representatives. Sidney Webb tried to convict private enterprise of inefficiency and called for the nationalization of the mines while the miners' leaders pressed for workers' control of the coalmining industry; the workers believed that "national ownership should be based, not on bureaucracy, but on a full participation of the organized workers, by hand and brain, in the management."[12]

The Webbs' opposition to the shop stewards' movement in 1920 made Lenin think they had sold out to the capitalist class.[13] But the Webbs never betrayed their anti-syndicalist ideas. Rather they lacked the tactical wisdom of Lenin who espoused the idea of workers' control of industry before the October revolution and disavowed it shortly after seizing power.[14] The Webbs lacked any revolutionary enthusiasm. They opposed the General Strike of 1926 as a disaster. The silver lining in this cloud was that the failure of the general strike would put an end to the "proletarian distemper" of the workers[1] control daydream.[15] Beatrice writes:

> The failure of the General Strike of 1926 will be one of the significant landmarks in the history of the British working class. Future historians will, I think, regard it as the death gasp of that pernicious doctrine of "workers' control" of public affairs through the Trade Unions, and by the method of direct action. This absurd doctrine was introduced into British working class left by Tom Mann and the Guild Socialists... In Russia it was quickly repudiated by Lenin and the Soviets, and the Trade Unions were reduced to complete subordination to the creed-autocracy of the Communist Party.[16]

The Webbs initially opposed Bolshevism on the mistaken impression that it was a Russian edition of syndicalism or guild socialism.[17] But later they came to see that the Soviet regime was in line with their ideas rather than their opponents, the libertarian socialists.

> ...The Soviet government had changed its basic ideal from workers' control and general anarchic freedom to rigid consumer's collectivism... The Soviet Government is the "servile state" in being — the very thought of which was denounced by the rebels of 1910-14.[18]

In fact, it was the shelving of the idea of workers' control, a friend noted, that "more than anything else roused in the Webbs a new interest in Soviet Communism."[19] Another friend of the Webbs writes:

> Beatrice Webb once told me that so long as the Russian revolution went in for any kind of nonsense like Workers' Control they had no interest in it. Once Lenin scrapped any element of Workers' Control in Russia, the Webbs began to show some interest in the great Revolution.[20]

116

Before the Webbs visited the Soviet Union, they anticipated that Russian communism would correspond to their model of socialism, described in *A Constitution for the Socialist Commonwealth of Great Britain*, in which trade unionist strivings are subordinated to the will of the consumer citizen.[21] Indeed, they found what they anticipated; the Soviet regime, they wrote in *Soviet Communism: A New Civilization*, placed ultimate power "in the hands of representatives, *not of any organizations of producers, but of organizations representing the consumers.*"[22] The dictatorship of the proletariat became, for the Webbs, the dictatorship of consumer representatives, and thus received their support.

To be sure, the Webbs championship of the Soviet Union was never unqualified, despite the affinity they felt between Soviet practice and Webbian principle. They retained their doubts about the restriction of democratic liberties in the Soviet Union. However they believed that the suppression of legality and liberty in the U.S.S.R. in the 1930s was the result of the combined religious, political and industrial revolutions Russia was undergoing, each of which had produced comparable suffering in western countries during the process of their modernization. They did not believe such repression was inherent in a regime where the state was the sole employer of labour, for such "state capitalism" was the necessary result of their aim to subordinate the interests of the producer to those of the consumer. The syndicalist spokesman, Tom Mann, opposed the Webbian conception of socialism as it culminates in a "centralized official bureaucracy giving instructions and commands to servile subordinates."[23] The guild socialist, G.D.H. Cole, insisted that "a society which organizes its industry on the basis of consumption will be inevitably servile."[24] What the libertarian socialists take to be servility, the Webbs take to be a sense of service. The spirit of socialism requires service and obedience to the state as collective consumer.

Since the Webbs consistently opposed syndicalism, an examination of their reasons for doing so might provide a sense of continuity in their thought. They found the idea of the self-governing workplace both impracticable and undesirable. Self-governing workplaces had hitherto failed because of a lack of capital, of managerial ability, of knowledge of the market and of workshop discipline.[25] Attempts of workers to control the operation of the shops, yards and mines in which they work would set back the clock; if they were to succeed, this would run counter to the need of all industrial countries for a co-ordinated national economy; it would upset the standardization of production, inherent in industrialism, and fostered by national trade unions.[26] Moreover syndicalism fosters "trade-sectionalism", "egoistic materialism", "the old Adam of Individualism" which conflicts with collectivism and the spirit of disinterested service that Webbian socialism requires.[27] "From beginning to end it is diametrically opposed to the socialist ideal."[28]

The Webbs did not believe that the lack of capital or managerial talent were insuperable obstacles to syndicalism; the needed "capital" could be obtained through a socialist transformation, and organizational ability could be learned from practical experience. The major obstacles are that workers lack the knowledge of consumer needs, of the standards required in other sectors of production, of the amount to be produced, etc.[29] In *Soviet Communism: A New Civilization*, the Webbs write:

> In any highly evolved industrial society, whatever its economic or political constitution, the citizen as producer, whether by hand or by brain, in the hours of work, must do what he is, in one or another form, *told* to do; for the very purpose of being able to receive, along with the other producers, in the rest of the day — the consuming hours — that which they all need and severally desire. And if the consumers' needs are to decide the producers' work, there must be — where the guidance of profit-making in a free market is abandoned — some organization, outside the factory, outside the trade union, outside the industry itself, by which the spokesmen or representatives of the whole community of citizen consumers can instruct each factory... exactly what it is to produce.[30]

But, as the Webbs were aware, such considerations do not dispose of the syndicalist claims, for industrial decision-making does not pertain just to what is produced (the amount and kind of produce) but also to how it is produced (the methods, machinery, materials, personnel organization and training) and to the conditions of working (wages, hours, safety measures, etc.).[31] In *What Syndicalism Means*, the Webbs cited the syndicalist spokesman, Tom Mann, who called for a national planning and marketing board to ascertain what is to be produced and to distribute the produce but "leaving to the men to determine under what conditions and how the work should be done."[32] Thus the Webbs did not confront the central point of contention between the syndicalists and themselves. The former did not disagree with the Webbs contention that socialism requires national planning boards to determine the amount and kind of produce. The contention arose over the issue of who should determine methods and conditions of work. The Webbs did not believe, as the syndicalists did, that workers had a right to decide how the required goods are to be produced.

While the Webbs opposed workers' participation in decisions relating to working methods, they continually insisted that trade unions had a role in bargaining for better working conditions, even in socialist societies (although they were perhaps more relaxed in this insistence regarding their observations on Soviet Russia). However, the popularity of the syndicalist demand for workers' self-determination of working methods led them to pay lip-service to the demand.[33] But they eliminated any content to the demand for workers' control of production methods by means of the following Jesuitical argument presented in *A Constitution for the Socialist Commonwealth of Great Britain:*

> It must be observed that the "right of self-determination" for any vocation does not include the right to determine the conditions under which any other vocation—such as that of the directors or those of several kinds of the technicians—shall carry out its own social function.[34]

Thus the Webbs did not believe that socialism involves any transformation of the capitalist division of functions between labour and management. Management must retain the prerogative of determining the kinds and uses of machinery and materials, the nature of work relationships, job training, schedules and routines.

If the workers were to control their working procedures, establish their own routines, work teams and training requirements, and select the foremen, technicians and managerial personnel, the effect would be a marked drop in productivity and a slackening of work discipline. The Webbs felt, as Taylor did, that manual workers were ignorant of alternative working methods and biased against any technical or organizational innovations.[35] Moreover the Webbs shared Taylor's belief that efficient production must be organized from the point of view of the consumer, who wishes maximum output and lower prices, rather than that of the producer, who aims to restrict output and raise prices. The

Webbs' advocacy of the introduction of Taylorism into Britain is a manifestation of the pattern of authority they felt to be inherent in industry. To be sure, the Webbs recognized working class hostility to scientific management. But, they believed, the difficulties of introducing micro-motion studies in capitalist society would be overcome in a socialist common-wealth where the workers would participate in the efficiency studies, thus facilitating the task of efficient management.[36]

The Webbs later came to believe that the Soviet effi-ciency movement in the 1930s, Stakhanovism, was the oppo-site of Taylorism, since the initiative for efficient innovation came from the workers rather than capitalist managers.[37] To some extent, this contention is valid because numerous young workers spearheaded the efficiency movement and received great benefits for introducing reforms similar in conception to Taylor's. However the Webbs did not mention the fact that in the 1930s the Soviet state had to purge 70-80 percent of trade-union officials, that trade union congresses were suppressed from 1932 to 1949 while the All-Russian Congress of Stakha-novites was held yearly, that a number of Stakhanovites were murdered by fellow workers, that severe penal measures were taken against industrial sabotage and breaches of discipline, that piece-rates were lowered as a result of the introduction of Stakhanovite innovations, reducing the income of one third of the labour force, and increasing wage disparities.[38] These measures indicate that there was not unanimity in the working class, as there came to be in the ruling class, on the desirability of Soviet Taylorism.

In contrast to Soviet trade unions which, the Webbs thought, admirably promoted productivity or national effi-ciency, western trade unions had merely a negative or restric-tive function. Western trade unions had served to limit the depredations of the capitalist class but did not participate in the promotion of increased productivity. The Webbs viewed trade unions as having been born from the decline in status of independent artisans who had become dependent wage-earners.[39] Workers, who no longer owned the materials, tools and products of their labour or controlled the processes of their work, were forced to combine to secure their livelihood. The earliest trade unions were divided vertically by trades, "instead of horizontally between employers and wage-earners."[40] But the tramping* arrangements of artisans with-

---

* In Britain, from the late eighteenth to the early twentieth century, artisans would feed, lodge, and provide tramping allowances to

in a trade gave way to national trade-unions. Industrial organization and technical progress made older trade demarcations obsolete and stimulated the integration of the working class. During the nineteenth century, the trade union movement indirectly furthered national efficiency by standardizing wages and working conditions through collective bargaining. The Webbs felt the trade unions would have a continued progressive function to fulfill if they would only concentrate on the establishment of common national standards of wages and working conditions.[41]

However, trade unionism retained its craft heritage, its division of the working class along trade demarcations. Trade unionists, especially the skilled and highly paid elements of the union movement, all too often were solely concerned with the interests of their particular trade, and neglected the socialist mission of equalizing the conditions and wages of industrial production.[42] They thus failed to give leadership to the less skilled and less organized sections of the working class. Moreover, craft unions attempted to follow the practice of professional occupations and establish their own standards of competence for a trade, and, in so doing, blocked technological progress and restricted entry into a trade. The apprenticeship system, through which craft unionists controlled the quality and quantity of its membership, was a restrictive practice, artificially maintaining a high standard of remuneration for trade service.[43] Within the trade union movement, custom, conservatism, hierarchy and inefficiency pre-dominated.[44] In those trades in which the apprenticeship system was retained, many of the characteristics of the leisure class could be observed. The Webbs noted:

> ...we find an unusual prevalence, among the rank and file, of what we may call the "gentle" nature — that conjunction of quiet dignity, grave courtesy, and consideration of other people's rights and feelings, which is usually connected with old family and long-established position.[45]

---

fellow members of a trade who were moving around the country to find employment, to subsist during a dispute with an employer or, in effect, to strike against an employer. The tramping arrangements combined a system of unemployment insurance with the continental practice of journeymen touring around a country to complete their craft education. See E. Hobsbawm, *Labouring Men*, ch. 4, for a more complete account of this practice than is to be found in the Webbs.

However, the efficiency movement is incompatible with the kind of economic security in which a leisured style may flourish. Those monopolies or vested interests which block the competitive flow of "capital, brains and labour" sap collective efficiency. Thus trade unionism is to be judged, the Webbs asserted.

> not by its results in improving the position of a particular section of workmen at a particular time, but by its effects on the permanent efficiency of the nation. If any of the Methods and Regulations of Trade Unionism result in the choice of less efficient factors of production than would otherwise have been used; if they compel the adoption of a lower type of organization than would have prevailed without them; and especially if they tend to lessen the capacity or degrade the character of either manual laborers or brain-workers, that part of Trade Unionism however advantageous it may seem to particular sections of workmen, will stand condemned.[46]

The criteria of efficiency condemn the trade-union demand to control their methods of work.[47] Working class participation in industrial decision-making should be restricted, in socialist as well as capitalist societies, to the safeguarding of working conditions by the trade unions and works committees whose concern "would be primarily the discussion of grievances and the making of suggestions."[48]

Beatrice explained why the workers' role in industrial policy should be limited to the voicing of grievances and suggestions.

> ... we have little faith in the "average sensual man", we do not believe that he can do much more than describe his grievances, we do not think that he can prescribe the remedies.[49]

The "average sensual man" played a role comparable to Taylor's Schmidt in the Webbian drama of industrial life; he required the direction of social engineers to prevent degeneration into idleness, vice and folly. The Webbs' belief in the sensual sloth of the average man is not only the basis of their view that workers would cease to work in worker-managed enterprises, but also is the foundation of the extraordinary Draconian measures the Webbs believed to be essential if proposals for a welfare state were implemented.[50]

122

The Webbs' distaste of the sensuousness of the average man was as notable as Taylor's asceticism, and their attempts to repress impulsiveness or sensuous inclination in man and beast were as illustrative of the spirit of scientific management as were Taylor's efforts. Beatrice had a running war with her beloved pet dog Sandy who insisted on barking with excitement, despite constant remonstrations to maintain decorum, whenever the Webbs were about to set out on a walk. No device succeeded in repressing his average sensual canine nature, and in anarchist rebellion, he bit Beatrice and consequently had to be destroyed.[51] Kingsley Martin relates the shock that befell a social gathering at the Webbs when he asked to use the lavatory. Harold Laski later "declared that my (Martin's) request had been an extraordinary act of courage which no one had ever dared perform before in the Webb household. He said that the week before he had dined there with Ramsay MacDonald, and that he and the Premier had had to make use of a timber yard on the way home."[52] Luckily, since guests of the Webbs were nourished more on stimulating and edifying conversation than on drink and food, these unfortunate occurrences could be kept to a minimum.

It was doubtless a felt affinity with the sober, Spartan outlook of Stalinism that contributed to the Webbs' admiration of the Soviet regime. Mrs. Webb admired the sexual puritanism of communists; they do not, she wrote, "waste energy, time or health on sex, food and drink."[53] One is reminded of her dictum that "marriage is the waste-paper-basket of the emotions,"[54] a Pauline aphorism for the age of F.W. Taylor. While in Russia, Mrs. Webb wrote newspaper articles counselling young ladies to avoid the use of lipstick,[55] but she was gratified to observe that "there is no spooning in the Parks of Recreation and Rest...."[56] In general, Mrs. Webb concluded, Soviet Russia would not please "the average sensual man" as its achievements pertain to the advance in morals, literacy and learning.[57]

Thus the first society to organize production entirely from the standpoint of the consumer, his "objective needs, mind you, not appetites,"[58] is not attractive to "the average sensual man". The efficiency movement used the perspective of the consumer to attack syndicalism and to justify the scientific management of the working class. But it did not adopt the consumerist perspective in order to enhance licentious consumerism in the working class.

The scientific management movement did not advocate the election of bodies of consumers to oversee production. Nor did the scientific managers, who determined the "objective needs" of the citizen-consumer, aim at the emancipation of sensuality. If Taylor was a prototype of the worldly ascetic and Veblen was the antithesis of a consumerist, the Webbs made a religion of austerity.

The efficiency movement, for the Webbs as for Taylor, was more a religion of self-denial than a means for material satisfaction. Beatrice writes:

> But I cling to the thought that man will only evolve upwards by the subordination of his physical desires and appetites to the intellectual and spiritual side of his nature. Unless this evolution be the purpose of the race, I despair — and wish only for the extinction of human consciousness. Without this hope — without this faith — I could not struggle on. It is this purpose, and this purpose only, that gives a meaning to the constantly recurring battles of good and evil within one's own nature — and to one's persistent endeavour to find the mass of men. Oh! for a Church that would weld into one living force all those who hold this faith, with the discipline and the consolation fitted to sustain this endeavour.[59]

Beatrice describes her god as follows:

> It is far nearer the thought of an abstract Being divested of all human appetite but combining the quality of an always working Intellect with an impersonal Love. And when I do think of the future man as I strive to make him in myself and in others, I forecast an Impersonality... casting out all feelings, all other sensations other than that of an all-embracing beneficence. Physical appetites are to me the devil: they are signs of the disease that ends in death, the root of the hatred, malice and greed that makes this life of man a futility.[60]

This religion, which Mrs. Webb conceived as "the art of mental hygiene" was not to be a form of Protestantism, where every man is his own priest.[61]

> I do not believe that the ordinary man is capable of prescribing for the diseases of the soul any more than they are for the diseases of the body. We need the expert here as elsewhere.[62]

It is from this perspective that we are to understand the Webbs' conception of efficient industrialism as prosaic religion. Factory discipline and subordination to managerial authority provide "the average sensual man" with the restraint, direction and purpose he cannot impose upon himself. For example, the Webbs noted in *Industrial Democracy*, that the pre-industrial artisan (or outworker in industry societies), who is the master of his time, lacks regularity in his work and restraint in his leisure. Unless driven to constant work by low wages,

> he may break off when he likes to gossip with a friend or slip round to the public-house; he may, in the intervals, nurse a sick wife or child; and he can even arrange to spend the morning in the garden, or doing odd jobs around the house... For good or for evil his working hours are determined by his own idiosyncrasies. Whether he desires to earn much, or is content with little; whether he is a slow worker or a quick one; whether he is a precise and punctual person governing himself and his family by rigid rules, or whether he is "endowed with an artistic temperament", and needs to recover on Monday and Tuesday from the "expansion" of the preceding days—these personal characteristics will determine the limits and distribution of his working time.[63]

This portrait of a varied working day determined by individual inclination should not however be considered more attractive than a standardized working day governed by the factory clock. For to be master of one's time is to be given over to self-indulgence. The Webbs deplored:

> the injurious effect upon the personal character of the "average sensual man" of this freedom to stop working whenever he feels inclined... The axiom that the vast majority of the manual workers, like other men, are the better for a certain degree of discipline, would not find ready acceptance among the rank and file of Trade Unionists... But the more thoughtful workmen would concur with the dictum... that when operatives were "obliged to be more regular in their attendance at their work, they became more orderly in their conduct, spent less time at the ale house, and lived better at home."[64]

For these reasons, it is dangerous to promote a wage-earner to a salaried position within a trade union.[65] The union official, not subject to the discipline and regularity of factory life, would fall prey to sloth and drunkenness. "Instead of being confined to the factory or the mine, he is now free to come and go at his own will, and drink is therefore accessible to him at all hours."[66] The working class movement is more effectively led by the less sensual, more scientific individuals from outside that class. However the widespread dislike of leadership by efficiency experts presented an obstacle to the scientific management of society. Beatrice wrote:

> The Webb conception of the relative spheres of intellect and emotion on the one hand, and, on the other, of the right relation of the leaders to the average sensual man, is vehemently objected to by all the "As," by the artist, the anarchist and the aristocrat.[67]

Beatrice went on to bemoan that the "As" comprise the bulk of the population.[68]

The artists, anarchists and aristocrats within the working class are the particular objects of humanitarian concern for scientific management. The syndicalist man must be overcome; "the old Adam of Individualism", the pride in work, the impulsive character, the enjoyment of ease are aspects of "the average sensual man" who needs externally imposed discipline and expert management to regulate his life.

The efficiency movement may appear to many to be a tiresome creed. However, for the Webbs, it is the substance of socialism; namely, people working for the optimal development of the productive forces, concerned solely with their function in the productive collectivity and not with their particular material interests. The efficiency movement is a form of self-abnegation or idealism; the workers are to set aside their inclinations and follow the iron discipline of the factory clock and the authority of the scientific managers; the leaders are to labour hard and impersonally to serve the masses, and by their service, obtain a sense of purpose or meaning to life. Of course, in obtaining a sense of purpose in their dedication to national efficiency, the Webbs did not think they were devouring the working class to satisfy their spiritual hunger. Their intentions were humane, directed only to alleviating the condition of those who are, they thought, incapable of helping themselves.

126

The Webbian management of the "average sensual man" contains as much of the thought of that unbalanced genius, Thomas Carlyle, the arch anti-utilitarian, as it does of the consumerist perspective of Benthamite utilitarianism. The principle of "work, and despair not" was the gospel that Carlyle preached to the leisured class.[69] The conversion of the leisured into "captains of industry" would provide meaning to the lives of the upper class, redeeming them from a purposeless indolence.

Carlyle thought that contemplation cannot disclose order in a chaotic world. Only through work can order be imposed upon that chaos of inconsistency and sensuality which is nature and human nature.[70] Philosophic meditation, he thought, not only is impotent, but is destructive. He wrote that "the mere existence and necessity of a Philosophy is an evil. Man is sent hither not to question, but to work", and if people fail to work, the vain and painful spirit of sceptical inquiry will assert itself.[71]

It is the fear of death, of the yawning abyss, that prompts the best to turn against the sensual component of their nature, to transcend the meaningless flux of sense experience into a life of duty, of service, of work which sheds this mortal coil and adorns itself in the permanence of principle.[72] Those who can overcome their sensuality in dedication, in service, in work are fitted to lead those lacking self-command who remain on the level of sensuous nature. Such a natural aristocracy in an age of industry will suppress "the cash nexus" of market relations with the working class, convert "nomadic into permanent contract", and introduce the drill of army life into the industrial world.[73]

The Webbs avoided the extremism of Carlyle but they were practitioners of his secular idealism, his religion of work which imposes purpose on the meaningless world of sense experience. The Aristotelian view of the inherent sweetness of life, the basis of the good or leisured life which does not turn in on, or oppose, life itself, was as antipathetic to the Webbs as to Carlyle.[74] For them the good or civilized life is in conflict with mere life or sensuous existence; one transcends material existence only through work, through a struggle with one's sensuous nature which forever tends to degrade one into barbaric idleness.

Moreover, the Webbs shared Carlyle's extension into industrial relations of the duality between the working intellect (which if not working, degenerates into the slough of

127

Despond) and idle sensuality. The duality between intellect and sensuality becomes the division between management and labour. The overcoming of the sensuous appetites becomes the management of the working class whose working time must be organized to prevent its nature from manifesting itself. The Webbs' admiration for Soviet methods of organizing leisure time into wholesome channels completes the management of idle sensuality by working intellect.[75] The intellect becomes the governing class, freed from the meaningless decadence of leisure activities, and given a purpose in the full time occupation of managing the working class.

Doubtless Carlye's work ethic, which Taylor and the Webbs shared, is not an essential component of ruling-class consciousness. Perhaps members of the ruling class can hold on to their positions of power without the adoption of this unleisurely creed. Indeed, British executives seem to be least affected by the Webbian gospel of redemptive management of any ruling class in the industrial world. Perhaps competitive pressures of global technique and the standards of the Common Market will generate increased demand for the scientific management of the British working class. If so, the decreasing leisure of British executives will not be a direct result of "the rise of the masses", as liberal and conservative writers have asserted. Rather the decline of the leisure class has been, and will continue to be, a result of the demand to control and manage the rising masses.

To the Webbs nothing could have appeared as perverted and degenerate as the first sentence of Oscar Wilde's *The Soul of Man Under Socialism:*

> The chief advantage that would result from the establishment of Socialism is, undoubtably, the fact that Socialism would relieve us from that sordid necessity of living for others which, in the present condition of things, presses so hardly upon almost everyone.

Wilde, in short, thought socialism to be the precondition of leisure for his class as well as the working class. The Webbs thought "living for others" to be a socialist aim rather than a "sordid necessity".

Wilde overlooked the possibility that socialism could increase the work load of the ruling class. Whether or not socialists accept the Webbs' ethic of work for the ruling class, the fact remains that the ruling class of state socialist regimes toil at least as long and hard managing their workers as do capitalist executives.[76] Those who are more concerned about the over-worked members of the ruling class than the under-managed members of the working class might re-open the syndicalist option which the Webbs tried to close off.

The central contradiction of the Webbs' thought is the adoption of the consumerist perspective of scientific management with less than a foster parent's love of the offspring of scientific management, namely, the increasing orientation of "the average sensual man" towards leisure and consumption. Contemporary sociology tends to view increased income and time off work as just compensation for the kind of working experience which scientific management fought to introduce and which is now deemed inherent in an industrial civilization. But whether or not contemporary sociology resolves the contradictions of scientific management is the question to be examined in the next chapter.

Chapter 7

Schmidt's Leisure:
The Problem of the Sociologists

The growth of leisure-time. Its uneven distribution; the over-worked ruling class and underworked proletariat. The "problem of leisure" as misused potential of workers' leisure-time. Impoverished work and impoverished leisure; greater variety, activity and participation in leisure activities corresponding to position in productive hierarchy. "Solution" to "problem of leisure" in scientific management of leisure activities. The leisure-as-compensation thesis: the necessity of education. The fallacies of the thesis: the servile automaton and the superabundant player not supported by empirical research; the possibility of creating a purely leisure-oriented educational system conflicts with empirical data. Alternatives either job enlargement or extension of scientific management into leisure activities. The latter not an inherent impossibility.

The Uneven Distribution of Work and Leisure

A bull market in the sociology of leisure has arisen since Veblen and the Webbs applied the principles of scientific management to sociological investigation. Although less overtly political than Veblen and the Webbs, contemporary sociologists of leisure tend to make the same technocratic assumptions that informed the politics of scientific management. However, beginning with the great depression of the thirties, sociology has increasingly turned from Veblen's and the Webbs' focus on the realm of production to the realm of leisure. The earlier emphasis on an efficient use of Schmidt's working time gives way to an emphasis on the productive use of Schmidt's time off work.

This new branch of sociology has been fostered by the increased free time made possible by scientific management and mass production. Our century has witnessed a shortened work week, longer vacations, later entrance into productive employment, and earlier retirement. An estimated 27% of a lifetime in 1900 was devoted to leisure activities, with 34% in 1950 and an anticipated 38% of a lifetime in 2000 will be free of the necessities of work, job related activities and travel, domestic necessities and sleep.[1]

However these percentages of time devoted to leisure have not been evenly distributed amongst the population. The youth and the retired, needless to say, have more spare time than the employed. Of the employed population, the married have less free time than the unmarried; those with children have less than those without; married men have considerably more leisure time than married women; apartment dwellers have more free time than home owners.[2] Housekeeping and child care are important items in time budgeting which, in large part, fall on women's shoulders. Non-working women have roughly the same amount of free time as working men. Employed women in capitalist and socialist countries generally work one to two hours less per day than men but do two to three hours more housework. In short, despite technological advances in domestic appliances, women have less free time than their husbands who, in all societies, contribute less than an equal share of the housekeeping and childrearing activities.[3]

Labour and leisure are unevenly distributed on class as well as sexual lines. While most workers have obtained a shorter working week since the second World War, an increasing percentage of Americans are working longer hours.[4] Managerial, professional, sales and service workers are most smitten by the work ethic whereas "...low income groups such as labourers and Negro workers include a smaller than average proportion working longer hours."[5] H.L. Wilensky writes:

> On balance, the female work week may be as long as it was a century ago, while pace-setting elites, the main carriers of cultural traditions and values, have likely increased their time at work. The uneven distribution of work among those working and the incidence of involuntary retirement and unemployment suggest that men who have gained most leisure need and want more work. The "lei-

131

sure stricken" are not replacing the poverty stricken; the two are becoming one.[6]

Wilensky's conclusion that those with most time off work want more work is supported by many other studies.[7]

As we have seen, the thrust of Taylorism was the attempt to transfer much of the work load from labour to management, in effect to overturn the social division between a leisure class and a working class. To a large extent, this aspiration has been realized. The industrial proletariat have more free time than ever before and the professional and executive strata, who comprise the ruling class in industrial societies, work longer hours and are more involved in their work than ever before.

It has been stated that:

> The executive possessed more leisure within his work situation and less outside while the blue collar worker enjoyed more leisure outside the work situation and less inside.[8]

However it would be incorrect to deduce that the worker has a more rewarding life of leisure than the executive who has less free time. For studies reveal that whatever the indices of the richness of leisure activities, sociologists of leisure are in general agreement that the professional and executive strata of capitalist and socialist countries have more of it than the working class, although some assert that individual, ethnic, religious or sexual differences are more significant than class differences. For example, a Hungarian study revealed that "people doing qualified intellectual work are attracted by active mental rest" whereas passive rest predominates with those doing routine, monotonous work in industry and agriculture.[9] Other studies demonstrate that, although the intelligentsia in Eastern Europe works considerably longer hours than the proletariat, it has more varied and active leisure life, with broader and deeper cultural interests.[10] Numerous studies reveal that wage-labourers in both capitalist and socialist countries have a lower rate of participation in social organizations and political activities than other strata of the population.[11] Participation in cultural as well as social organizations in the U.S. bears a direct relationship to one's position in the social hierarchy.[12] Furthermore, an extensive survey of the mass media in the U.S. demonstrated that those persons who work the longest hours tend to have higher quality of exposure to mass media and those who work shorter hours tend to have more trivial tastes in magazines, books, television, etc.[13] French workers express less interest in science, art, literature and philosophy than do other strata within industry.[14] British professionals and executives watch less television, participate more in active recreation and have broader and more diverse cultural interests than the proletariat.[15] In short, executives "were more 'involved in their work and some of this 'involvement' spilled over into their life at home. They had wider leisure interests than other people."[16] Thus empirical studies support the conclusion that:

> For those who are likely to have most free time in the high-technology society are also those who, through no fault of their own, are often least trained by education and environment to use free time wisely and creatively — to convert free time into genuine leisure.[17]

However it is not simply class differences that shape the form of leisure activities. For within the working class, individuals have differing work experiences which seem to influence their involvement in leisure activities. A study of Canadian workers found a direct correlation between the amount of discretion workers exercise on the job and the variety of leisure activities enjoyed off the job. It concluded that the ability or inability to exercise judgment on the job is carried over to leisure activities, and that "lack of opportunity to talk on the job is associated with dramatically reduced rates of participation in associations."[18] Similar results were found in investigations on American and East European workers.[19] French workers too, who find their work interesting, display more intellectual curiosity, read more, and participate more in cultural, social and political activities.[20]

Job satisfaction seems to be a major factor in mental health. Studies indicate that better mental health is to be found in workers holding more skilled and responsible jobs, and that this relationship of mental health to skill level "does not appear to be caused in any large degree by differences of pre-job background or personality of the men who remain in the several types of work."[21] Not surprisingly, "workers with the lowest mental health and job satisfaction were often escapist or passive in their non-work activities: they watched television: did not vote: and did not participate in community organisation."[22]

Not only do wage-labourers participate less in cultural and social associations, political or civic organizations than other strata of the population but also the amount of working class involvement in these activities appears to be decreasing. Although increasing numbers of workers have been organized into unions and vote for labour or social democratic parties, there has been a decline in working class participation in union and political activities in the last half century.[23] J. Habermas characterizes our age of "alienated leisure" as one of "civil privatism."[24] Even J. Dumazedier, the foremost champion of the contemporary 'man of leisure', concedes that he is not "a conscientious citizen."[25] Time budget studies conducted in the Soviet Union in 1924 and 1959 undermine the traditional socialist expectation that a reduction of working hours will lead to a greater degree of participation in public life. Between 1924 and 1959, participation "in all social activities, including political and union activities, decreased from 109 to 17 hours a year for urban manual workers, in spite of the increase in spare time."[26]

The Solution to "the Problem of Leisure"

The mass of empirical research which we have briefly surveyed reveals an important direct effect of the adoption of scientific management, namely, the increased work load for the "Taylors" and increased free time for the "Schmidts". An indirect effect is that Schmidt's leisure time has become a problem for sociologists. Taylor's leisure is not a problem for the sociologist of leisure. To be sure, psychologists and theologians deprecate the "workaholism" of contemporary professionals and executives, and conservative writers such as T.S. Eliot, J. Pieper and S. De Grazia bemoan the lower standard of culture enjoyed by the increasingly hard working upper class in relation to earlier, more leisured ruling classes.[27] However, such concerns are not refuted by the sociologists of leisure; they are simply ignored; for it is Schmidt's leisure and not Taylor's which is subjected to the science of sociology.

Or rather leading socioloists of leisure do not contradict the conservative writers but make a counter-assertion that the level of popular culture is steadily rising. In support of this contention, J. Dumazedier cites a list of the most popular books sold by wandering pedlars in France in the mid-nineteenth century, many of which were sentimental or pornographic. The novels borrowed from contemporary public libraries or on the best-sellers lists, "are not of the same kind."[28] Although we may find this insufficient proof for the assertion of an improvement in popular culture, Dumazedier does at least provide some evidence (in distinction to other sociologists, such as M. Kaplan and N. Anderson, who do not support their contentions). However, we might note that Dumazedier says that, in modern factories with a worker-run leisure programme, workers read more books than average, but of a lower quality.[29] Thus the low or high quality is, for Dumazedier, not so much to be correlated with the difference in general taste between the nineteenth and twentieth centuries as with the difference between working class and non-working class selections of reading material. The alleged improvement in popular culture might be seen as simply a change from class cultures to a mass culture, that is, one provided to the working class by the magnates and social workers of the leisure industry. The so-called problem of leisure is integrally bound up with the sociologists' solution; Schmidt's problematic leisure time can be increasingly productively employed under the tutelage of the scientific managers of leisure. Although there may have been an improvement in popular culture, the improvement is seen as the effect of external direction of Schmidt's judgment.

Since "authorities are agreed that the chief need in recreation is competent leadership,"[30] authoritative "leisurists" call for a greater role for a social science elite in the organization and management of leisure activities.[31] For "most people do not know what they want, when it comes to developing their intellects, their personalities, and their bodies. They should be encouraged or compelled to learn to like things they presently dislike."[32] Moreover

> Since the average citizen is unable to invent new uses for his leisure, a professional elite shares a heavy responsibility for discovering criteria for ways of employing leisure and creating enthusiasms for common ends within the moral aims of the community.[33]

Such a professional elite of recreation leaders, or leisurists, are to "create and mold taste, communicate purposes and skills, encourage the development of faculties, and accept the responsibility for cultural initiative and the development of cultural traditions."[34] The leisurist does not consider whether the elite might develop a stake in the dependency of the average citizen, whose leisure activities are to be planned and controlled by the elite. Certainly he intends to provide greater scope for the employment of a managerial elite in the full-time servicing of the masses, thereby occupying the minds of the

135

elite with useful purposes rather than idle thoughts and keeping it as busy as those whose lives will be managed. Doubtless the acceptance of this "heavy responsibility" would keep the professional elite from hanging around street corners.

A junior executive in the leisure industry explicitly calls for the scientific management of leisure.

> ...leisure has become a part of life in industrial societies; and as such it has to be considered not only as a field of theoretical study for the sociologist or as a field of spontaneous action for each citizen, but as a sector of life which must be studied, understood, and organized, as was work throughout the last decades. For in industrial societies, people have leisure on their hands...[35]

Thus sociologists tend to conceive of "the problem of leisure" in a technicist manner. The problem of leisure is not simply that the class with the most free time lacks the resources to dispose of it other than in "other-oriented" or conformist "pass-times", in the passive consumption of the mass-media, in the activities of *'idiotes'* (those preoccupied with the realm of their own, the *'idion'*) rather than of *'polites'* or citizens. We do not intend to deny the sociological findings that workers lack the resources for full citizenship in contemporary culture. What we wish to stress is that the way in which the problem is conceived presents the leisurists in the same relation to Schmidt in his free time as Taylor was to Schmidt in his working time. Further, if Taylor's solution to the problem of Schmidt's working time led to a separation of thinking and doing, the leisurist's solution to the problem of Schmidt's leisure time leads to the separation of leisure planning and recreational execution. The technicist perspective of the leisurist blinds him to the consequences of his own research, prevents him from assessing seriously the data revealed in his own empirical studies. It is not that sociologists of leisure are wrong to think that many workers are incapable of expansive enjoyment off work but rather that they do not take sufficiently seriously the view that incapacity for leisure is a "spillover effect" of externally managed work.

The dominant theme of the sociology of leisure, around which most empirical studies are centred, is that leisure activities can be made to compensate for the vicissitudes of Taylorized jobs. That is, the leisure-as-compensation thesis accepts as unalterable the effects of scientific management —

the separation of planning and doing, initiative and execution, the minutely subdivided tasks co-ordinated from above, the lack of variety and challenge in most industrial operations, regimentation and externally imposed routines and methods of working. However the thesis proposes that workers will react to the inherently oppressive character of industrial work and will, in conjunction with the direction of the sociologists of leisure, discover new sources of satisfaction and personal development in their hours off work. The emptiness of unattained job satisfactions is to be filled by new sources of pleasure in a creative life of leisure.

To be sure, the more thoughtful exponents of the thesis have reservations about the possibility of enjoying an enriched life of leisure when workers' abilities are cramped in an impoverished life of work. An early edition of *The Lonely Crowd*, one of the most interesting studies of American patterns of leisure activities, advanced the leisure-as-compensation thesis. But in a subsequent preface to the book, D. Riesman admitted that he, N. Glazer and R. Denney were wrong to think "that autonomy in the post-industrial culture was to be found in play and leisure, and not in work." Riesman continued: "In fact, we soon realized that the burden put on leisure by the disintegration of work is too huge to be coped with; leisure itself cannot rescue work, but fails with it, and can only be meaningful for most men if work is meaningful...[36]"

R. Aron argues that "a full, balanced life presupposes that work is a source of joy", but since this is impossible for most workers in an industrial society, "they demand or should demand of leisure not only rest, not only entertainment (no longer thinking of their jobs), but joy and enrichment." Unfortunately, what workers should demand of leisure is not what they in fact do demand. Thus the state has a special responsibility to educate its citizens to find in leisure the compensatory satisfactions they cannot obtain in work. Otherwise leisure will "appear to millions of men as potential boredom or a burden to bear."[37] G. Friedmann considers the desirability of "humanizing" work but concludes that this objective is technically impossible for many jobs in an industrial society and thus it becomes imperative to create "a new centre for human development" outside the work world to compensate for the inherent drudgery within.[38]

J. Dumazedier, the acknowledged *doyen* of the sociologists of leisure, is a strong exponent of the leisure-as-compensation thesis. Despite his empirical research which found that dissatisfaction with work tends to breed conformist leisure activities.[39] Dumazedier does not conclude that more satisfactory work is the condition of fulfillment in leisure activities. Despite his view that decreasing participation of the mass of workers in social, political and cultural affairs is the central problem of our civilization of leisure, Dumazedier does not follow up his conclusion that "intellectual and social leisure time activities are related to a manifest interest in work."[40] He does not infer that "the problem of leisure" might be alleviated by making work more interesting to those who have produced this leisured society. We may conclude that Dumazedier's adherence to the leisure-as-compensation thesis is grounded in Aron's and Friedmann's assumption that Taylorism is an inexorable necessity in industrial production.

The leisure-as-compensation thesis also informs the politics of the 'new left', the followers of the Frankfurt School and of E. Mandel and the British Trotskyists. To be sure, they think that leisure cannot compensate for Taylorized work in capitalist societies but that it will compensate for such toil in a future socialist state. For example, H. Marcuse asserts that leisure time is not at present a consolation for the vicissitudes of wage-labour, as leisure time activities are closely integrated into exploitative productive collectivities. But socialism, in Marcuse's view, does not aim to make working experience more fulfilling in order to vitiate an adverse spillover effect upon leisure. Rather it aims to restrict inherently oppressive working time to a minimum, and thus enlarge the options available after hours.

> Necessary labour is a system of essentially inhuman, mechanical, and routine activities; in such a system, individuality cannot be a value in itself. Reasonably, the system of societal labour would be organized rather with a view of saving time and space for the development of individuality *outside* the inevitably repressive work world.[41]

Such an economizing of time involves an overcoming of trade-unionism and its restrictive mentality, as well as of workers' aspirations for greater autonomy in, or greater control over, their working experience. "Self-determination in the production and distribution of vital goods and services would be wasteful."[42] The technical structure of industrial capitalism, shorn of trade-union opposition, would remain in Marcuse's socialist society, with no qualitative changes in working methods and relationships, but with a more centralized control of the means of production in the hands of a technical elite. Such an elite would, for a transitional period, direct the educational system and recreational and entertainment facilities until the masses could make rational use of their leisure time.[43] At such a time, a qualitatively different, non-repressive culture, governed by the pleasure principle, would emerge; free instinctual play would be emancipated from external mangement and from the restraints of a civilization governed by the necessities of toil.[44]

A Marxist might object to the utopian character of Marcuse's socialism, to his aspiration to liberate people independently of any structural changes in production. For Marxism insists that relations of dominion and servitude are rooted in the economic structure or in the relations of production. A projected emancipation from servitude which leaves intact the roots of that servitude — the capitalist use of machinery and capitalist forms of productive organization — is, for the Marxist, destined to failure. Also one might object to the potential for political domination inherent in Marcuse's proposal for an unchecked elite wielding centralized control over the means of production, communication, education and entertainment. In addition, if Marcuse's belief that work is inherently repressive were correct, one would have to worry that the elite, working long and hard to service the butterflies flitting about outside the iron cage of technical rationality, will resent the easy playfulness of the masses and turn on them in an awful revenge. Of course, the managerial and professional strata existing today, despite Marcuse's theory of work, do not look upon their work as a burden.

Rather than concentrating on these objections to Marcuse's variant of the leisure-as-compensation thesis, let us focus on two contentions which are common to all the proponents of the thesis. The first assumption is that individuals can be servile automatons during the working day (which the hopeful believe can be reduced to two hours) and spontaneous, superabundant players in their free time. The second is that people can be educated to enjoy a culture which is entirely unrelated to their vocation.

The Mindless Worker and the Dynamic Player

The assumption that individuals can be servile automatons at work and expansive players off work is based on the expectation that the working day can be sufficiently shortened to prevent any adverse effect of working experience upon leisure time. However there has been a tendency in industrialized countries for hours of work to flatten out when they drop below forty hours weekly.[45] Aside from the preference for increased income to increased leisure from increased productivity, coupled with the difficulty of workers to maintain income levels in a period of fiscal, trade and energy crises, there is a more fundamental structural reason for the retardation in the reduction of working hours. That is, the service sector is the most rapidly expanding area of advanced industrial economies and this sector is more labour intensive and less susceptible to automation than the extractive, manufacturing and construction sectors of the economy.[46] This tendency then limits the process of automating production which is the ground of shortened working time and enlarged leisure time.

A more profound difficulty in the assumption of the mindless worker and the dynamic player, who alternately reside in the body and soul of the proletarian, is of a psychological nature. K. Mannheim inadvertently exposes the folly of this assumption of the leisure as compensation thesis.

> The mechanization of industry and its schematized routines deny creative outlets and personal initiative to the many, and demand compensation in leisure-time pursuits. Leisure, besides the natural balance to man's work, becomes the place for personality development and self-expression.[47]

However he also notes that:

> The worker can hardly be expected to put up with the ugliness of an outmoded factory and unsatisfactory work conditions if during his leisure he learns to appreciate beauty and the art of self-expression.[48]

Thus, if leisure really does compensate for work, it would render intolerable those conditions which require compensatory leisure. The sense of beauty and the art of self-expression learned off work cannot be exercised during work, as even the cleanest and best decorated factories and offices "deny creative outlets and personal initiative to the many." The split between self-expressive, appreciative leisure and regimented, servile labour might well engender derangement or personal disintegration. What Mannheim sees as the requirements of work renders untenable what he sees to be the required function of leisure.

Marcuse apparently recognizes the psychological impossibility of individuals slaving in the realm of necessary toil (even when the working day is much shorter than at present) and liberating their playful instincts in culture and social relationships during their leisure time. He foresees that, with a substantial (although unspecified) reduction of working time, the pleasure principle governing leisure time activities would inform working experience, providing it with an aesthetic dimension and making it more playful.[49] Marcuse's prospect of transforming work into play may be foolishness but it is born from the avoidance of the folly of Mannheim. It is not foolish for Marcuse to reject the liberal leisure-as-compensation assumption that a cramped working life, devoid of skill and initiative, can be complemented by a varied and enterprising life of leisure.

In order to assess the possible co-existence of the passive, unreflective and repressed worker and the active, considerate and expansive player, we might consider whether the individual, as worker and player, is really two different personalities or an integral whole exhibiting a unified personality in different forms of activities. Empirical studies cannot be decisive on this question but they do contribute to an answer. A study of 806 students in technical and educational institutions in Quebec found a remarkable correlation between work values and leisure values, leading to the conclusion that there are unified beliefs within the person which express themselves in both work and leisure.[50]*

Sociologists have studied different occupations to see whether individuals' working and non-working activities converge or diverge. These studies conclude that a convergence of vocational and leisure interests is more common in some occupations (such as social workers, architects, railwaymen and professors) than in others; dentists, clerks, and assembly line operatives are less likely to extend professional relationships and vocational interests into their leisure activ-

---

* Such lofty ideals as utilizing knowledge and skills, developing oneself toward personal goals, self-improvement and extending oneself through challenge and effort were highly valued for both work and leisure. Similar correlations were found for the values least cherished in work and leisure. Some divergence pertaining to the value of pride in accomplishment which rated more highly in work than in leisure and to that of pleasant companionship which was deemed more important for leisure than for work.

ities.[51] The unsurprising conclusion of most of these empirical studies is that when a person considers his job to be his central life interest, his hobbies, reading, friends, etc. are more work-related than those whose life interests are centered on the family or on leisure activities. The most elaborate model of the relationship between work and leisure activities is that of S.R. Parker who distinguishes leisure as an extension of work, as opposition to it, or as complementary to it.[52]

	Spheres	Demarcation	Attitude to Work	Main Function of Leisure
Extension	Similar	Little	Involved	Development of personality
Complementarity	Somewhat different	Some	Indifferent	Relaxation
Opposition	Very different	A lot	Ambivalent or hostile	Recuperation

However, Parker's model might give the misleading impression that a critical attitude toward work is not likely to correspond to a discriminating choice of leisure activities (those conducive to the development of personality). Moreover, the model incorrectly suggests that "a busman's holiday" (or the extension into leisure of working interests) is necessary to personal integrity and individual development. Leisure activities which are very different from working activities are quite compatible with personal growth. Nor is it necessarily the case that when the leisure activities are very different from working activities, as Parker indicates for miners and fishermen,[53] the attitudes and abilities brought to bear on both spheres are markedly different. Another observer of the leisure activities of miners writes: "Used to managing their own affairs in the chapels and their Trade Unions, the miners and steel workers have also organized their own choral societies, brass bands, orchestras, dramatic societies, educational courses and institutes for recreation."[54] That is, although these leisure activities are quite different from mining, the initiative British miners have displayed in resisting scientific management and in managing their own working lives corresponds to their self-management of leisure activities. Thus the fact that the leisure activities of groups such as miners are different from their working activities does not imply that such persons are distinct personality types at work and at play. Revision of Parker's model in line with the above considerations would strengthen his overall contention regarding "the spillover effect" of working experience upon leisure. Parker's conclusion, based on his own and on others' research, is that a varied and challenging working environment is conducive to an enterprising and satisfying life of leisure.[55] Thus empirical studies conflict with the first assumption of the leisure-as-compensation thesis, the expectation that one can be a slave at work and a free man at play.

The Permanent Revolution in Leisure Education

The second assumption of the leisure-as-compensation thesis follows from the first assumption that people's time and psyches can be neatly divided into the realms of necessary work and of free play, of cramped servility and expansive superabundance. In order to endow the uninvolved, manipulated worker with sufficient energy and judgment to be a discriminating, spontaneous player, the process of education must be broadened in scope and lengthened in duration so as to result in a more intense and personal involvement in cultural and social activities. This second assumption, more explicitly formulated by the proponents of the leisure-as-compensation thesis, is that a system of avocational training can be devised to equip the working class for a civilization of leisure. J.L. Hammond clearly expounds the new programme:

> ...under modern conditions the part played by intelligence and imagination in the mass of work done by mankind is steadily reduced as routine methods become more common. The more a man loses in interest, variety and scope in his self-expression in his work, the more necessary is it to give him interest, intelligence and scope for self-expression outside... A century ago our fathers educated a small class for leisure and the rest of the population for work. We now have to educate a whole society for leisure.[56]

H.L. Wilensky concludes his intelligent study of the use Americans make of the mass media with the observation that "among men not accustomed to the wider universe made available by demanding work, it takes a long, expensive education to avoid an impoverished life."[57] J. Dumazedier also emphasizes the need of a long, expensive education to prepare for our age of leisure. "Let us not deceive ourselves into thinking that spontaneous activities compensate for the dullness of daily work. Awareness of a style of life and a general education are required; otherwise, dull work is most often accompanied by dull leisure."[58] Thus Dumazedier calls upon us "to invent a new system of permanent education for both youth and adults that is oriented toward the self-development of the personality of every age, creating a new relation between obligation and free choice, between study and leisure."[59]

However Dumazedier presents us with sufficient empirical data to demonstrate the impracticability of this permanent educational revolution. His observations illustrate the usefulness of empirical research to the same degree that his lack of thought manifests the limits of empiricism. The reasons for his advocacy of a permanent revolution in a "leisure-oriented education" pertains to marked class inequalities in public involvement and cultural attainment, and to the inability of existing educational institutions to answer the needs of leisured citizens. The folly of his proposal pertains to a systematic ignoring of educational motivations.

Dumazedier estimates that 8% of French wage-earners, 17% of craftsmen, and 35% of middle management are members of social clubs and organizations.[60] In addition, only 4% of wage-earners belong to a cultural organization (concerned with music, painting, literature or the like) compared to 16% of small businessmen and craftsmen and 20% of salaried employees. Manual workers "show little interest in science, art, literature or philosophy"[61] whereas interest in these subjects is more pronounced as one mounts the hierarchy of industry.

> The percentage of workers interested in art and literature is five times smaller than that shown by executives. The commitment of French education to equality is well known. Prolongation of mandatory school attendance, from this viewpoint, is essential for the progress of a common culture that would reduce the imbalances...
> Each job makes its demands, but the different evolution in each social group implies a difference in training which, in certain cases, could be compensated for. Sharing in popular culture would then become a life-long acquisition.[62]

Dumazedier's conclusion is by no means clearly intelligible. He calls for a prolongation of mandatory school attendance even though what is presently in the school curriculum is of little interest to adults. In his study of the leisure activities of the citizens of Annecy, Dumazedier found that "there is only a rather remote connection between what interests adults and what is taught in school."[63] Thus a new educational system for "continued culture" must be devised to promote a better understanding of the world and the means to solve the problems individuals confront in their daily lives. The French system of adult education, Dumazedier feels, is not as well developed as those in Britain, North America and the Soviet Union and thus most French citizens must do their own reading when they wish to improve their knowledge of subjects that interest them. Dumazedier's proposed new educational system for continuous culture is expected to complement the existing form of self-improvement.[64]

However the interests expressed by individuals, in their choice of reading material, render the kind of education Dumazedier proposes for the age of leisure highly questionable. "Only three kinds of subjects managed to escape their indifference: practical matters, technical questions, and geography."[65] Given Dumazedier's definition of leisure as those activities distinct from vocational and domestic usefulness, the educational interests of the adults Dumazedier studied are markedly unleisurely. "First, we note the preferred topics are connected to *utilitarian* preoccupations, answering a need for information about matters affecting daily life. As one would expect, one of the chief concerns of a man is the kind of work he does."[66] Thus, although the leisure-as compensation thesis entails an education system which is not called into being by, or even related to, vocational requirements, the facts appear to be that educational motivations are rooted in the realm of necessity. The view that an enlarged cultural horizon is compatible with a circumscribed working experience does not find support from Dumazedier's research.

However the lack of realism in Dumazedier's proposal for a permanent educational or cultural revolution is not that work and education are inherently inseparable. The disassociation of education and work is not only possible for the future, but also, in large part, exists in the present. Much of the time spent in schools and universities does not prepare individuals for the world of work. As people are obtaining more and more education, most jobs require less vocational preparation. I. Berg's *Education and Jobs: The Great Training Robbery* states unequivocally that there is no basis for the popular assertion that technical advance demands better educated workers. In fact, areas with the greatest increases in productivity are sectors with the lowest educational level.[67] With longer schooling for increasing numbers of people, there is an increasing tendency for workers to be in jobs that utilize less education than they have. Greater education than is needed for the fulfillment of a job is a major source of worker dissatisfaction.[68] Moreover, in numerous occupations, the level of education is totally unrelated to standards of work performance and opportunities for advancement.[69] Also, increasingly of late, educational attainments do not help in securing employment; in 1959, the median education of the employed in the U.S. was 12.0 years, of the unemployed, 9.9 years: in 1971, the median education of the employed and unemployed was 12.4 years and 12.2 years respectively.[70]

Since many jobs require only literacy and practical experience with a short period of on-the-job training, one does not need to be an efficiency expert to see that the more than twelve years schooling for employed and unemployed alike is wasteful, i.e., not put to a productive use. Such schooling may be indirectly productive as a babysitting service for working parents, as a means to save employers from using Rorschach tests to determine an individual's perseverance and industry, or as a method to habituate students to industrial discipline. However it certainly does not provide future workers with intellectual command over their instruments or production, or with a sufficiently broad scientific and technical training to enable workers to move to allied areas when the structure of demand changes or when a technical innovation is introduced. The rapidity of technical change and the relative simplicity in learning most jobs make a short vocational training, and then retraining whenever necessary, much cheaper than a thorough apprenticeship in an occupation.

Thus there is reason to suppose that the more than twelve years education that the average American receives is only peripherally related to securing a job and acquiring the skills to do so. The proposal of the leisurists to orient education to leisure does not require a radical disassociation of education from work because most of the time presently occupied in school systems is not preparation for an occupation. Since the present trend is to increase the period of schooling and to decrease the amount of time requisite to mastering a trade, one might think Dumazedier's proposal to create a leisure-centered educational system reasonable.

The difficulty with the proposal to orient education exclusively to leisure is that most people have been motivated to achieve an education upon the expectation that it is useful for social mobility and earning a livelihood. A recent survey in England revealed that 90 percent of parents and children thought that education pertains to earning a living and acquring the skills to do so.[71] As the remaining 10 percent expressed educational ideals as well as real motivations, it is not unreasonable to suppose, in the absence of other information, that the vast majority of students acquire an education on the expectation that they will put it to some practical purpose. The failure of educational systems to meet this expectation may well be a major source of discontent with existing educational institutions.

The assumption that an educational system with no vocational orientation can serve to prepare people for cultural and political citizenship runs counter to existing expectations of the purpose of an education. To be sure, schools, universities and institutes for adult education do, to a greater or lesser degree, provide opportunities for cultural growth as well as vocational training. The results may be assessed in the fact that 42 percent of Americans in 1969 admitted that they had, at some time during their life, finished reading at least one book, besides text books and the Bible.[72] In 1961, the National Publishers' Syndicate found that "forty-two percent of the French read books."[73] Statistics Canada revealed that 57% of Canadians in 1979 do not read books.[74] A study of Britain in 1967 revealed that fifty-eight percent of the youth do not read books.[75] However perhaps two-thirds of the adult population of Britain have read a book in the previous year.[76] When one considers the relative ease by which the fifty-eight percent of Americans, Canadians, Frenchmen and British youth could join the aristocracy of book readers, one wonders why the serious endeavours of educationalists have not borne greater fruit.

Some hypotheses might be advanced to account for this. It might be suggested that culture is not necessary for most occupations; technical competence rather than cultural attainment is what is needed, honoured and rewarded in public life. Further, it might be asserted that the separation of what C.P. Snow popularized as the two cultures of art and science is such that art no longer mirrors our scientific-technical life, no longer reveals the injustice and necessities of our work-a-day life. It might also be advanced that the streaming of many working-class children into vocational programmes or technical schools neither provides these students with a taste for the culture enjoyed by the ruling classes, nor reinforces popular culture or working-class self-understanding. Since the most productive sectors of capitalist economies tend to be those with the lowest educational levels and since educational attainments cannot be considered a sure passport to securing work and job advancement, we must consider the industrial stagnation and potentially revolutionary situation that would arise if educationalists were to succeed in imparting a liberal education universally. But even the students who are not streamed into technical education may find that the liberal principles informing Western educational systems—namely, freedom of choice, respect for the individuality of the young, non-imposition of the values of teachers upon students, etc.— make problematic the role of culture in an education. To conceive of culture as a standard of attainment, as an objective of education, as a form to guide students growth, as a mould for character, as a nucleus to give coherence and meaning to the factual knowledge imparted, etc. runs counter to profoundly held liberal principles. These principles inhibit the forming of students' character according to an odious mould or type, in fact leaving the forming of personality to "the invisible hand" of socio-economic determinants, but, in doing so, render the role of culture largely unintelligible to the student.

A combination of such factors as these may help to explain the relatively unfruitful results of so much education. On the one hand, it may be argued that neither the economic nor the educational systems are responsible for the level of mass culture. Rather it is simply that a large number of students are incapable of being educated. Such a viewpoint may be adopted by those who wish to apply the results of I.Q. tests in order to rationalize the system of education but is clearly untenable for the sociologists who wish to use education to create a rewarding leisure life to compensate for the monotonous drudgery of industrial work.*

---

* The "socialist" H. de Man, in *Joy in Work*, (London, 1921, p. 121) believes that intelligence tests have proved Taylor's and Ford's theory that most Americans prefer, and are only capable of performing, unskilled repetitive work. "On the basis of information derived from intelligence tests, American statisticians declare that in the United States there is an especially large percentage of morons, that is to say of persons who, though they cannot be classed as idiots, have not attained a level of intelligence fitting them for more than the simplest kinds of work." We still await a *Joy in Leisure* calling for an organization of leisure activities, and an educational system to prepare for it, determined by the results of intelligence tests.

The above considerations have been predicated on the assumption that a low level of general culture is indicated by the fact that a majority of the adult population does not read books. However the assumption is perhaps not warranted, especially in an age of electronic media, since there are many forms of cultural expression that do not depend on the printed word. Indeed, besides the mass media, Americans in 1960 spent 300 million dollars for art museums, a similar amount for libraries, 200 million buying paintings, prints, colour reproductions and art materials, 90 million on classical records, 590 million for musical instruments, 26 million for symphony orchestras, 1 billion for books, 375 million for theatre, opera and concert halls.[77] However studies reveal that the consumption of these commodities is more marked in the executive and professional strata of the population.[78] It is probable that many of the 58 percent who have never read a book rely on the mass media, and in particular television, for their entire cultural consumption.

Although, as we have already seen, Dumazedier and other sociologists of leisure believe the level of popular culture is steadily rising, it is not sufficiently high to do without the educational or organizational direction of the leisurist. Dumazedier stresses education rather than organization as the means to elevate workers to the standards required by the theory of compensatory leisure. Indeed he is adamant that a revolution in education is necessary to invent new forms of social involvement which have atrophied with the technicist organization of society in this century. A preparation for social and cultural citizenship to replace declining professional, familial, religious and political involvements is essential "so that the masses, not only the elite, increasingly participate in the elaboration of their own destiny."[79]

The difficulty with Dumazedier's scheme of avocational training is not just that it would be immensely costly. More importantly, it is not in accord with existing educational motivations and thus has little promise of bearing fruit. For Dumazedier's own research demonstrates that educational goals are rooted in the realm of necessity or utility.

While Dumazedier favours a prolongation of school attendance and a continuing cultural education to prepare "the masses" for the dawning civilization of leisure, he foresees an alternative—managed leisure. That is, rather than educating individuals up to the level where their leisure could compensate for the vicissitudes of Taylorized work, the

149

leisurist accepts individuals as they are, and organizes their leisure. Perhaps recognizing the impracticability of his prescription for a permanent cultural revolution, Dumazedier asserts that if workers are not educated to assume responsibility in our age of leisure

> the masses could hand over this fascinating but tiresome power to an oligarchy of intellectual specialists, technocrats, or bureaucrats in order to enjoy their increased time of leisure and the consumption of goods which will be distributed in growing quantities to a growing number of individuals.[80]

Thus the leisurist's managerial skills become indispensable to the extent that avocational training proves ineffective. Since the necessity of the leisurist, in his educational or organizational capacity, is integral to the leisure-as-compensation thesis, Dumazedier ignores the implications of his own research on the "spillover effect" of work upon leisure.

> It is among the workers who find their work interesting that intellectual curiosity and the need for complementary education are most lively. They read more serials and novels. They show more desire to participate in cultural vacations, aimed at general culture or preparation for social responsibilities.[81]

To be sure, the leisurist would be in less demand if the majority of workers found their jobs interesting. But the conclusion is inescapable—not only is educational motivation but also cultural attainment is rooted in the demands of the job. The less narrowly jobs are defined, the less circumscribed one's education or culture is likely to be.

The proposal to create a leisure-centred educational system is required by leisure-as-compensation theory but is rendered untenable by the facts revealed by the sociology of leisure.

Closing the Iron Cage

The scientific management of leisure may be thought to be an inherent impossibility. Conflicting interests within the leisure industries of capitalist societies, according to Soviet leisurists, preclude the possibility of "the rational utilization of the workers' free time."[82] Moreover, leisure may be thought to be less susceptible to technicist organization than work. For technique is a means to a given end. By reducing work to production (which has the one purpose of maximal output), Taylor's technical imagination found the means to achieve that end. By conceiving of sports as contests (which have the one aim of victory), Taylor's problem-solving mentality eliminated many of the obstacles to his joyless victories. But is it possible to conceive of one end or function of leisure? Leisure activities are frequently thought to serve a plurality of ends, such as restoring and recreating energies for the task ahead, diverting attention from burdensome cares, "raising consciousness" or "mind expansion", having fun or harmless enjoyment, keeping people off the streets and so forth. The difficulty in establishing one end of leisure, to which methods of achievement are to be integrated, would seem to block the application of technical or means-ends rationality. Productive activities may be standardized and organized into a hierarchy of specialized performances, as all such activities can be understood as a means to the end of maximum productivity. If the plurality of ends of leisure cannot be reduced to a common end, leisure activities will elude the iron cage of technical rationality.

Perhaps however a single end or function of leisure can be inferred from the pertinent literature.

> Organized recreation, if properly directed, has a tendency to prevent the occurrence of social disorganization and personal demoralization. Recreation affords opportunities for the achievement of fair play, respect for law and order, and the inculcation of co-operative participation.[83]

Thus by a reduction of leisure to wholesome recreation, similar in nature to Taylor's reduction of work to production or sports to contests, we arrive at a unitary purpose for leisure—namely, social integration. Through this reduction of leisure to wholesome recreation, the leisurist can assume his proper place in the "technostructure". Leisure activities, "properly directed", will bear such a relation to productive activities as to reinforce efficient performance and thus will be integrable into a totally managed collectivity.

Within the sociology of leisure, there is widespread acceptance of the proposition that our civilization of leisure depends upon the efficient performance of the productive collectivity. The leisure-as-compensation thesis regards

Taylorism not only as inevitable, but also as desirable, as the goose that lays the golden eggs. Thus the function of leisure is seen to reinforce or support the organization of production that maximizes leisure time and the income to enjoy it. To ensure the perpetuation and growth of leisure time, leisure activities, subject to the educational and organizational skills of the leisurist, become socially productive recreations. Leisure activities, like productive activities, serve to enhance the productive collectivity. Productive and recreational activities are integrated within a system of total management.

The separation of thinking and doing in the planning and execution of wholesome recreations extends the principles of scientific management from the realm of necessity into the realm of freedom. The extension of scientific management from the realm of production to the realm of leisure is the closing of Weber's iron cage of technological rationality.

The problem of Schmidt's leisure time derives from the increased time off work made possible by "the managerial revolution", coupled to the atrophy of abilities in those subjected to scientifically managed jobs. The solution to "the problem" advocated by the leisurist is to complete the work of Taylor in the total management of Schmidt's time. The prospect of a totally managed or totalitarian society cannot be ignored within the horizon of assumptions constituting the leisure-as-compensation theory.

Before assessing this prospect, we shall examine a radically opposed solution to that of scientific management — that of the syndicalists. The major alternative to the thesis that leisure can compensate for Taylorized jobs is the thesis that only job enlargement can avoid a negative spillover effect from work onto leisure. Syndicalism is job enlargement from below. The syndicalist demand for self-management represented for Max Weber a force opposed to technological rationality. In *Politics as a Vocation*, Weber portrayed syndicalism as noble futility in an age of ignoble utility[84]. The subsequent chapter will examine the grounds of the futility of the syndicalist hammerings on the iron cage.

Chapter 8

Job Enlargement from Below

Conceptual and historical opposition of syndicalism and scientific management. Syndicalism defined in relation to anarchism and business unionism. The antagonism of syndicalism and Leninism. Leninism as state capitalism or state-sponsored Taylorism.

The Party State as Capitalist Versus the Union Federation as Merchant. A Merchant does not buy labour-power and thus does not determine methods of work. Why federal monopoly of mercantile functions does not restrict autonomy of producers. The deproletarianization of producers and the proletarianization of commercial functionaries. Tentative steps towards the abolition of wage-slavery.

Alleged technological imperatives and non-mechanical machine labour. Technology in leisure industry. Alternative production relations. Job enlargement from above and below; solving "the problem of leisure" and dis-solving it.

Syndicalism and Leninism

In 1919, following the introduction of scientific management throughout the capitalist world as well as Soviet Russia, W. Gallacher and J.R. Campbell, two of the leaders of the British shop stewards' movement in the second decade of this century, wrote:

> Under the guise of "scientific management" the Capitalists are introducing into industry schemes for dividing operations, and making the labour of workers more automatic. The results of this tendency are to deny the worker responsibility, to rob him of initiative, and to reduce him to the level of

153

> some ghastly, inhuman, mechanical puppet. The
> capitalist idea of more "automatic" workers is
> bound to conflict with the workers' aspirations for
> greater responsibility, greater initiative and
> democratic control of industry. The two are abso-
> lutely incompatible...[1].

These aspirations for "greater responsibility, greater initiative and democratic control of industry" which are "absolutely
incompatible" with scientific management are what we have
called syndicalism. Syndicalism has been presented as the
conceptual opposite, and the historical antagonist, of scientific
management.

However syndicalism requires a more definite charac-
terization than as the antithesis of Taylorism. Yet syndicalism
evades precise definition as it has taken different forms in
England, France, Russia, Scandinavia, Italy, Spain, Latin
America, the United States, western Canada and Québec.
From the outset of the 'new unionism' in Britain and the
formation of the Confédération Générale du Travail in the
1890's until the 1920's when syndicalism waned in Europe and
North America, with many defections to communism (and, in
Italy, to fascism),[2] a variety of militant union movements,
dedicated not only to the improvement of wages and working
conditions but also to the abolition of the wages system, sprang
up around the industrialized world.

George Woodcock has defined syndicalism as "the
industrial manifestation of anarchism."[3] This bold definition
linking syndicalism and anarchism is useful, in spite of the
fact that anarchism is no easier to define than syndicalism.
For the untamed spirit, common to the men and women in the
anarchist and syndicalist traditions, prevented the growth of
either systematic doctrine or definitive organizational practices. The syndicalist hostility to industrial authoritarianism
might be thought to be simply a species of the genus, anarchic
anti-authoritarianism.

Indeed, the link between anarchism and syndicalism is
manifest in the term 'anarcho-syndicalism'. Yet this link
establishes the difference as well as the similarity between
anarchism and syndicalism. For 'anarcho-syndicalism' would
be a redundancy if they were identical. Indeed, Errico
Malatesta considered 'anarcho-syndicalism' a bastard term;
"either it is the same as anarchy, and is therefore a term which
only serves to confuse matters, or it is different from anarchy
and cannot therefore be accepted by anarchists."[4] However,

the logical rigour of Malatesta's either anarchism or syndicalism did not impede the historical development of anarcho-syndicalist movements. Anarcho-syndicalism then results from a dialectical unity, not a simple identity of anarchism and syndicalism.

Malatesta explains that because trade unions "for pressing reasons, are often obliged to engage in negotiations and accept compromises" in order to retain the allegiance of their mass following, syndicalism is "essentially" or "necessarily reformist."[5] Although Malatesta rightly directs our attention to the difficulties of wedding an intellectual sect to a mass movement, he is surely one-sided in understanding syndicalism as essentially a reformist movement. Murray Bookchin, on the other hand, defines syndicalism as inherently revolutionary and having identical goals to anarchism.[6] But, just as the term 'anarcho-syndicalism' suggests that there is a non-anarchic as well as an anarchic form of syndicalism, so the ascription 'revolutionary syndicalism' suggests that there is a reformist as well as a revolutionary form of syndicalism. Indeed, the French syndicalist Confédération Générale du Travail split in 1910-11 between revolutionary and reformist elements and the Spanish Confederacion Nacional de Trabajo divided on the same lines in 1929-1930.

Thus anarchists and syndicalists must be regarded as no more than fellow travellers with a common destination of overturning capitalist relations of production enforced by the modern state. But the syndicalist, unlike the anarchist, "opposes the state not because all government is objectionable, but because this particular form of government is suited only to capitalist society, and is utterly incompatible with the economic society which he proposes to introduce."[7] Further, efforts to link syndicalist movements with political parties (for which Daniel DeLeon was kicked out of the American I.W.W. and Angel Pestana was removed from the Spanish C.N.T.) are inconsistent with anarchist, but not necessarily syndicalist principles. Since syndicalists believe that real power is based on control over production, they have tended to repudiate the parliamentary or the party political path to power. But this stance for the syndicalist as distinct from the anarchist is more a matter of strategy than of principle.

The parameters for defining syndicalism then are anarchism on the one side and business unionism on the other. Syndicalists are not purely anarchists because they have to compete with business unions to retain the allegiance of the rank and file and they are never purely bread and butter unionists, concerned with wages and working conditions, or they lose the characteristically syndicalist concern to overthrow capitalist authority relations in the mines, shops and yards. Syndicalists were reluctant to institute collective bargaining because, they felt, such a process inherently sells out the goal of industrial self-management and authorizes the capitalists' right to manage industry in return for agreed conditions of work. Moreover, collective bargaining procedures were seen to be an institutionalization of class conflict which undermines militancy, restricts wildcat strikes and plant occupations. Further, contracts binding on workers for specific periods of time limit the ability of union locals to act against employers in a timely way and prevent contractually bound workers from joining in the strike activities of others. Although some syndicalists tried to combine revolutionary with business unionism, they were united in their opposition to bread and butter unionism; they wanted "bread and roses too."[8]

The pattern of recruitment of syndicalist movements varied from country to country. Whereas the French C.G.T. and the British shop stewards were recruited largely from skilled urban mechanics, the North American I.W.W. organized mainly unskilled, and often rural, workers.[9] The British industrial syndicalist movement was made up of both skilled and unskilled workers, as were the Unione Syndicale Italiano and the Spanish C.N.T. which organized farm workers as well as urban wage-labourers.[10] The I.W.W. refused to follow the practice of the British syndicalists in amalgamating with, and "boring from within" existing mass unions; the union preferred "hammering from without", attacking the American Federation of Labour for the exclusivity and sectionalism of its craft unionism and for the class-collaborationist ideas of its leader, Samuel Gompers. The I.W.W. concentrated on strata of the labour force neglected by the A.F.L. (Blacks, women, immigrants and migratory workers). The 'Wobblies' thus organized a more heterogeneous labour force than European syndicalist organizations: "it opened its doors to all: Negro and Asian, Jew and Catholic, immigrant and native."[11] Because of this un-American propensity, the I.W.W. conformed perfectly to Taylor's and Ford's idea of the outside agitator, the foreign element corrupting the naturally loyal hands, instilling into the Schmidts' of this world alien ideas of class conflict. The opposition of the I.W.W. to America's participation in World War I led to the successful prosecution of the I.W.W. leadership by the federal government during the war, and lynch mobs as well as official repression, under the Criminal Syndicalist legislation in the post war years.[12] Although repression of syndicalist movements in Europe was not as brutal as in the U.S.A., only in Spain, which maintained neutrality during the war, did syndicalism enter the post war years in a position of strength.

Whether syndicalists were skilled workers who wished to preserve craft control of production, or unskilled workers who aspired to the protection of an industrial union, they were united in the spirit of the Wobbly song, "Dump the Bosses off Your Back". With their aim of industrial self-management, the syndicalists stand out, in this epoch of scientific management, as the masterless men and women of the twentieth century.

If syndicalism can be characterized more by its end or goal than by its constituency, it can also be distinguished by its means or methods. Syndicalists employed the tactics of "direct action" — wildcat strikes, factory occupations and "sabotage" — to combat the power of employers and to stimulate the resolve of fellow workers to participate in class warfare and to join syndicalist organizations. Although most syndicalists preached and practiced "sabotage" (from *sabot*, or wooden shoe), what was meant by sabotage varied from country to country, and also within the national syndicalist movements. It varied from deliberate slow-downs, restrictions on output or what Taylor called "systematic soldiering" (producing as if one were wearing heavy wooden shoes) to theft, and the destruction of property (putting the wooden shoe into the machinery). "Direct action" also could be either non-violent or violent, legal or illegal. By "direct action" was meant undelegated activity, action of the rank and file unmediated by what syndicalists thought to be undemocratic leadership of trade union hierarchies and political parties. Syndicalists felt that union "mis-leaders" were cut off from the concerns of the rank and file in their official positions and moreover were ill-situated, because of their desire to be recognized as official bargaining agents, to deal with the issues of control over the shop, mine or yard. As a result, even when not practicing "dual unionism", syndicalists often created organizations parallel to trade union bureaucracies, such as shop or factory councils or committees of shop stewards, which sprang into action at times of crisis to challenge the more conservative leadership of national trade unions. The Russian factory soviets, the British shop stewards' committees, the I.W.W., the German shop steward movement of 1918, the Italian factory councils, the

157

One Big Union at the time of the Winnipeg General Strike, were examples of syndicalist organizations in the years prior to, during, and following World War I. Many of the syndicalists who subsequently joined the Communist party did so from an enthusiasm for the soviet idea, from the impression that the Soviet regime was the actualization of the aspirations and the organizational forms syndicalists had adopted in Europe and America.[13] Those who continued in the Communist party after the Soviet Union had abandoned its syndicalist character, had subordinated the soviets and the unions to a party controlled state, and had promoted a state sponsored form of Taylorism, no longer held to the syndicalist principles they had earlier espoused.

What distinguishes syndicalism from both communism and social democracy pertains to the higher priority syndicalists gave to the union over the party in social transformation. While many syndicalists were associated with parliamentary or revolutionary political parties and thus did not share the principled opposition of the anarchists to party politics, syndicalists generally did not see political parties to be the primary vehicles for the abolition of wage-slavery. The departure of the DeLeonites from the I.W.W. shortly after its founding exhibits the uncertainty about the place of political parties, even among those sympathetic to syndicalist aims, in a syndicalist movement. Politicians, such as Daniel DeLeon, were often regarded with suspicion, as middle class intellectuals who wished to use the labour movement for objectives other than workers' control or management of industry. But the main reason for the primacy of the union over the party was the syndicalist view that political power did not reside in parliament but in the ownership and control of the means of production. The state apparatus merely enforced the interests of those with economic power. To contest political power in electoral politics was thus to concern oneself with a mere symptom of the structure of domination which emerges at the point of production.

Parliamentary politics, from the standpoint of syndicalism, cannot by itself bring about industrial democracy. After all, "parliament was not brought into existence to enable the working classes to obtain ownership and mastery over the means of production."[14] Syndicalists saw unions and factory committees rather than labour parties or socialist representation in parliament as their primary weapons in the fight against capitalism. In addition, workers' management of industry, rather than simply the nationalization of production, served as the focus of syndicalist objectives.[15] Indeed mere nationalization, without workers' control of industry, is likely to consolidate the power of the capitalist exploiter over the worker.[16] The Fabian or state socialist programme would not emancipate the wage-labourer but would merely constitute "a centralized official bureaucracy giving instructions and commands to servile subordinates..."[17] As Tom Mann asserted in 1911:

> The industrial syndicalist declares that to run industry through Parliament, i.e., by the State machinery, will be more mischievous to the working class than the existing method, for it will mean that the capitalist class will, through Government departments, exercise over the natural forces, and over the workers, a domination even more rigid than is the case to-day.[18]

The Russian syndicalists expressed a similar distaste for state controlled industry after the Communist Party had suppressed the factory committees and subordinated the unions to the party. The controversy between Lenin and Russian syndicalists, R.V. Daniels wrote, turned on the question:

> Were the factories to be turned into autonomous, democratic communes, or were the industrial workers to be subjected again to managerial authority, labour discipline, wage incentives, scientific management—to the familiar forms of capitalist industrial organization with the same bourgeois managers, qualifed only by the state's holding title to the property.[19]

Thus what distinguished syndicalists from Fabians and Communists was not just differing assessments of the efficacy of industrial versus political action, the primacy of the union or the party, or of organization at the place of production or in parliament, but also to differing views of the nature of a post-capitalist society and state. If syndicalism offered a genuine alternative to state socialism, it also lacked a clear strategy for contesting capitalist hegemony on the political level and a clear vision of how self-managing industrial collectives would plan and co-ordinate production on a national and international basis. That is, syndicalists concerned themselves with the creation of power centres and nuclei of industrial democracy within "the shell" of capitalist society but were not prepared for the contestation of power in World War I and the post-war period when the power of various states was brought to bear on European and North American syndicalist organizations, suppressing and dispersing them. The use of political parties, and the programmes of state socialists, appeared more effective for attaining their objectives than the apolitical approach of the pre-war syndicalists.

With the assumption to power of the Bolsheviks, the syndicalist character of Lenin's writings, which was extremely marked in the period just prior to the October revolution, disappeared. In *Can the Bolsheviks Retain State Power?* Lenin supported the workers' movement to take over factories and manage them by workers' councils. The socialist regime, he asserted, will be based upon self-management in industry. In fact, Lenin denounced as "bourgeois-reformist" any attempt to replace the doctrine of workers' control with the programme of state control of industry.[20] His celebrated *State and Revolution*, also written just before the October revolution, also advocated workers' self-management of industry. But this authoritative text on the Leninist theory of revolution and the dictatorship of the proletariat appears syndicalist precisely because Lenin's major contribution to Marxism, namely, the theory of the party, is in this one work strikingly absent. In the absence of an account of the role of the party in the central planning and coercive construction of a socialist society, Lenin's emphasis on self-administration and factory councils as the basis of the Soviet regime stimulated the syndicalists whom Lenin was to attack after the October revolution.

Shortly after the revolution, Lenin reversed himself and advocated state control rather than workers' control of industry. He called for the replacement of collegiate management vested in factory councils by the unitary management of "bourgeois specialists" overseen by the communist party, a state sponsored form of Taylorism (time-motion studies, "socialist competition", piece-wages, wage-differentials) and a rigorous system of punishment to enforce "proletarian discipline" or the unquestionable authority of management in relation to the workers within an enterprise.[21] Lenin tirelessly denounced all left or syndicalist opposition as "petty-bourgeois" and "infantile"; "petty-bourgeois" because they manifested the individualism associated with artisans or small proprietors, their hatred of bosses and of the discipline of externally regimented work and "infantile" because they failed to see the alleged technological necessity for the authority of bourgeois' management in industry and the political necessity of a centralized party governing all aspects of the construction of a socialist society. In *Left Wing Communism: An Infantile Disorder,* Lenin declared that it is nonsense to attempt to implement "the dictatorship of the proletariat, without a rigourously centralized party, with iron discipline, without the ability to become masters of every sphere, every branch, and every variety of political and cultural work."[22] Indeed, he asserted to the ninth party congress that all important decisions in the political and economic institutions of Soviet Russia are made under the direction of the central committee of the party.[23] Syndicalist "infantilism" is to be superseded by what syndicalists considered Leninist paternalism.

In *The Party Crisis,* Lenin asserted: "Syndicalism hands over to the mass of non-Party workers, who are compartmentalized in the industries, the management of their industries, ("the chief administrations and central boards"), thereby making the Party superfluous..."[24] The reason for the suppression of the syndicalist faction of the Communist party in 1921 is evident in Lenin's rhetorical question: "Why have a Party, if industrial management is to be appointed... by the trade unions, nine-tenths of whose members are non-Party workers?"[25] Indeed Lenin came to believe that "all direct interference by trade unions in the management of factories must be regarded as positively harmful and impermissible."[26]

It is not our concern to assess the merits of Lenin's position and of the syndicalist position in the context of the economic devastation of World War I, the revolution and the civil war and of the political tensions of a party, with only minority support within Russia, attempting to govern in the face of external and internal hostility. Our concern is simply to distinguish the position of syndicalism in relation to "state socialism". The difference pertains to the capacity or incapacity of workers for self-management; the party's guiding role in the dictatorship of the proletariat is necessary to the extent that the "self-government of the immediate producers" in factory committees and unions is deemed to be impractical. Lenin's opposition to syndicalism is not purely political, namely, that the majority of workers are not Bolsheviks and thus that an administration of elected soviets and unions would supplant the "iron discipline" and leadership of the communist party. Besides being politically undesirable, syndicalism is technically unfeasible. The technological requirements of modern industry, together with Lenin's aim to turn

161

Russia into one large factory and office, do not accord with workers' self-management of industry.

Justifying his policy in April 1918 of introducing the Taylor system of management and of replacing soviet management of industry by capitalist managers under the direction of the communist party, Lenin wrote:

> ...large-scale machine industry — which is precisely the material source, the productive source, the foundation of socialism — calls for absolute and strict *unity of will*, which directs the joint labours of hundreds, thousands and tens of thousands of people... But how can strict unity of will be ensured? By thousands subordinating their will to the will of one... *unquestioning subordination* to a single will is absolutely necessary for the success of processes organized on the pattern of large-scale machine industry.[27]

In *Left Wing Childishness and the Petty-Bourgeois Mentality*, Lenin denounced the syndicalist opposition who failed to see that socialism is equivalent to German state capitalism, subordinated to the Communist party rather than to "Junker bourgeois imperialism."[28] That is, socialism is based upon the technical infrastructure of state organized capitalism, but the machine is to serve new masters. Lenin wrote that "socialism is merely state-capitalist monopoly *which is made to serve the interests of the whole people* and has to that extent *ceased* to be capitalist monopoly."[29]

Lenin then considered socialism to be a party-dominated state performing the functions of a capitalist class. The syndicalist opposition held that "wage-slavery" is not abolished when the state becomes the sole employer of labour power.

Marxism holds that relationships of domination and subordination arise from the economic structure or the manner in which production is organized. The Russian revolution did not arise from, or give birth to, fundamentally different production techniques or relations of production than those regulating the subordination of wage-labour in capitalist societies. Russian socialism was based upon a centralized development of capitalist techniques and productive relations, and thus did not actualize the Marxist and syndicalist aspiration to abolish the wages system. For Marx, socialism was to be the de-proletarianization of economic life. But since Russian socialism did not emerge in a predominantly industrial society with a majority of industrial wage-labourers, educated for, and habituated to, the discipline of factory life, the task for socialism became the repressive proletarianization of the Russian economy. For Marx, socialism was to abolish wage-slavery; for Lenin, socialism was to universalize it.

The aim of syndicalism was, and is, to abolish the wages system by the creation of an industrial democracy based upon unions and factory committees. The efficacy of this apolitical approach was severely challenged with the suppression of syndicalist movements in western Europe and America after World War I and the success of Leninism in the Soviet Union. The repudiation of party politics amongst syndicalists was associated with their rejection of "the servile state" or the form of socialism advocated by the State socialists, whether parliamentary or communist. Support for the party political approach was tantamount to support for the statist form of socialism.

The Party State as Capitalist Versus
The Union Federation as Merchant

We have seen that syndicalists connected party politics with support for the statist form of socialism. Their repudiation of "politics" was associated with their rejection of "the servile state" of both Fabians and Bolsheviks. Conversely, syndicalist political strategies have been blocked by their inability to provide a fully developed alternative model of a socialist society. The basic difficulty is to indicate how the syndicalist goal of industrial self-management is compatible with socialism, namely, the public ownership of the means of production and centralized planning. If ownership is vested in the state, rather than a workers' collective, are not workers just employees of the state? If an economy is centrally planned, how is it possible for the workers to plan and organize their working lives? Conversely, if ownership is not vested in the state, how is it possible to eliminate inequalities between one collective and another or if the economy is not centrally planned, how is it possible to avoid the chaos of the market-place? This section will attempt to sketch an outline of a socialist society which is compatible with the syndicalist goal of self-management.

The model of an alternative to the Leninist state derives partly from the ideas of French, British, and North American syndicalists and partly from the theory and practice of

Catalonian syndicalists in the Spanish Civil War. However, the lessons derived from reading of syndicalist thought and practice are mine. The following systematization of selective syndicalist practices does not correspond entirely to the ideas of any anarcho-syndicalist that I have read.

The conceptual distinction that I wish to make pertains to the difference between a capitalist and a merchant. As Marx pointed out, whereas a capitalist purchases labour-power and thus has a right of executive command over the labourer in the time purchased, a merchant buys finished products, and is thus not in a position to undermine the independent producers, that is, to determine the methods of production of the artisan or farmer whose product is bought. Not the medieval merchant, but the urban guildsman or the rural peasant determined the standards and method of working. A labourer, subject to an industrial or agricultural capitalist, on the other hand, has the same choice that a horse does in choosing its bit and bridle, its pace and its destination (although perhaps, if unionized, the labourer has the right to bargain on the quantity of oats, the materials of the whip, spur, shoes, blanket etc.) The state as capitalist, on our Animal Farm, deprives the horse of the benefit of unions.

The alternative model of socialism to the party dominated state fulfilling the function of a collective capitalist is for the One Big Union, or a federation of unions*, to play the role

---

* It could be objected that the proposed union or federation is in reality a state, and thus the antithesis should be between the state as capitalist and the state as merchant. And, to be sure, to the extent that the union federation cannot incorporate all strata of the population, that is, to the extent that it excludes non-proletarians (as was generally envisaged by the syndicalists), an alternative public authority, such as a parliament or national congress of people or regions, would be necessary to represent those elements of society excluded from the unions and to co-ordinate the activities of unionists and non-unionists. However, since the term 'state' has the connotation, for anarcho-syndicalists, of command, of military-like authority, I use the term union to emphasize that the 'state' is the workers' own institution, with authority constituted from the bottom up rather than the top down. Anarchists doubtless would think that greater detail is in order about the structure of the socialist 'union' or 'federation', namely, about the composition of popular courts, of a citizens' militia, of the relation between legislation and administration, etc. These matters are crucially important but fall outside my theme of the syndicalist opposition to industrial authoritarianism or scientific management. To ex-

of collective merchant. Not functioning as a capitalist, the federation of unions is thus not in a position to undermine the independence of self-managing collectives in determining their methods of working. What is involved here is a strict division between what Veblen called workmanship and salesmanship; the union federation as collective merchant is to do all the buying and selling of products but is to leave the entire control over the work process in the hands of the workers involved.

We have seen in Chapter 6 that syndicalists like Tom Mann, whom the Webbs attacked, favoured national planning and marketing boards, while strongly insisting on the autonomy of workers at the coal face or shop floor. Thus the separation of workmanship and salesmanship is compatible with the aims of British syndicalism and also obviates one of the Webbs' arguments against syndicalism, namely that workers cannot be expected to know enough about market conditions to estimate the quantities and qualities demanded in the domestic and world market.

The other objections the Webbs had to syndicalism were being disproven in the practice of Spanish syndicalists at the same time that the Webbs trumpeted Stalinism as the embodiment of Fabian anti-syndicalism. Within forty-eight hours of seizing control of the factories in Barcelona in July 1936, workers had the tramways and buses, telephones and the utilities (water, gas and light) operating with at least the level of efficiency prior to the uprising (and the killing or fleeing of entire managerial staffs, including senior engineers).[30] So it is not only the fascists who got the trains running on time. The success of these self-managing factories until parts or raw materials became scarce in the Spanish Civil War refutes the Webbs' view that workers lack the discipline and ability to manage and co-ordinate their working lives. However, the Webbs' view that workers are unable to assess accurately market conditions was not put to the test because the manufacturing sector in Catalonia lost its markets inside and outside Spain with the outbreak of civil war.[31] None of the self-managing factories produced for "the free market". A number of industries were successfully retooled into munitions for the war effort, with the financing of operations done, and the arms

pand the theme to encompass all the political and cultural conditions of a libertarian society would diffuse the central ideas of this book and would ride roughshod over some of the more cherished aspects of libertarian doctrine.

purchased, by the central government. F. Borkenau was amazed that factories were running as smoothly as if nothing had happened. Buses were built in five days as compared with seven before the revolution and industrial self-management. He attributes the success of the bus construction enterprise to the fact that the former repair shop had stock, with little need of raw materials, and with a certain income from bus fares. "Thus there was no problem of marketing its produce."[32] Anarchists might think that workers' self-management implies autonomy in merchandizing as well as producing goods and services. Vernon Richards writes of the self-managed industries in Barcelona:

> Government interference from Barcelona and from Madrid succeeded in preventing the experiment of collectivization of industry from developing to its limits. Nevertheless, there is enough evidence to show that given a free hand, that is by controlling the finances as well as occupying the factories, the Spanish workers, who showed a spirit of initiative and inventiveness and a deep sense of social responsibility, could have produced quite unexpected results. As it was, their achievements in the social services — in which they were not so dependent on government finances or raw materials and were much freer than industry from government blackmail — have been acknowledged by all observers of the Spanish scene in its earliest phases.[33]

Thus Richards and other anarchists might object to the separation of salesmanship and workmanship. However, first, Richards is speculating about what *might have been*, had the syndicalists had a free hand in financing its operations, purchasing raw materials and selling products whereas my concern is to establish what *in fact* the syndicalists did do, and thus to demonstrate that the model of a public authority performing the function of a merchant, but not a capitalist, accords with anarcho-syndicalist practice. In addition, one might question Richards' implication that workers are freer or nobler when involved with salesmanship as well as workmanship. One might also question whether Richards' view is consistent with his view that plant seizures led to differential income amongst workers since "the prosperous factories with large stocks of raw material and modern equipment had therefore an unfair advantage over the uneconomical factory struggling to keep going on small stocks."[34]

That is, without some public body, outside the factory, to finance operations, to provide materials and purchase produce, it is difficult to see how the disparities Richards deprecates could be minimized.

The separation between productive and mercantile functions in a syndicalist society would involve the decentralization of technical decision-making to the place of production while centralizing financial and commercial policy in federal banks and marketing agencies. The federation, while the owner of all property, would have possessions limited to banking, insurance and marketing facilities.[35] For public ownership is not inconsistent with co-operative or even private possession of the means of production, as Marx noted in his analysis of pre-capitalist economic formations and as the Spanish syndicalists recognized in the social construction of the civil war period.[36] Indeed most languages distinguish ownership from possession in a manner similar to English (propriété-possession, Eigentum-Besitz) so that no linguistic absurdity exists with reference to a private possession being common property or publicly owned. Ownership connotes greater exclusivity than possession; what is one's own (*eigen, propre* or other Romance derivatives of the Latin *proprius*) inheres in *owne*rship, *Eigen*tum and *propr*iété and not in possession or Besitz.

Ownership pertains to the right to use and abuse, and the right to sell or otherwise alienate something, while possession pertains to a less absolute right to use, one which is subject to the conditions imposed by the lease. The factories in Catalonia were possessed and managed by the workers, but they were forbidden to sell or rent any part of the factory.[37] The means of production were owned by the C.N.T. (whose members jointly decided on industrial policy and general regulations governing the operations of factories and workers' collectives) but the factories were possessed by self-managing workers at the point of production.[38] The methods for creating the produce distributed by the C.N.T. were left to the self-managing collectives.

A syndicalist federation would thus allot land and implements to individual families and agricultural co-operatives, a boat and gear to fishermen, a plant and machinery to self-managing industrial co-operatives, subject to certain vocational attainments and laws which prohibit, on penalty of forfeiture, sale of such property or employment of persons who are not co-possessors of the means of production. The workers would then have security of possession, subject to the laws and

167

general regulations of the commonwealth, while the federation would be the sole owner of the means of production but an owner which would possess only that which is necessary to carry out its mercantile function. Since the property seized by workers or granted to co-operatives by the federation would have unequal values because of the differential technical composition of various spheres of the economy, the value of the means of production seized by workers or leased to individuals and co-operatives would be amortized with a federal bank to minimize inequalities from differential fertility, productivity or advantages of location. Part of the value of the produce sold to a central marketing agency could repay the federation for the property leased. Workers' co-operatives might be able to trade produce directly to one another, but any buying or selling must be done through federal marketing boards. Although the federal monopoly of mercantile functions may be thought to restrict the freedom of producers, it is perhaps to be noted that many small producers in various sectors of capitalist economies find their security of tenure and income enhanced by state marketing boards replacing the free market.

There are various ways in which federal agencies could put into effect a system of central planning. The setting of quotas at fixed prices is not the sole means by which a central plan could be implemented. Fixed prices for a definite quantity of produce often leads to the ignoring of quality considerations and inhibits incentives to innovation, efficiency and industry. A plan which provides a margin between minimum and maximum goals and which has a flexible pricing system as a means to reward quality or marketability, and to equalize advantages of location, would enable producers to profit from enterprise or industry. The federation's monopoly of mercantile functions, necessary to economic planning, would leave the workers free to decide for themselves whatever technical innovations to introduce, to establish their own organization and methods of work, to set their own schedules, pacing and routines, and generally to determine whatever means are desirable to meet the quotas of the marketing board and to profit from efficient performance.

The federal planning and marketing agencies would be staffed by employees of the union federation, many of them former capitalists whose assets have been socialized. The de-proletarianization of the workers would involve a proletarianization of commercial functions. As functionaries of the union federation, former capitalists would exercise their financial talents and carry out commercial functions while ceding their managerial and control functions to the workers who would organize and discipline themselves. Thus commercial employees would work a "nine-to-five" day with the rewards for abnormal industry, enterprise or innovation which are customarily given to civil servants. Although their income would be reduced, the members of the formerly overworked ruling class would receive increased leisure and thus would provide an Aristotelian object lesson in the higher order of leisure to consumption. In short, the burden that Taylor placed on the shoulders of contemporary ruling classes would be removed.

The liberation of capitalists from managerial burdens is simultaneously the de-proletarianization of workers. The separation of workmanship from salesmanship would be an abolition of the wages system. The workers would share in the income of the co-operative or collective; that is, they would receive a given proportion of the difference between the value of the products sold to the federal marketing agencies and the value of the materials purchased from the federal bank. Thus the workers' income is neither derived from wages, nor from the alienation of labour power. For the federation does not buy labour power or potential labour; it buys products or actualized labour, and thus does not undermine productive self-actualization. As distinct from the relation of employer to employee, (where the selling of labour power involves the alienation of productive potential to the employer, where the potential for working is actualized under the direction or management of the employer), the relation of federation to producers is similar to that between a merchant and an independent artisan or farmer. The so-called problem of leisure would dissolve not because workers would be working longer hours, but because the co-operative skills, organizational competence and initiative of self-managing enterprises would spill over into the hours off work.

In a syndicalist society, where the federal monopoly is limited primarily to commercial functions, the trade unions and professional associations comprising the union federation would have a larger function than they do where the state is the sole employer of labour power, and unions function largely to stimulate productivity and to administer welfare benefits. In addition to electing delegates to oversee the commercial functionaries of the federation, they would enter into negotiations with civil servants or representatives of consumers on the establishment of price schedules for goods and services, although the civil service and federal delegates would retain, in order to give effect to an incomes policy, the final authority to set prices if negotiations could not be satisfactorily concluded. More importantly, vocational associations would have the power to establish standards of performance and a code of conduct for a trade, as guilds once did, and professional associations are supposed to do. They would appoint members to sit on the governing boards of relevant educational institutions and, wherever possible, run their own training programmes. They would set the qualifications necessary for workers to join a co-operative or to obtain access to the federation's grant of instruments of production, thus being in a position to regulate, together with the central marketing agencies, the number of persons in a trade. Although they would not have the power to impose organizational and technological methods on co-operatives or individual workers, they would have the power to establish standards for the final products and could employ efficiency engineers and disseminate information about improved performance.

The above is not an attempt to draft a detailed utopia which is magically to dissolve existing traditions or to circumscribe developing practices into a preconceived scheme. The aim of sketching the outlines of a new society, where the state is not a monopoly employer of labour power or where there are economic power centres independent of the state, yet consistent with central planning and public ownership of the means of production, is to present alternatives to capitalist and Soviet modes of production, and to facilitate the formation of renewed syndicalist strategies.

If this alternative were not espoused by the workers as a means to transcend the wages system, and the details not modified or developed in accordance with particular traditions and transformative practices, the alternative would be a utopian or impracticable attempt to impose theory upon practice. The alternative may well be dismissed as utopian since there is no certainty that, were such a system to come into existence, the income of workers would increase relative to capitalist and state socialist systems, even considering the increasing repression of trade unionism within capitalist countries and the inefficient centralized direction of socialist countries. What the alternative does offer is the abolition of "wage-slavery".

Two immediate trade union demands might constitute steps towards a syndicalist society. First, syndicalists might demand that no representatives of management be allowed on the shop floor, in the mine shafts, in the typing pools, etc. Secondly, they might demand that all workers be paid for their travelling time to and from work.

The first is a more radical demand than those for higher wages and improved working conditions. F.W. Taylor proved conclusively that increased wages and increased profits were not incompatible, that trade union struggles with capital are not a "zero sum game" (as are struggles for workers' control of the workplace). The adoption of a resolution barring access of management to the shop floor, stipulating that production orders are to be handed to a shop steward and the methods for meeting these orders are to devolve on the workmen themselves, would be a first step towards industrial democracy. Such a step is, I believe, essential, as concern with control issues is most lively at the immediate work place.[39] Experience has shown that, without democratic involvement of workers in their work situation, there is little enthusiasm for workers' participation in the governing of an enterprise or a national industry.[40]

The second proposal—that workers be paid for their time travelling to and from work, as well as for their time on the job—accords with the consensus amongst the sociologists of leisure that travelling time is to be reckoned as working time, in distinction to leisure time and time for personal needs, domestic cares and civil obligations. An interesting fact revealed by time budget studies, which ought to be of concern to both unions and "quality of life" groups, is that the further one lives from one's place of work, the less free time one has at one's disposal—a diminution which is only in part accounted for by the greater amount of travelling time. In Jackson, Michigan, those who live 10-20 kilometers from place of work have 30 minutes less free time per day than those 7-10 kilometers from work, although they have only 6 minutes more travelling time. Also they have 54 minutes less than those living 1-2 kilometers from their work place, although there is only a difference of 18 minutes in travelling time.[41]

The adoption of a proposal to pay workers for their travelling time in trade union demands might facilitate an alliance between the working class and the "ecological" and citizens' groups whose concerns have hitherto been opposed to one another. Environmental groups, or concerned citizens such as Ralph Nader, often adopt the one-sided perspective of the consumer, leading to a hostility to trade unionism, which limits potentially significant opposition to contemporary capi-

171

talism. That enterprises presently find it cheaper to concentrate production near large urban marketing centres (since the costs of transporting workers to and from the place of work is not borne by the enterprise as distinct from the cost of transporting goods) is of concern to "environmental" and "conservationist" groups as well as the workers directly involved. Reversing the principle that people are cheaper to move than other commodities would contribute to the decentralization of industry. The espousal of this bread-and-butter demand which has wider social implications might be a step towards minimizing the relative isolation of workers from intellectuals in North America.

It would perhaps be unseemly in a book on leisure not to join the 'leisurists' in calling for a shortening of the work week. Unions need no prompting in putting forth this worthy demand. Indeed, since it is in line with the principles of scientific management, shortening the work week is quite a plausible reform. Indeed, syndicalists might well support it, as long as this reformist demand is not used as a trade-off against genuinely syndicalist aims for structural change in industry. For, as the previous chapter indicated, there is no reason to think that increased time off work will in itself enrich the experience of work or of leisure.

Dissolving the Iron Cage
Of Technological Imperatives

Max Weber, writing during the ascendancy of scientific management, asserted that syndicalist aspirations to create an industrial democracy were doomed to failure. For while industrial society opens up vistas of democracy with its promise of wealth for all, the organizational techniques necessary to obtain such wealth create a world of specialized technicians whose limited functions must be coordinated hierarchically by a managerial elite. Thus the democratic aspiration of universal abundance, inherent in the employment of industrial techniques, is effectively blocked by the hierarchical means to bring that aspiration into effect. Technical imperatives for the Weberian replace what Marxians consider political determinants; repetitive, mechanical toil is required by machine industry and is not just a facet of the capitalist use of machine technology; command and subordination are inherent in the employment of industrial techniques *per se*, and are not just a legacy of capitalist exploitation. That the Soviet Union has not changed the character of

172

most proletarian jobs or the hierarchical infrastructure of industry might be thought to substantiate the Weberian view of technological imperatives rather than the Marxian conception of the politics of industrial organization.

The idea of technological imperatives underlying the structure of industrial societies suggests that the uses of machinery, and the methods and relationships of production, will become standardized wherever industrial society becomes established. Let us first consider the alleged imperative regarding the type of machinery employed in industrial societies. We might note at the outset that the types of machines employed in production are quite different from those used in leisure. Machines for hobbies fulfill a different function than industrial machinery. One machine designed for the "do-it-yourself" crowd can cut, turn, drill, screw, sand, and in short do all the 57 operations necessary to build a sailboat. Machines with a sufficient number of replaceable parts to perform a comparable number of operations are not used in industry. Industrial technology is designed solely to maximize productivity; unlike leisure technology, it is not designed to take into account the needs and capacities of workmen. Repetitive mechanical toil is not an inherent consequence of machine design, given the different technology of the leisure industry. The imperative to design industrial technology solely to maximize productivity is based as much on political as on technical determinants.[42]

Nor can the notion of technical imperatives account for the different patterns of industrial organization existing within the industrial world. The replacement of assembly line techniques in Volvo, Saab, Phillips Electronics, etc. by work teams of skilled operatives indicates that the minute subdivision of labour is not necessarily "the one best way" of getting the job done. Impressive results in terms of morale (lower turnover rates, absenteeism, sickness, etc.) and of productivity have been achieved by "job enlargement" and job enrichment schemes.[43] P. Drucker notes the example of 60 workers who took six weeks planning a new eleven acre shop building for the Chesapeake and Ohio Railway at a cost of 2.5 million dollars. Management thought that "a similar planning job would take from 30 months to three years" and would cost 10 to 15 million dollars.[44] The separation of managerial thinking from proletarian doing in this case would have been highly inefficient.

Although "job enlargement" has been discussed as an antidote to simple, repetitive proletarian jobs, it has been estimated that three quarters of the applications of these schemes pertain to "white collar" rather than "blue collar" occupations.[45] Often, within the latter category, workers have taken it upon themselves to enlarge their jobs. The reaction of British coalminers to the introduction of scientific management in the mines resulted in the workers assuming most of the functions Taylor assigned to management. Comparisons of yearly figures of managed versus autonomous work groups demonstrated that autonomous groups of miners "rated better in measures of output, turnover, absence, accidents and stress illness."[46] 5000 workers at the Pirelli tire factory at Torino established new working speeds without assistance from technicians and engineers. Moreover they rerouted the factory in the opposite direction and ran it at varying speeds.[47] Examples could be multiplied of workers encroaching on managerial prerogatives without any detriment to production. But perhaps the most telling argument against Weberian theory and Taylorite practice was the success with which self-managing syndicalist factories and industries operated until supplies became scarce in the Spanish civil war.

Syndicalism is job enlargement from below. As such, it stands opposed to scientific management's job constriction from above. The alleged imperatives of technological development, the subdivision of labour co-ordinated from above, the separation of thinking and doing, the use of machinery which makes productive labour mechanical, will dominate modern industry to the extent, and only to the extent, that they are not challenged by workers. Technical imperatives rest on political decisions.

We have shown that Taylor never attempted to test the hypothesis on which scientific management is based; namely, that workers are incapable of organizing production with a level of efficiency comparable to that of capitalist management. Syndicalism is precisely the crucial experiment lacking in the Taylor system and in the assumptions governing the sociology of leisure. The leisure-as-compensation theorists, as we have seen, accept Taylorized production as an unalterable given and see in the sphere of leisure an opportunity for fulfillment denied at work. But because of the negative "spillover effect" of the job onto leisure, self-managing leisure is deemed to be as much of a waste of time as the unmanaged productive efforts of "Schmidt" were assumed to be.

In the sociological literature on leisure, the alternative to the leisure-as-compensation thesis is the job enlargement thesis, or the elimination of the cause of "the spillover effect".

174

W.E. Moore writes:

> Leisure, then, is a problem where work is a problem, and probably proportionally. The 'constructive' use of leisure is likely to depend in considerable measure on the constructive definition of the job.[48]

However, we do not mean to suggest that 'the problem of leisure' could be solved by 'the constructive definition of the job' even if we assume the reclassification of jobs comes as the result of labour's, and not management's, initiative. Problem-setting and problem-solving presuppose the (technicist) perspective of the engineer. Taylor, as we have seen, tried to solve his own problem of leisure by turning play into contests just as he attempted to solve the problem of production by reducing work to labour. In so doing, he established the one end of games to be victory and the one end of production to be maximal productivity. Thus, to designate work or leisure as a problem is to posit a specific end in terms of which the particular means required to achieve the end are considered the solution to the problem.

Therefore, we are not trying to suggest that 'the constructive definition of the job is *the* means to *the* end of an enriched life of leisure. Certainly a prime function of factories is to turn out automobiles, shoes or whatever and not just the kind of workers that will be better players. Thus the 'definition of the job' cannot simply be conceived to be a method for resolving 'the problem of leisure'. Syndicalism is not so much a technical but a political alternative to scientific management. The aim of syndicalism is not to solve problems but to enable the workers to assess alternatives, to judge for themselves the methods and goals of production, the kinds of technological innovations needed for efficient performance and job satisfaction, the amount of the surplus to be re-invested and consumed, the length of the working day to balance demands for increased income and leisure, for the quantity of production and the quality of life, etc. In short, syndicalism entails the re-politicization of the relations of production.

Technicist organization, the homogenizing de-politicization of social relations, is possible only because producers do not determine the methods and aims of production. In opposing itself to the one-sided perspective of the scientific manager and leisurist, syndicalism does not adopt the problem-setting and problem-solving mentality of the social engineer. Syndicalist job enlargement from below does not aim to solve 'the problem of leisure' but to dis-solve it.

Chapter 9

Dis-closing the Iron Cage

Whether industrial work is inherently repellent. Empirical findings. "Central life interests". The significance of work; its relation to hobbies; as social connectedness. Scientific management as "soulless" socialism; technique replaces communitarian disposition. Why scientific management must invade the realm of leisure. The untenability of the leisure-as-compensation thesis reviewed. Why the liberation of leisure requires the emancipation of the worker from Taylorised production.

In Chapter 7, we examined the leisure-as-compensation thesis. The thesis might be condensed into the following propositions:

(1) Work is onerous toil from which no enjoyment, personal development or sense of purpose can be derived.

(2) The jobs required by a mass technological society and employing the bulk of the population cannot be substantially changed.

(3) As a result, maximal automation to reduce to a minimum necessary toil and to maximize leisure time is the goal; scientific management or rationalization from above should be unhindered in its task of shrinking the realm of necessity.

(4) The quantitative reduction of time on the job, and increase of time off the job, will, without fundamentally new productive methods and relationships, engender a qualitatively new culture.

(5) Necessary work, rationalized to a minimum, will not have an adverse effect on the spontaneous and

expansive activities enjoyed in the new culture of leisure.

(6) An educational system, disassociated from occupational concerns and geared to the employment and enjoyment of leisure, is possible and also necessary to prevent leisure activities from degenerating into trivial, unwholesome or anti-social entertainments.

We have already dealt with propositions 2 to 6. We should now like to assess the first proposition from which the others derive.

First of all, it is by no means clear that all work is shunned, or even that a majority of factory and office jobs are thought repellent. The incidence of strikes, absenteeism, sickness, job turnover, etc., would suggest that, indeed, work is not our favourite recreation. Yet studies reveal that an overwhelming majority of workers in North America, Europe, Japan and Australia report satisfaction with their jobs.[1] However, when pressed, the respondents usually make some negative comments about the lack of variety or skill called for in their occupation and indicate that, although satisfied, they are not deeply involved with or committed to their work and, given the opportunity, would choose a different occupation.[2]

Work is reported to be "a central life interest" for select occupations, such as nurses, railwaymen, farmers, architects, professors, etc., and even for the bulk of the population in certain regions of the industrialized world.[3] Yet it appears that, for a majority of job-holders in industrialized countries, work is not considered a central life interest.[4] However, studies rarely indicate a majority expressing a vital involvement in their leisure activities.[5] Rather vague statements indicating a preference for more leisure are common in sociological studies, perhaps more so for Europeans than North Americans.[6] But concrete proposals, such as for the desirability of a 32 hour working week, frequently are repudiated by a majority of respondents.[7] The preference for income over leisure is fairly wide-spread. Working overtime, or holding a part time or second full time job, perhaps occupies one quarter of the labour force in industrialized countries.[8]

The central life interest of most people, studies report, is not their work or their leisure but their home life.[9] Indeed, the curious pervasiveness of the institution of marriage might be said to constitute a popular devaluation of leisure time. All

177

studies agree that marriage, even before the raising of children, drastically cuts into leisure time, especially for women.[10] Further, marriage tends to curtail the development of new leisure interests.[11] The settled character of the marital state may promote tranquillity or 'leisureliness' but it restricts the growth of cultural interests, enlarges the realm of necessity and diminishes leisure time. Clearly, the scientific management of sexual love and reproduction would be a major step towards increasing "the realm of freedom".

The central importance of family life to most persons appears to be that it provides the most elementary meaning to life and work. Domestic concerns and activities constitute a transcendence of narrow egoism in love and care, a link with the past and an orientation to the future, a reason to work and strain "to provide", etc. Yet work is not valued exhaustively in terms of family life. Those who have had the choice rarely confine themselves exclusively to the domestic realm and increasingly choose work rather than other forms of non-domestic activity, not only for the money but also for the variety, society, public recognition and sense of accomplishment lacking in familial engagements. Job-holding (regardless of the objective usefulness of the job held)* confers a sense of citizenship in the wider economy, of identity, of participation in common purpose, of service or doing something useful for others, of public recognition of worth in the form of money, and, occasionally, of challenge or accomplishment.[12] Thus caution is warranted in assessing the reports that work is not a central life interest but is instrumental in providing a comfortable private life for oneself and one's family. The public recognition of individual worth that one hopes a working experience will provide complements the stability, identify and sense of purpose of family life.

Although the work in modern factories and offices is considered by many intellectuals to be inherently alienating, many women and oppressed minorities consider that the

---

* Working is not necessarily a virtuous activity. It is so only when the job fulfills some social need, when the worker understands the purpose of his activity and engages himself in it from that understanding. Often work is, as Tolstoy says, (*Essays and Letters*, London, 1903, p. 108) "a moral anaesthetic, like tobacco, wine, and other means of stupifying and blinding one's self to the disorder and emptiness of our lives..." Our intention here is not however to determine when work is a virtue or a vice but to clarify its meaning to the worker (whether an addict or a saint).

ability to obtain such work lessens their feelings of alienation. A political movement based on the proposition that work is odious, as Marcuse proposes, will likely remain marginal as most people consider their "liberation" (or at least a tolerable degree of satisfaction) to consist in securing a job. Most workers want full employment, not just to improve their financial position. Studies reveal that a substantial majority of Americans said that they would continue to work even if they were guaranteed a satisfactory outside income.[13] Thus it is a considerable oversimplification to say that work is inherently alienating or repellent.

Whatever the reasons for working, the experience of work provides a subjective and objective connection with society. Even if one works solely for money or the means of subsistence and comfort, the work objectively exists for others. The difference between a hobby and work pertains to its social significance. Both may involve strain and pain and both may be enjoyable and challenging, but in a hobby, one does something for oneself; it may be an amusing pastime, a form of relaxation, or an activity deemed personally significant. But hobbies lack the seriousness of work, the feeling that what one is doing is of value to others as well as to oneself. A hobby is not just unpaid or unrecognized work. Work matters to others besides the worker; its meaning to the worker derives from its anticipated importance to others.[14]

Socialist thought has often emphasized the centrality of work in its conception of a new society. In free work, Marx thought, the interest of the individual and society are united. There is no inherent conflict of interest between individuals if "life's prime want" is indeed the expression of one's capabilities in work; the fulfillment of one's highest interests serves others or complements their interests. On the other hand, if work is considered to be merely a means to consumerist ends, competition for scarce consumer resources will be the dominant principle. Thus Marx's "work ethic" is part of his socialism; one works both for others and for oneself.

Marxian materialism thus rejects the materialism of the consumerist perspective as it rejects the idealist ethic of renunciation. Idealist conceptions of work, perhaps most beautifully portrayed in S. Weil's *The Need for Roots*, conceive of it as a living death, a punishment, an atonement, a painful sacrifice, which can be only made tolerable or meaningful through the understanding of one's daily participation in the experience of the crucifixion and through the redemption which graces voluntary renunciation of the ego in daily work.

179

For Marx, no act of renunciation or alienation is necessary to give meaning to an individual's life, although idealistic justifications are common in a society based on wage-labour, where work is conceived to be primarily a means to income and leisure. Any demand for a change in values, whether a return to a work ethic or an advance to a socially involved leisure ethic, which is independent of any transformation in the way people work, is, for the Marxist, just empty chatter. Without a radical transformation in the methods and relationships of production, work will remain a toilsome means to the aimless diversity of consumption and leisure, or else, during the temporary enthusiasms of war and revolution, an idealistic sacrifice to the service of the nation or class.

While Marx's work ethic is an integral part of his advocacy of socialism, the production ethic of scientific management has also been considered to be socialistic. The emphasis on the development of productive forces to provide wealth for all, on the standardization of procedures, relationships and products, on the adherence to the scientifically established "one best way" of producing which transcends the conflict born of selfish particularisms, etc., has frequently been held to be socialistic in character. The efficiency movement creates a rationalized productive collectivity which transcends the restrictive practices and interests of both trade unions and capitalists.

The beauty of the system is that it does not require the participants in the productive collectivity to have a consciousness of the social goals to be achieved by the system. It is a form of socialism that does not require communitarian awareness or disposition; the socialism inheres in the system and not in the individuals who comprise it. Egoism in production is suspended by the transcendence of the personal or "the human element" in routine formalism. Scientific management produces the type of person who is a collectivist as a producer and an individualist as a consumer — in his leisure and "private life." The individual submits to a system which denies all autonomy, initiative and capacity for co-operation in his working life, which subdivides all jobs and re-integrates them from above, which imposes all methods and pace of work contrary to his instincts and rhythms, which, in effect, transforms the individual into a replaceable part in the productive collectivity*, in order to have an enlarged and

---

* That many workers feel their work (and themselves) to be un-
important or superfluous is not unconnected with the fact that they

enriched sphere of life off work. Collective life is a means to individual life.

The new individualism exhibited in the civilization of leisure has been shaped by scientific management. 'Civil privatism' and conformism, that is, declining social and political involvement coupled with increasing "other-orientedness", characterize contemporary leisure activities. Sociologists often conclude that the 'leisurist', in his educational or organizational role, is essential to re-orient individuals from asocial amusements to cultured citizenship. However what is thrown into question in this book is whether the alleged incompetence of the "masses" to enjoy expansive leisure is not the effect of scientific management's assumption that workers are incapable of organizing their working time productively.

Underlying the technological imperatives which constitute the bars of our iron cage is the assumption that workers are incompetent, incapable of working productively without outside management. The Weberians believe that repetitive mechanical toil is required by machine industry and that industrial authoritarianism is necessary to co-ordinate large-scale factory production. The fact that the Soviet Union has not changed the character of most proletarian jobs or the hierarchical infrastructure of industry seems to support the view that it is technique itself, and not just the capitalist use of it, that determines the character of modern industry. Yet, the affinity of Taylorism and Leninism has been demonstrated. What is a stake is whether a syndicalist alternative to scientific management will contest the alleged imperatives of technique.

If initiatives challenging managerial prerogatives fail to come from unions, the Weberian characterization of industry as structured by the iron of technological imperatives, rather than the rubber of political determinants, will likely become accepted as conventional wisdom. But we should like to emphasize a mistaken assumption common in the sociology of leisure, namely that technical imperatives pertain only to the realm of necessary production and not also to the realm of freedom or leisure. To accept that determinate methods and relationships are inherent in industrial production is to accept the form of consumption dictated by such production, and the

---

are performing operations which are, as yet, unautomated; they are a stop-gap and imperfect bits of machinery, like pieces of wire or string upon which one's motor depends until one gets a new part.

pace, schedules and synchronization required throughout society by such techniques. It is in effect to accept the regulative subordination of leisure to scientifically managed production.

The structural dominance of production over leisure is not merely a matter of 'the day shift' or work being prior in time to 'the night shift' or leisure. The temporary priority is but a manifestation of the wider priority in the allocation of vital energies; our best is to be put into production so that 'the night shift' will be longer and more colourful. However 'the leisurist' must see that 'the night shift' is not such as to disturb the uniform grind of production upon which our civilization of leisure rests. The iron bars of technological imperatives must not be corroded. The character of the realm of freedom is a function of the necessity to keep "the iron cage" in a good state of repair. The shape and substance of leisure is thus determined by the rigid structure of technical imperatives it encompasses.

Our emphasis on the re-organization of production does not derive from our evaluation of the greater worth of productive activities than leisure activities. Rather the insistence on the relevance of productive organization to the understanding of leisure activities is a question of facts rather than values. We have no quarrel with those who 'value' leisure more highly than work. But when 'thinkers' assert that the Marxist and syndicalist goals are obsolete in our dawning civilization of leisure, and that workers should demand "freedom from work" rather than self-managed work, we would point to the empirical data refuting the leisure-as-compensation thesis. There is no empirical support for the expectation that a qualitatively new culture of spontaneous and expansive leisure activities can emancipate itself from "the spillover effect" of Taylorized production or that a new system of avocational training can prepare workers for the enjoyment of leisure without a vanguard of leisurists organizing their leisure time. The realistic alternative to syndicalism is the scientific management of leisure, the extension of Taylorism from the realm of production to the realm of leisure.

Our emphasis on a re-organization of production is then related to, but not a function of, the desire to liberate leisure from its regulative subordination to work. The complement to enhanced social relatedness in work would be the emancipation of leisure from social work. The social worker's desire to prevent social marginalization or atomisation through the public organization and control of leisure activities, the task of converting them into wholesome recreations, or the impetus to make what is an individual concern into a social function, corresponds to the diminished sense of responsibility and social connectedness arising from the routine, mechanical and passive execution of managerial directives. A transformation of production which would make possible a commitment to work by the bulk of producers may be the only means available of relieving leisure from the expectation that it too should be made socially productive. The commitment to society through work would then liberate the personal dimension of leisure.

Such a transformation of production would certainly provide the ruling classes of contemporary societies with more leisure time. Perhaps even the leisurists, who wish to assume executive and clerical responsibility in our civilization of leisure, might even experience what they are so busy writing about. Leisure, in short, would cease to be regarded as a problem — by laymen and even by leisurists. William Wordsworth anticipated the syndicalist objection to the scientific managers of the age of mass leisure:

> These mighty workmen of our later age
> Who with a broad highway have overbridged
> The froward chaos of futurity,
> Tam'd to their bidding; they who have the skill
> To manage books, and things, and make them work
> Gently on infant minds, as does the sun
> Upon a flower; the Tutors of our Youth
> The Guides, the Wardens of our faculties
> And Stewards of our labour, watchful men
> And skilful in the usury of time,
> Sages, who in their prescience would controul
> All accidents, and to the very road
> Which they have fashion'd would confine us down,
> Like engines, when will they be taught
> That in the unreasoning progress of the world,
> A wiser Spirit is at work for us,
> A better eye than theirs, more prodigal
> Of blessings, and more studious of our good,
> Even in what seem our most unfruitful hours?[15]

FOOTNOTES

Introduction

1. M. Weber, *The Protestant Ethic and the Spirit of Capitalism*, London, 1965, p. 181-2.
2. ibid., p. 181.
3. M. Heidegger, 'Die Frage nach der Technik' in *Vorträge und Aufsätze*, Pfullingen, 1959, p. 13-44; H. Arendt, *The Human Condition*, Chicago, 1958; M. Oakeshott, *Rationalism in Politics*, London, 1962; L. Strauss, *Thoughts on Machiavelli*, London, 1969; J. Ellul, *The Technological Society*, London, 1965; H. Marcuse, *One Dimensional Man*, Boston, 1964; J. Habermas, *Knowledge and Human Interests*, Boston, 1971.
4. G.P. Grant, *Empire and Technology*, Toronto, 1969.
5. C.B. Macperson, *Democratic Theory: Essays in Retrieval*, Oxford, 1973, p. 24-5.
6. Marcuse, 1964, p. 154.
7. H. Marcuse, *Eros and Civilization*, Boston, 1961, p. 142.
8. J. Child and B. MacMillan, 'Managers and their Leisure' in M.A. Smith, S. Parker and C.S. Smith, *Leisure and Society in Britain*, London, 1973. See also footnote 36 of chapter 2.
9. G. Lundberg, M. Komarovsky and M.A. McInery, *Leisure: A. Suburban Study*, New York, 1934, p. 81-2.
10. See P.S. Foner, *History of the Labor Movement in the United States*, New York, 1964, vol. 3, ch. 1; V.R. Lorwin, *The French Labor Movement*, Cambridge, Mass, 1966, ch. 3; B. Pribicevic, *The Shop Stewards' Movement and Workers Control, 1910-22*, Oxford, 1959, ch. 1-2.

Chapter 1

1. J. Dumazedier, 'Leisure', *International Encyclopedia of the Social Sciences*, (New York, 1968), Vol. 9, p. 250; *Towards a Society of Leisure* (London, 1967), p. 16-7; 'La dynamique du loisir dans les sociétés industrielles avancées' in *Une nouvelle civilisation? Hommage à Georges Friedmann*, (Paris, 1973) p. 239-40; 'Travail et loisir', in G. Friedmann et P. Naville, *Traité de Sociologie du Travail*, (Paris, 1962), Vol. 2, p. 341; *Sociologie empirique du loisir*, (Paris, 1974), p. 82, 90-2; J. Dumazedier and N. Latouche, 'Work and Leisure in French Sociology', *Industrial Relations* (February 1962) 1:2:20.
2. B.M. Berger, 'The Sociology of Leisure: Some Suggestions', *Industrial Relations*, (February 1962) 1:2:38; A.W. Bacon, 'Leisure and Research: A Critical Review of the Main Concepts Employed in Contemporary Research', *Society and Leisure* (1972), 2:87; A. Giddens, 'Notes on the Concept of Play and Leisure', *The Sociological Review* (March 1964), 12:1:82.
3. E. Barker, 'The Uses of Leisure', *The Journal of Adult Education* (September 1926), 1:1:31.
4. Lin Yutang, 'The Importance of Loafing'. *Harper's Magazine*, (July 1937), 175:144.
5. Dumazedier, 1968, p. 251.
6. Aristotle, *Politics* (New York, 1962) Bk. 8, ch. 3, 5; *Ethics* (London, 1965) Bk. 10, ch. 6-7; E. Barker, *Reflections on Leisure*, (London, 1947) p. 2-4; M.J. Adler, 'Labour, Leisure and Liberal Education', *The Journal of General Education*, (October 1951) 6:1:37; T.W. Adorno, 'On Popular Music', *Studies in Philosophy and Social Science*, (1941) 2:38; D. Bell, *The End of Ideology*, (Glencoe, Ill., 1960), p. 250; M. Clawson, 'How Much Leisure, Now and in the Future', and P. Weiss, 'A Philosophical Definition of Leisure', in J.C. Charlesworth, ed., *Leisure in America: Blessing or Curse*, (Philadelphia, 1964) p. 3, 21; I. Craven, 'Leisure', *Encyclopedia of the Social Sciences*, (New York, 1935) Vol. 9, p. 402; S. DeGrazia, *Of Time, Work and Leisure*, (New York, 1962), ch. 4; J.M. Domenach, 'Loisir et travail', *Esprit* (Juin 1959) 27:1105; A.R.C. Duncan, *The Concept of Leisure*, (Kingston, Ont., 1963) p. 4-5; J. Farina, 'Towards a Philosophy of Leisure' in *Leisure in Canada*, (Ottawa, 1969) p. 4,9; A. Giddens, 1964, p. 81; F. Govaerts, *Loisir des femmes et temps libres*, (Brussels, 1969), ch. 8-10; H. Lefebvre, *Critique de la Vie Quotidienne* (Paris, 1958), Vol. 1, p. 42; G.A. Lundberg, M. Komarovsky, M.A. McInery, 1934, ch. 1; J. Pieper, 'The Social Meaning of Leisure in the Modern World', *The Review of Politics* (October 1950) 12:4:415; G. Soule, 'The Economics of Leisure', *The Annals of the American Academy of Political and Social Science*, (September 1957), 313:16.

7. *Ethics*, Bk. 7, ch. 7; *Politics*, Bk. 8, ch. 7.

8. *Ethics*, Bk. 4, ch. 8.

9. *Politics*, Bk. 8, ch. 7.

10. *Ethics*, Bk. 3, ch. 10, Bk. 6, ch. 2, Bk. 7, ch. 14, Bk. 10, ch. 7; Politics, Bk. 7, ch. 2-3, 14; Bk. 8, ch. 3, *Metaphysics* (London, 1857) Bk. 1, ch. 1,2.

11. *Ethics*, Bk. 10, ch. 5.

12. Lin Yutang, 1937, p. 147; c.f. T.S. Eliot, *Notes Toward the Definition of Culture* (London, 1948), p. 27.

13. This accurate if illiberal description is provided in M. Kaplan and P. Bosserman, *Technology, Human Values and Leisure* (New York, 1971), p. 7.

14. Dumazedier, 1962, p. 343-5; 1967, p. 14-15; 1968, p. 251; 'Leisure in Post-Industrial Societies', in Kaplan and Bosserman, 1971, p. 211; 'Current Problems of the Sociology of Leisure', *International Social Science Journal*, (1960), 12:4:526-7.

15. Dumazedier, 1967, p. 242; c.f. 1974, p. 82.

16. Dumazedier, 1962, p. 345.

17. Dumazedier, 1968, p. 251.

18. J. Bentham, 'The Rationale of Reward', in J. Bowering, ed., *The Works of Jeremy Bentham*, (Edinburgh, 1843) Vol. 2, p. 253-5.

19. J. Locke, *Some Thoughts Concerning Education*, (London, 1964), p. 202-4

20. J. Bentham, *Fragment on Government and Principles of Morals and Legislation*, (Oxford, 1948), p. 111.

21. Plato, *The Republic*, (Indianapolis, Ind., 1974), 357 b-d.

22. N.C. Morse and R.S. Weiss, 'The Function and Meaning of Work and the Job', *American Sociological Review*, (April 1955), 20; 2:191-8; R. Carter, 'The Myth of Increasing Non-Work vs. Work Activities', *Social Problems* (Summer 1970), 18:1:53.

23. H. Arendt, 1958, p. 72.

24. Dumazedier, 1962, p. 359; 1967, p. 18-9, 73-4; 1974, p. 78-9.

25. I. Kant, *Lectures on Ethics*, (New York, 1963), p. 189-90. For a critique of Kant's conception of philosophy as labour, see J. Pieper, *Leisure, The Basis of Culture*, (London, 1952) p. 30.

26. B. Russell, *In Praise of Idleness*, (London, 1935), p. 31.

27. L. Stone, *The Crisis of the Aristocracy*, 1588-1641, (Oxford, 1965), p. 677.

28. P. Lafargue, 'Le droit a la paresse', in *Textes Choisis*, (Paris, 1970), p. 100-45; B. Russell, 1935; Lin Yutang, 1937; G. Santayana, *The Idler and His Works* (New York, 1957); C.E.M. Joad, *Diogenes or the Future of Leisure*, (London, 1928)

29. A.R. Orage, *Social Credit and the Fear of Leisure*, (London, 1934), p. 18; W. Beveridge, *Planning under Socialism*, (London, 1936), p. 99; C. Bell, *Civilization*, (London, 1928), p. 205-19; J. Larrue, 'Loisirs ouvriers et participation sociale', *Sociologie du Travail*, (1963), 5:1:55.

30. J. Field, *An Experiment in Leisure*, (London, 1937), ch. 10, 12; A.R. Martin, *A Philosophy of Recreation*, (Chapel Hill, N.C., 1957), p. 6-11; W. Oates, *Confessions of a Workaholic*, (New York, 1971), p. 21-8; S. DeGrazia, 1962, p. 7-8; R. Glasser, *Leisure, Penalty or Prize*, (London, 1970); J. Pieper, 1952, p. 40-3; T.F. Green, *Work, Leisure and the American Schools*, (New York, 1968), p. 138.

31. Pieper, 1952, p. 43.

32. A.R. Martin, 1967, p. 8, *Leisure Time; A Creative Force*, (New York, 1963), p. 3.

33. R. McIver, 'The Great Emptiness', in E. Larrabee and R. Meyersohn, *Mass Leisure*, (New York, 1958), p. 119.

34. B. Wolfe, 'The Real-Life Death of Jim Morrison', *Esquire*, (June 1972), 77:6:110.

35. Dumazedier, 1967, p. 13.

36. Ibid.

37. DeGrazie, 1962, p. 327.

38. A. Heckscher and S. DeGrazie, 'Executive Leisure', *Harvard Business Review*, (July-August 1959), 37:4; 6-16, 144-56; DeGrazie, 1962, p. 66-140; 'The Uses of Time', in R.W. Kleemeier, *Aging and Leisure*, (New York, 1961), p. 113-41.

39. R.J. Havighurst, 'The Nature and Values of Meaningful Free-Time Activity', in Kleemeier, 1961, p. 316; J.P. Robinson, 'Television and Leisure Time', *Public Opinion Quarterly*, (Summer 1969), 33:2:214; K.K. Sillitoe, *Planning for Leisure*, (London, 1969), p. 17, 41.

40. R.J. Havighurst, p. 316; c.f. N. Anderson, *Work and Leisure*, (London, 1961), p. 116.

41. See, for example, W.R. Torbert, *Being for the Most Part Puppets*, (New York, 1974); A. Touraine, 'Leisure Activities and Social Participation', in M.R. Marrus, *The Emergence of Leisure*, (New York, 1974) and H.L. Wilensky, 'Mass Society and Mass Culture: Interdependence or Independence', *American Sociological Review*, (April 1964), 29:2:173-97.

42. DeGrazia, 1961, p. 142-3.

185

Chapter 2

1. L. Mumford, *Technics and Civilization*, (New York, 1963), p. 14-16; E.P. Thompson, 'Time, Work-Discipline and Industrial Capitalism', *Past and Present*, (December 1967, 38:56-97; DeGrazia, 1962, p. 305-15; J. Ellul, 1965, p. 328-9; S. Weil, 'Factory Work', *Politics* (December 1946), 3:11:369-71.

2. C. Babbage, *On the Economy of Machinery and Manufacturers*, (London, 1832), p. 43.

3. Thompson, 1967, p. 60; c.f. M. Maget, 'Les ruraux', *Esprit* (Juin 1959), 27:919; K. Thomas, 'Work and Leisure in Pre-Industrial Society', *Past and Present* (December 1964, 29:52; P. Bourdieu, 'La Société traditionnelle', *Sociologie du travail*, (1963), 5:1:30.

4. See E.C. Rodgers, *Discussion of Holidays in the Later Middle Ages*, (New York, 1940), ch. 1; C.R. Cheney, 'Rules for the Observance of Feast Days in Medieval England', *Bulletin of the Institute of Historical Research*, (November 1961) 34:90;117-8; J.A.R. Pimlott, *Recreations*, (London, 1968), ch. 1; DeGrazia, 1962, p. 89.

5. H.L. Wilensky, 'The Uneven Distribution of Leisure: The Impact of Economic Growth on Free Time', *Social Problems*, (Summer 1961) 9:1:33; C.D. Burns, *Leisure in the Modern World*, (London, 1932) p. 190; G. Glotz, *Ancient Greece at Work*, (London, 1926) p. 283-7.

6. H.L. Wilensky, 'The Impact of Change on Work and Leisure', *Monthly Labour Review*, (September 1967) 90:9:21.

7. Thompson, 1967, p. 60; c.f., Bourdieu, 1963, p. 30.

8. K. Thomas, 1964, p. 50-2; C. Greenberg, 'Work and Leisure Under Industrialism', *Commentary*, (July 1953) 16:1:58-9; DeGrazia, 1962, p. 307-16; R.J. Smith, 'Cultural Differences in the Life Cycle and the Concept of Time', in Kleemeier, 1961, p. 92-3; R.W. Malcolmson, *Popular Recreations in English Society*, (Cambridge, 1973), p. 15; M.R. Marrus, *The Emergence of Leisure*, (New York, 1974) p. 5-8; B. Dhingra, 'The Spirit of Asian Leisure', *Way Forum*, (December 1957) 26:6-7, 54-5; R. Firth, 'Anthropological Background to Work', *Industrial Psychology*, (April 1948) 22:2:94-7.

9. K. Buecher, *Arbeit und Rhythmus*, (Leipzig, 1897) ch. 4.

10. Glotz, 1926, p. 279-80.

11. Buecher, 1897, p. 114-5.

12. Marx wrote (*Capital*, Vol. 1, Moscow, 1959, p. 422-3): "At the same time that factory work exhausts the nervous system to the utmost, it does away with the many-sided play of the muscles, and confiscates every atom of freedom, both in bodily and intellectual activity. The lightening of the labour, even, becomes a sort of torture, since the machine does not free the labourer from the work, but deprives the work of all interest."

13. F. LeGros Clark, *Work, Age and Leisure*, (London, 1966) p. 102-7.

14. Dumazedier, 1968, p. 249; 1974, p. 25.

15. Dumazedier, 1968, p. 249; 1974, p. 24-5; 1962, p. 350.

16. Ibid.

17. Rodgers, 1940, p. 117-19.

18. Ibid., p. 109-10.

19. S. Pollard, 'Factory Discipline in the Industrial Revolution', *The Economic History Review*, (December 1963) 16:2:256; E.P. Thompson, *The Making of the English Working Class*, (New York, 1963) p. 305-6; B. Harrison, *Drink and the Victorians*, (London, 1971), p. 40; T.S. Ashton, *An Economic History of England: The 18th Century*, (London, 1959) p. 204.

20. Dumazedier, 1968, p. 249; 1974, p. 26, 1962, p. 350.

21. E. Katz and M. Gurevitch, *The secularization of Leisure: Culture and Communication in Israel*, (London, 1976) p. 35.

22. Rodgers, 1940, ch. 3; Cheney, 1961, p. 117-8; Pimlott, 1968, p. 15-6; J. Strutt, *The Sports and Pastimes of the People of England*, (London, 1830) p. 344-55; Malcolmson, 1973, ch. 1.

23. Dumazedier, 1968, p. 249.

24. Ibid; 1974, p. 24-6.

25. Marrus, 1974, p. 8.

25a. R. Brown et. al. 'Leisure in Work: the 'occupational culture' of shipbuilding workers', in Smith, Parker and Smith, 1973, p. 99.

26. Thompson, 1967, p. 93-7.

27. Green, 1968, p. 58-9.

28. B. Franklin, *Collected Writings*, (New York, 1905) Vol. 2, p. 370-2.

29. Ibid., Vol. 3, p. 412. Franklin continues: "Not to oversee Workmen, is to leave them your purse open."

30. Harrison, 1971, p. 46-53, 297-300, 319; G. Best, *Mid-Victorian Britain*, (London, 1971) p. 173, 198, 220-1; J.L. Hammond, *The Growth of Common Enjoyment*, (London, 1933) p. 4-10.

186

31. F.R. Dulles, *America Learns to Play*, (New York, 1952), VIII-IX; Thompson, 1967, p. 88-93; S. Pollard, *The Genesis of Modern Management*, (London, 1965) p. 195-7; Malcolmson, 1973, p. 98-100.

32. Thompson, 1963, p. 40 1-10; B. Harrison, 'Religion and Recreation in Nineteenth Century England', *Past and Present*, (December 1967) 38:98-125; Best, 1973, p. 200, 209-11; W.E. Houghton, *The Victorian Frame of Mind, 1830-70*, (London, 1957), p. 242-62: Pollard, 1963, p. 254-70; 1965, p. 181-97; Ellul, 1965, p. 382-3; J. Huizinga, *Homo Ludens: A Study of the Play Element of Culture*, (London, 1949) p. 197-9; Malcolmson, 1973, ch. 6-7.

33. F.D. Copley, *F.W. Taylor: The Father of Scientific Management*, (New York, 1969) Vol. 1, p. 310.

34. A. Smith, *The Theory of Moral Sentiments*, (London, 1804) Vol. 1, p. 376-7.

35. H.G.J. Aitken, *Taylorism at Watertown Arsenal*, (Cambridge Mass, 1960) p. 19-20.

36. C.A. Andreae, *Oekonomik der Freizeit*, (Hamburg, 1970) p. 87-8; R. Bauer, 'The Sociology of Leisure Time', *Transactions of the Fourth World Congress of Sociology*, (Milan, 1959) Vol. 2, p. 133; Berger, 1962, p. 36-7; Carter, 1970, p. 62; A.C. Clarke, 'Leisure and Levels of Occupational Prestige', *American Sociological Review*, (June 1956) 21:3:306; DeGrazia, 1962, p. 131-6; R. Denney, 'The Leisure Society', *Harvard Business Review*, (May-June 1959) 37:3:47; Dumazedier, 1974, p. 72; A. Heckscher and S. DeGrazia, 1959, p. 6-16, 144-56; P. Henle, 'Leisure and the Long Workweek', *Monthly Labour Review*, (July 1966) 89:6:722-3; G.H. Moore and J.N. Hedges, 'Trends in Labour and Leisure', *Monthly Labour Review*, (February 1971) 94:2:7, 11; F.P. Noe, 'Autonomous Spheres of Leisure Activity for the Industrial Executive and Blue Collarite', *Journal of Leisure Research*, (Fall 1971) 3:4:220-4, 246-7; S. Parker, *The Future of Work and Leisure*, (London, 1971) p. 59-60; D. Riesman, *Individualism Reconsidered and Other Essays*, (Glencoe, Ill., 1954) p. 203; *Abundance for What and Other Essays*, (London, 1964) p. 242; Wilensky, 1961, 9:1:34-6, 42, 56; 1967, 90:9:21-2; M. Yanowitch, 'Soviet Patterns of Time Use and Concepts of Leisure', *Soviet Studies*, (July 1963) 15:1:22-3. Great Britain appears to be unique in that its managerial class seems to be less hard-working than the ruling classes of other industrial countries. P. Willmott found that, although executives were "more involved" in their work than British workers, they had shorter working hours. ('Family, Work and Leisure Conflicts Among Male Employees', *Human Relations*, (December 1971) 24:6:577,583.) K. Roberts (*Leisure*, London, 1970, p. 10) and S. Parker *(The Sociology of Leisure*, London, 1976, p. 31) assert that free time is equally distributed amongst the social classes of Great Britain. J. Child and B. Macmillan, (1973, p. 112-6) conclude, on the basis of studies other than the above, that British managers work between 42-44 hours per week, about the same as the men they manage. Child and Macmillan point out that the hours of work of British managers are shorter than those of American, Russian, Japanese and continental European managers and believe that this relative lack of devotion to work may jeopardize Britain's competitive position in the international economy.

37. P. Drucker, *Technology, Management and Society*, (London, 1970) p. 35.

38. Cited in D. Riesman, 1954, p. 321-2.

39. Parker, 1976, p. 34 5.

40. S.B. Linder, *The Hurried Leisure Class*, (New York, 1970) passim.

41. G.S. Becker, 'A Theory of the Allocation of Time', *The Economic Journal*, (September 1965) 75:299:514.

42. Linder, 1970, ch. 1.

43. Parker, 1976, p. 35.

44. Becker, 1965, p. 513.

45. Greenberg, 1953, p. 43.

46. G.A. Prudenski, 'The Concept of Leisure in the U.S.S.R.', *Industrial Relations*, (October 1962) 2:1:100.

47. P. Devinat, *Scientific Management in Europe*, (Geneva, 1927) p. 62-9; R. Bendix, *Work and Authority in Industry*, (New York, 1956) p. 207-10.

48. See I. Deutscher, *Soviet Trade Unions*, (London, 1950) p. 99-116; M. Dobb, *Soviet Planning and Labour in Peace and War*, (London, 1942) p. 70-98; V.G. Afanasyev, *The Scientific Management of Society*, (Moscow, 1971) p. 103-13; G. Bienstock, S.M. Schwarz and A. Yugow, *Management in Russian Industry and Agriculture*, (London, 1944) p. 92-118.

49. Prudenski, 1962, p. 100; c.f., N. Ignatiev and G. Osipov, 'Le communisme et le problème des loisirs', *Esprit*, (Juin 1959) 27:1061-2; Y. Frolov, *Work and the Brain: Pavlov's Teaching and Its Application to Problems of Scientific Organization of Work*, (Moscow, 1963) p. 28, 179-82; Yanowitch, 1963, p. 18, 33.

50. Prudenski, 1962, p. 100; c.f., B. Grusen *et al*, *Die freie Zeit als Problem*, (Berlin, 1970) ch. 1; V.A. Artemov, B.P. Kutyriov and V.O. Patrushev, 'Free Time Problems and Perspectives', *Society and Leisure*, (1970) 3:44-6; P. Hollander, 'Leisure as an American and Soviet Value', *Social Problems*, (Fall 1966) 14:2:182-3.

51. K. Marx and F. Engels, *Collected Works*, Vol. 4, (New York, 1975) p. 415-6, 422-4, 466-7.

52. I. Howe, 'Notes on Mass Culture', in B. Rosenberg and D.M. White, *Mass Culture*, (Glencoe, Ill., 1957) p. 497.

187

53. H. Dubreuil, *A Chance for Everybody*, (London, 1939) p. 199.

54. Copley, 1969, Vol. 1, p. 189.

55. Wilensky, 1964, p. 188.

56. See D. MacDonald, 'A Theory of Mass Culture', in Rosenberg and White, 1957, p. 59-73; Howe, 1957, p. 496-503, Marcuse, 1964, ch. 3; Touraine, 1974, p. 102-115.

57. See chapter 7.

58. E. Andrew, 'Work and Freedom in Marcuse and Marx', *Canadian Journal of Political Science*, (June 1970) 3:2:241-56.

59. G. Burck, 'There'll Be Less Leisure Than You Think', *Fortune*, (March 1970) 81:3:87-8; Moore and Hedges, 1971, p. 9-11; M. Clawson and J.L. Knetsch calculate that 27% of a lifetime in 1900 was leisure time, 34% in 1950 and 38% of an American's life in 2000 will be leisure time. ('Leisure in Modern America', in J.F. Murphy, *Concepts of Leisure*, Englewood Cliffs, N.J., 1974, p. 87.)

60. K. Marx, *Grundrisse*, (London, 1973) p. 712.

61. V.I. Lenin, *State and Revolution*, in *Collected Works*, (Moscow, 1961) p. 474.

62. See Hollander, 1966, p. 182-3; J.R. Azrael, 'Notes on Soviet Union Attitudes Toward Leisure', *Social Problems*, (Summer 1961) 9:1:69-70, 75-6; Yanowitch, 1963, p. 18, 33-7; H. Marcuse, *Soviet Marxism*, (New York, 1958) p. 233-6; Artemov, Kutyriov and Patrushev, 1970, p. 35, 44; Ignatiev and Osipov, 1959, p. 1061-3; Prudenski, 1962, p. 97-100; Frolov, 1963, p. 121-5; A.V. Darinski, 'Present-Day Problems of Evening Schools in the U.S.S.R.', *Society and Leisure*, (1972) 1:149-66.

Chapter 3

1. H. Braverman, *Labor and Monopoly Capital*, (New York, 1975) ch. 4; G.R. Seale, *The Quest for National Efficiency*, (Oxford, 1971) ch. 1; C.S. Maier, 'Between Taylorism and Technocracy: European Ideologies and the Vision of Industrial Productivity in the 1920s', *Journal of Contemporary History*, (1970) 5:2:27-48.

2. Copley, 1969, Vol. I, XIX-XX.

3. Drucker, 1970, p. 25.

4. Copley, 1969, Vol. 1, XX; W.G.H. Armytage, *The Rise of the Technocrats*, (London, 1965) p. 200; D.S. Landes, *The Unbound Prometheus*, (London, 1969) p. 297.

5. M.J. Nadworny, *Scientific Management and the Unions*, (Cambridge, Mass., 1955) p. 21-3; R.F. Hoxie, *Scientific Management and Labor*, (New York, 1915) p. 134-5; Copley, 1969, Vol. 1, p. 210; S. Haber, *Efficiency and Uplift: Scientific Management in the Progressive Era, 1890-1920*, (Chicago, 1964) p. 69; H.B. Drury, *Scientific Management: A History and Criticism*, (New York, 1915) p. 176; F.W. Taylor, *Shop Management*, p. 183 and *Testimony*, p. 149-51, 287 in *Scientific Management Comprising Shop Management, The Principles of Scientific Management, Testimony Before the Special House Committee*, (London, 1964).

6. S. Kabar, *Frederick Taylor: A Study in Personality and Innovation*, Cambridge, Mass., 1970) p. 44.

7. Ibid., p. 71.

8. Copley, 1969, Vol. 2, p. 224.

9. Ibid., p. 438.

10. Ibid.

11. Ibid., p. 446.

12. Ibid., Vol. 1, p. 185.

13. Ibid., p. 87-8.

14. Ibid., p. 188.

15. Ibid., p. 172; Vol. 2, p. 225; Taylor, *Shop Management*, p. 198-9.

16. Haber, 1964, p. 5.

17. Kakar, (1970, p. 26) and Haber (1964, p. 5) attribute Taylor's headaches to a subconscious rejection of his father's mode of life and a decision not to follow in his father's footsteps.

18. M.B. Calvert, *The Mechanical Engineers in America, 1830-1910*, (Baltimore, 1967) p. 67-8.

19. F.W. Taylor, 'A Comparison of University and Industrial Methods and Discipline', in *The Taylor Collection*, p. 6; 'Why Manufacturers' Dislike College Graduates', *The Electrician*, (October 1, 1909) 63:25:981.

20. Copley, 1969, Vol. 1, p. 75.

21. Ibid., p. 72; W.T. Morris, *Management Science in Action*, (Homewood, Ill., 1963) p. 38.

22. Copley, 1969, Vol. 1, p. 117.

23. Ibid., Vol. 2, p. 215-23.

24. Ibid., p. 433-4, 438; Vol. 1, p. 84; Kakar, 1970, p. 77, 130.

25. Taylor, 'A Comparison' p. 6.

26. Ibid., p. 3.

26a. Copley, 1969, Vol. 2, p. 262.

27. Kakar, 1970, ch. 3-6; c.f., Copley, 1969, Vol. 1, p. 134, 150.

28. Copley, 1969, Vol. 1, p. 214.

29. Ibid.; c.f. Kakar, 1970, p. 68-9, 120. Taylor referred to the threats to his life and the sabotage of workmen in *The Principles of Scientific Management*, p. 52 and in his *Testimony Before the Special House Committee*, p. 79-85.

30. Taylor, *Principles*, p. 40 51, *Testimony*, p. 85.

31. Taylor, *Testimony*, p. 146; Copley, 1969, Vol. 2, p. 420-1.

32. Taylor, 'Laws vs. Private Opinion as a Basis of Management' and 'Government Efficiency' p. 15-19, in *The Taylor Collection*; *Testimony*, p. 149, 189; Copley, 1969, Vol. 1, p. 175; Vol. 2, p. 420-1; Nadworny, 1955, p. 78.

33. Taylor, *Shop Management*, p. 185; *Testimony*, p. 32-3, 145; *Principles*, p. 72; Copley, 1969, Vol. 2, p. 67. Haber points out that Taylor refused to write for the National Association of Manufacturers as he had no intention of fighting the unions; his reforms would merely eliminate the need for them.

34. Taylor, *Principles*, p. 136.

35. Ibid., p. 10, 142-4; *Testimony*, p. 27-30, 93, 153, 250-6; Copley, 1969, Vol. 1, p. 312-2; Vol. 2, p. 420-2.

36. Taylor, *Shop Management*, p. 186-91; *Principles*, p. 139, *Testimony*, p. 118-20, 183-4; *A Piece-Rate System: Being a Step Towards a Partial Solution of the Labor Problem* (1895) in C.B. Thompson, *Scientific Management*, (Cambridge, Mass., 1914) p. 637-8; Aitken, 1960, p. 45.

37. In *Shop Management* (p. 56-7), Taylor declares that those who work in scientifically managed enterprises belong to a union which is paid for by the company and officered by the management. Compare with *A Piece Rate System*, p. 638-42; 'Laws vs. Private Opinion' p. 10-12. Kakar, 1970, (p. 185) writes: "Though pro-worker, Taylor was certainly anti-union, believing that unions had no place in scientific management, which could much better serve the true interests of the workers...."

38. Copley, 1969, Vol 1, p. 318.

39. Hoxie, 1915, p. 40.

40. R.F. Hoxie, *Trade Unionism in the United States*, (New York, 1920) ch. 7-8.

41. Copley, 1969, Vol. 2, p. 135.

42. Ibid., p. 79; W.H.G. Armytage, *A Social History of Engineering*, (London, 1970) p. 278.

43. Copley, 1969, Vol. 2, p. 46.

44. The reasons why Taylor was fired from the Bethelem works may be found in Kakar, 1970, p. 137-50, 184 and Copley, 1969, Vol. 2, p. 1-150.

45. Copley, 1969, Vol. 1, p. 159.

46. Ibid., Vol. 2, p. 166.

47. Haber, 1964, ch. 5-8.

48. Aitken, 1960, ch. 1-3.

49. Nadworny, 1955, p. 102 3; Drury, 1915, p. 141.

50. Copley, 1969, Vol. 2, p. 348. That Taylor agreed with Copley's assessment of the opposition can be seen in the fact that Taylor's testimony with union leaders in the House Committee meetings investigating scientific management had to be stricken from the record.

51. Copley, 1969, Vol. 2, p. 452.

52. Ibid.

53. Ibid., p. 387.

54. Searle, 1971, ch. 1; Haber, 1964, p. 120; L. Urwick and E.F.L. Brech, *The Making of Scientific Management*, (London, 1949) Vol. 2, ch. 7; E. Hobsbawm, *Labouring Men*, (London, 1964) p. 359; S. Pollard, *The Development of the British Economy*, (London, 1970) p. 6, 82; A.L. Levine, *Industrial Retardation in Britain 1880-1914*, (London, 1967) ch. 4.

55. Maier, 1970, p. 27-61; Devinat, 1927, p. 31-100; G. Friedmann, *Industrial Society*, (Glencoe, Ill., 1964) p. 42-5.

56. Copley, 1969, Vol. 1, XXIII.

57. Ibid., XXI; Kakar, 1970, p. 2.

58. Armytage, 1965, p. 200.

59. Devinat, 1927, p. 19.

60. Ibid., p. 100.

60a. E.L. Dowell, *A History of Criminal Syndicalist Legislation in the United States*, (Baltimore, 1939), p. 14; L. DeCaux, *The Living Spirit of the Wobblies*, (New York, 1978), p. 135; P. Renshaw, *The Wobblies*, (New York, 1967), ch. 8.

60b. DeCaux, 1978, p. 135; J.S. Gambs, *The Decline of the I.W.W.*, (New York, 1966), p. 29.

189

61. J.R. Conlin, *Bread and Roses Too*, (Westport, Conn., 1969), p. 140; Renshaw, 1967, p. 23; Gambs, 1966, ch. 1; Nadworny, 1965, p. 109; Haber, 1964, p. 137; R. Bendix, 1956, p. 282-5; J.H.M. Laslett, 'Socialism and the American Labor Movement', in D. Brody, *The American Labor Movement*, (New York, 1971), p. 67-82.

62. Nadworny, 1955, p. 122.

62a. G.D.H. Cole, *A History of Socialist Thought*, (London, 1958) Vol. 4, p. 430.

63. Copley, 1969, Vol. 2, p. 401-3; c.f. Devinat, 1927, p. 148; Hoxie, 1920, ch. 7-8.

64. Aitken, 1960, p. 241; c.f. Nadworny, 1965, p. 145.

65. B. Pribicevic, 1959, V-VIII, 108-150; Haber, 1964, ch. 8; Lorwin, 1966, p. 53-7.

66. Lenin, 1961, Vol. 27, p. 258-9.

67. Ibid., p. 348.

68. H. Braverman, 'Labor and Monopoly Capital', *Monthly Review*, (July-August 1974) 26:3:10.

69. H.A. Clegg, *A New Approach to Industrial Democracy*, (Oxford, 1960) p. 4-5.

70. E. Mayo, *The Human Problems of an Industrial Civilization*, (New York, 1933); L. Mumford, 1963, p. 385.

71. W.W. Daniel and N. McIntosh, *The Right to Manage?* (London, 1972) p. 9; P.F. Drucker, *The Practice of Management*, (London, 1961) p. 241-8; 1970, p. 25-6, 69-70; J.L. and H.L. Wilensky, 'Personal Counselling: The Hawthorne Case', *The American Journal of Sociology*, (November 1957) 57:3:268, 272-3; *Work in America: Report of A Special Task Force to the Secretary of Health, Education and Welfare*, (Cambridge, Mass., 1973) p. 18, 50-1.

72. D. Nelson and S. Campbell, 'Taylorism Versus Welfare Work in American Industry', *Business History Review*, (Spring 1972) 46:1:4.

73. Braverman, 1975, p. 87.

74. G. Friedmann, 'Leisure and Technological Civilization', *International Social Science Journal*, (1960) 12:4:516.

75. Devinat, 1927, XI.

Chapter 4

1. *Testimony*, p. 40; c.f., p. 48, 77; *Principles of Scientific Management*, p. 36, 85. R.F. Hoxie, (1915, p. 134) wrote that "the whole scheme of scientific management, especially the gathering up and systematization of the knowledge formerly the possession of the workmen, tends enormously to add to the strength of capitalism. This fact, together with the greater ease of replacement..., must make the security and continuity of employment inherently more uncertain". Also (p. 104) Taylorism "gathers up and transfers to the management the traditional craft knowledge and transmits this again to the workers only piece meal as is needed in the performance of the particular job or task. It tends, in practice, to confine each worker to a particular task or small cycle of tasks. It thus narrows his outlook and skill and the experience and training which are necessary to do the work. He is therefore, more easily displaced."

2. *Principles of Scientific Management*, p. 36; c.f., p. 85; *Testimony*, p. 42, 48, 77.

3. *Principles of Scientific Management*, p. 36; c.f., p. 85; *Testimony*, p. 42-3, 48, 77.

4. *Principles of Scientific Management*, p. 37; c.f., p. 85; *Testimony*, p. 44-5, 48, 77.

5. *Shop Management*, p. 66.

6. Drury, 1915, p. 84.

7. E. Wilkenson and R.S. Foster state, in *Management Principles and Practice* (London, 1963), p. 278: "When Taylor separated his planning bosses from the shop floor, the link by which their contact was preserved was the instruction. This replaced personal contact and oral communication, and introduced clerical activities into the factory."

8. *A Piece Rate System*, p. 642-3.

9. Drury 1915, p. 83.

10. J.J. Gillespie, *Dynamic Motion and Time Study*, (London, 1947), p. 10.

11. Hoxie, 1915, p. 40-87; A. Abruzzi, *Work Management*, (New York, 1952) p. 217-22; W. Rodgers and and J.M. Hammersky, 'The Consistency of Stop-Watch Time-Study Practitioners', *Occupational Psychology*, (April 1954) 28:2:61-71; Nadworny, 1955, p. 91; Aitken, 1960, p. 26.

12. Nadworny, 1955, p. 70-2; Hoxie, 1915, p. 90-2.

13. Nadworny, 1955, p. VI, 52. R.F. Hoxie writes (1915, p. 123) "Under the ordinary form of management found in industries, the machine operator is something more than a mere feeder of material into the machine, for he performs manual and mental labor as the result of his craft knowledge and skill, which is as essential to complete the product as in the work done by the machine. In addition to being a machine operator, he cares for the machine, corrects and repairs minor accidents, makes necessary adjustments, attends to the belting and grinds his own tools. He exercises also, within

reasonable limits which call for his initiative and dependence upon his craft knowledge, individual judgment in the laying out and setting up of a job, and in determining the method and feed and speed to be employed."

14. Taylor's views on "natural" and "systematic soldiering" are expressed in *Shop Management*, p. 30-2, 186-91; *Principles of Scientific Management*, p. 7, 13, 17-24; *Testimony*, p. 8-12, 24, 114-22, 183; *A Piece Rate System*, p. 637-8, 644-5; 'Laws vs. Public Opinion as a Basis of Management', p. 10-11.

15. *Shop Management*, p. 50, 188; *Principles of Scientific Management*, p. 15; *Testimony*, p. 10-21, 135.

16. *Testimony*, p. 176-7; 184-6; Nadworny, 1955, p. 65.

17. *Principles of Scientific Management*, p. 26, 38, 48, 59, 102-4, 114-5; *Testimony*, p. 49, 235-7; 'Laws vs. Public Opinion as a Basis of Management', p. 9.

18. *Principles of Scientific Management*, p. 54-5.

19. Hoxie, 1915, p. 94.

20. *Principles of Scientific Management*, p. 59.

21. Taylor provides his account of the development of the science of handling pig iron in *Shop Management*, p. 47-52; *Principles of Scientific Management*, p. 40-8, 57-64, 137-8; *Testimony*, p. 48-50.

22. *Principles of Scientific Management*, p. 59.

23. Ibid., p. 62.

24. Ibid., p. 40, 59, 62, 137; c.f. *Shop Management*, p. 147; *Testimony*, p. 49-50.

25. *Principles of Scientific Management*, p. 62-4.

26. Ibid., p. 64-77; *Shop Management*, p. 53-6; *Testimony*, p. 50-66.

27. Testimony, p. 221.

28. Ibid., p. 51.

29. *Principles of Scientific Management*, p. 69.

30. *Testimony*, p. 57.

31. Ibid., p. 56.

32. Ibid., p. 209-14.

33. *Shop Management*, p. 56, 131; *Principles*, p. 136-8; *Testimony*, p. 147, 228-36.

33a. *Principles*, p. 71.

34. Ibid., p. 137; *Testimony*, p. 233-6.

35. *Testimony*, p. 264-6.

36. *Aitken, 1960, p. 40*.

37. *Shop Management*, p. 27; *Principles*, p. 74; Copley, 1969, Vol. 2, p. 53.

38. Kakar, 1970, p. 6.

39. Friedmann, 1964, p. 195; A. Touraine, *Workers' Attitudes to Technical Change*, (Paris, 1965) p. 30.

40. *A Piece Rate System*, p. 637-8, 642, 665; *Shop Management*, p. 56-7, 186-91, 194; *Principles*, p. 28, 75-7, 93-5, 138-144; *Testimony*, p. 30-3, 57, 149-151, 156-7, 165, 265-6, 274-6, 284-5.

41. *Principles*, p. 68-9; *Testimony*, p. 55-8, 96; *Shop Management*, p. 64-6.

42. *Principles*, p. 77-85; *Testimony*, p. 66-77, 227-33.

43. *Testimony*, p. 75-6.

44. *Principles*, p. 83.

45. *Testimony*, p. 81-3.

46. 'On the Art of Cutting Metals', in Thompson, 1915, p. 242-67.

47. Ibid.; Kakar, 1970, p. 146; Copley, 1969, Vol. 2, p. 120.

48. *Testimony*, p. 262.

49. Hoxie, 1915, p. 123; G.B. Babcock. *The Taylor System in Franklin Management*, (New York, 1917) p. 48; Kakar, 1970, p. 146; Aitken, 1960, p. 22-3; Copley, 1969, Vol. 1, p. 268; Friedmann, 1964, p. 195.

50. Copley, 1969, Vol. 1, p. 412.

51. *Shop Management*, p. 85-91; *Principles*, p. 86-97.

52. *Principles*, p. 88.

53. Ibid., p. 92.

54. Ibid., p. 90.

55. Ibid., p. 87. F.B. Copley frequently reiterates (Vol. 1, p. 194-5, 450-1, 463; Vol. 2, p. 263, 272) Taylor's view that the disassociation of work and play is a central principle of scientific management.

56. Bendix, 1956, p. 289.

57. Copley, 1969, Vol. 1, p. 450.

58. *Testimony*, p. 258-60; Copley, 1969, Vol. 1, p. 230.

59. Drury, 1915, p. 101-2; Haber, 1964, p. 65-6; Copley, 1969, Vol. 2, p. 267.

60. *Testimony*, p. 200-2; Drury, 1915, p. 112; F.B. and L.M. Gilbreth, *Applied Motion Study*, (New York, 1917) p. 12; F.B. Gilbreth jr. and E.G. Carey, *Cheaper by the Dozen*, (London, 1949) p. 102-4.

61. Haber, 1964, p. 29.

62. *Principles*, p. 7. Taylor continued (p. 8) to express the hope that "the same principles can be applied with equal force to all social activities: to the management of our homes, the management of our farms; the management of the business of our tradesmen, large and small; of our churches, our philanthropic institutions, our universities, and our government departments."

63. 'Laws vs. Public Opinion', p. 9.

64. Copley, 1969, Vol. 1, p. 83.

65. Ibid., p. 178-9, 450.

66. *Principles*, p. 71.

67. Copley, 1969, Vol. 1, p. 62.

68. Ford's "sociology department" or network to spy on the domestic habits of employees is discussed in W.R. Burlingame, *Henry Ford*, (London, 1957) p. 83 and K. Sward, *The Legend of Henry Ford*, (New York, 1948) p. 59.

69. Dumazedier, 1967, p. 28.

70. Cited in Bendix, 1967, p. 208.

71. *Work in America*, 1973, p. XVII, 22, 50-1, 83.

72. Ibid., p. 83; A. Kornhauser, *Mental Health of the Industrial Worker*, (New York, 1965) p. 202; M. Kohn, *Class and Conformity-A Study in Values*, (Homewood, Ill., 1969) p. 190; M. Meisner, 'The Long Arm of the Job: A Study of Work and Leisure',*Industrial Relations* (October 1971) 10:3: 250-60; J. Rudas, 'Some Results of Research on the Connection between Work and Leisure Time Activities', *Society and Leisure*, (1971) 3:2:103-7; B. Filipova and V. Jestrab, 'Information on the Theoretical Conception of the Survey of Leisure in Ostravas', *Society and Leisure*, (1909) 1:1:32.

73. An exception might be R.J. Havighurst, 'The Nature and Values of Meaningful Free-Time Activity' in Kleemeier, 1961, p. 310, who states that "contemplation is viewed with suspicion as not being far removed from mere vegetation" and thus indicates that the absence of thinking in his classification of leisure activities is not an omission on his part.

74. N.H. Cheek and W.R. Burch, *The Social Organization of Leisure in Human Society*, (London, 1976) p. 43. Similar views will be examined in chapter 7.

75. Oates, 1971; Martin, 1957; Green 1968; Pieper 1952.

76. Rudas, 1971, p. 103; Sillitoe, 1969, p. 50, 63; Dumazedier and Latouche, 1962, p. 23-4; Willmott, 1971, p. 580-3; H.L. Wilensky, 'Life Cycle, Work Situation, and Participation in Formal Associations', in Kleemeier, 1961, p. 219-22; 1964, p. 187-8; M. Kaplan, *Leisure in America*, (New York, 1960) p. 183-4; Roberts, 1970, p. 27-9; Kohn, 1969, p. 190; R.J. Havighurst, 'The Leisure Activities of the Middle Aged', *American Journal of Sociology*, (September 1957) 63:2:158-60; R. Mayntz, 'Leisure, Social Participation and Political Activity', *International Social Science Journal*, (1960) XII:4:572-3; R. Bauer, 1959, p. 135; Clarke, 1956, p. 304-8; Touraine, 1974, p. 114; L. Riessman, 'Class, leisure and social participation', *American Sociological Review*, (February 1954) 19:82; R.J. Budge, 'Levels of occupational prestige and leisure activities', *Journal of Leisure Research*, (Summer 1969) 1:262-74; S. Parker, 'Work and Leisure: Theory and Fact', in J.T. Haworth and M.A. Smith, *Work and Leisure*, (London, 1975) p. 26.

77. Green, 1968, p. 90.

78. Hecksher and DeGrazia, 1959, p. 154.

79. H.L. Wilensky, 'Work, Careers, and Social Integration', *International Social Science Journal*, (1960) XII:4:558.

80. *Testimony*, p. 216.

81. *Principles*, p. 18. Aitken (1960, p. 175-7) demonstrates that Taylor continued to believe throughout the strike at Watertown Arsenal that the workmen favoured scientific management but were subject to tyrannical pressure from union "misleaders". Aitken also shows that there was not the slightest amount of truth in Taylor's belief in outside agitation. Nadworny (1955, p. 79-80) points out that over 90% of workmen polled at Watertown disapproved of Taylorism and also indicates that Taylor's view of demagogic unionists interfering with the willing Schmidts was inappropriate. Taylor's views on labour agitators are presented in Copley, 1969, Vol. 2, p. 348, 401-30.

82. H. Ford (with S. Crowther), *My Life and Work*, (London, 1922) p. 5.

83. Sward, 1948, p. 452; Burlingame, 1957, p. 139.

84. Babbage, 1832, p. 227, 246.

85. Ibid., p. 227, 247, 330, 332.

86. C. Dickens, *Hard Times*, (London, 1970) Bk. 2, ch. 5, p. 150.

87. Ford, 1922, p. 43, 103-5, 247, 279.

88. Ibid., p. 99.

89. Ibid., p. 250-2. Ford said (p. 255) "If the official personnel of labour unions were as strong, as honest, as decent, and as plainly wise as the bulk of the men who make up the membership", there would be no doctrine of class warfare. Explaining his refusal to hire unionized men, Ford referred to hidden influences and Bolsheviks corrupting the "sound judgment" of American workers (p. 261) and asserted that agitators and speculators are the cause of most strikes in American industry. (p. 260).

90. Sward, 1948, p. 157, 450-63.

91. Lenin, 1961, Vol. 7, p. 269, 286, 323-6, 392-403, 415.

92. J. Habermas, *Legitimation Crisis*, (London, 1976) p. 70.

93. Ellul, 1965, p. 255-91.

94. *Work in America*, 17-18, 50-1, 112-4; H.L. Sheppard and N.Q. Herrick, *Where Have All the Robots Gone?* (New York, 1972) VII-IX, XIX, XXX, 35.

Chapter 5

1. Haber, 1964, ch. 5-8; E. Layton, 'Veblen and the Engineers', *American Quarterly*, (Spring 1962) 14:1:64-72; J. Dorfman, *Thorstein Veblen and His America*, (New York, 1934); T.W. Adorno, 'Veblen's Attack on Culture', *Studies in Philosophy and Social Science*, (1941) 9:389-413.

2. Adorno, 1941, p. 401.

3. L. Fishman, 'Veblen, Hoxie and Labor', in D.F. Dowd, *Thorstein Veblen: A Critical Appraisal*, (Ithaca, 1958) p. 223.

4. T. Veblen, *(Theory of the Business Enterprise*, (New York, 1904) p. 354.

5. Ibid.

6. T. Veblen, The *Instinct of Workmanship*, (New York, 1914) p. 222-4, 345.

7. Ibid., p. 321.

8. Ibid., p 320.

9. Ibid., p. 226.

10. Ibid., p. 224, 345-55.

11. Haber, 1964, ch. 2-8; Layton, 1962, p. 66-71; Dorfman, 1934, p. 455.

12. Veblen, an ardent pacifist, predicted as early as 1904 (*The Theory* of Business Enterprise, p. 393-400) that a world war would retard the progress of industrialism; the 'dolicho-blonds' are not only the most efficient workmen but are also the best soldiers, destined to die out in imperial ventures. The alternatives for the twentieth century, Veblen held, are militarism or socialism.

13. T Veblen, *The Engineers and the Price System*, (New York, 1921) p. 79, 88-9.

14. Ibid., p. 88, 133-7, 166.

15. Ibid., p. 69; c.f., p. 51-4, 79-81, 134-6, 144-52, 166.

16 T. Veblen, *The Vested Interests and the Common Man*, (London, 1924) p. 179.

16a. Veblen, 1914, p. 313.

17. T. Veblen, *The Place of Science in Modern Civilization*, (New York, 1919), p. 387; D. Riesman, *Thorstein Veblen*, (New York, 1953) p. 19; Adorno, 1941, p. 391; R. Hofstadter, *Social Darwinism in American Thought, 1860-1915*, (Philadelphia, 1945) p, 129-31.

18. This evolutionary scheme is found in most of Veblen's writings but it is most fully elaborated in *The Theory of the Leisure Class*, (New York, 1899) and *The Instinct of Workmanship*.

19. Veblen provided the most extensive discussion of the instinct of workmanship in *The Instinct of Workmanship*, of the desire for status or the need to make 'invidious comparisons' in *The Theory of the Leisure Class*, and of the thirst for disinterested knowledge or 'idle curiosity' in *The Higher Learning in America*, (New York, 1918). However references to these three "instincts" are common throughout Veblen's works.

20. T. Veblen, *Absentee Ownership*, (London, 1924) p. 107.

21. Veblen, 1899, p. 340-2.

22. Ibid., p. 15.

23. Ibid., p. 93-8; 1914, p. 40-1, 194, 345-8.

24. Veblen, 1899, p. 14.

25. Ibid., p 38.

26. Ibid., p. 43.

27. Ibid., p. 45-6, 93-8, 393-6.

28. Ibid., p. 255-7, 270; *Imperial Germany and the Industrial Revolution*, (New York, 1918a) p. 136-44.

29. Veblen, 1918a, p. 132-6; 1899, p. 46-7.

30. Veblen, 1899, p. 60-5.

31. Ibid., p. 396.

32. Ibid., p. 386-90.

33. Ibid., p. 390.

34. Ibid., p. 330, 386-7; 1918, p. 6-10; 1914, p. 310-11; 1919, p. 17-8.

35. Veblen, 1899, p. 334-5.

36. Veblen, 1918, p. 5.

37. Ibid.

38. Veblen, 1899, p. 389-90.

39. F. Bacon, *Of the Advancement of Learning*, (London, 1906) p. 39-40.

40. Veblen, 1904, p. 7, 307-10; 1914, p. 310-14.

41. Veblen, 1918, p. 24-5, 32-9.

42. Ibid., p. 25.

43. Ibid., p. 32-4.

44. Ibid., p. 6, 8-10.

45. Ibid., p. 5, 15.

46. Veblen, 1899, p. 389-90.

47. Ibid., p. 393.

48. Veblen, 1904, p. 14.

49. Veblen, 1914, p. 313.

50. See Wilensky, 1964, p. 193-5. However S.C. Florman, in *Engineering and the Liberal Arts*, (New York, 1968), advocates liberal education, and selects some edifying books, sights and sounds, for engineers. Interestingly, Hegel is rejected (p. 175-6) as anti-engineering, one who is guaranteed to alienate all practical persons, whereas in a subsequent classic, *The Existential Pleasures of Engineering*, (New York, 1976, p. 8), Florman depicts Hegel as embodying the engineering ethos.

51. Adorno, 1941, p. 394.

52. B. Rosenberg, in *The Values of Veblen*, (Washington, 1956, ch. 3), exposes Veblen's "Olympian pose". D. Riesman (1953, p. 47) considers Veblen's "pretense at impersonality" to be a weakness of character rather than a scholarly method. H. Laski viewed Veblen's cynical detachment as "merely a protective colouring beneath which he concealed deep emotions he did not like to bring to the surface." (in Dorfman, 1934, p. 451.) Adorno (1941, p. 393-4, 405-7) refers to the "grandiose misanthropy" and "malicious glance" of Veblen which is thought to arise from "spleen" or "a hatred for thinking". In short, the interpretations of Veblen, however disparate, rightly discount his pretensions to be a dispassionate spectator of human affairs.

Chapter 6

1. S. Webb and A. Freeman, *Great Britain After the War*, (London, 1916) p. 59-63; S. Webb, *The Restoration of Trade Union Conditions*, (London, 1917) ch. 5; S. Webb, *The Works Manager Today*, (London, 1917a) p. 131-9. On the attachment of the Fabian society to the efficiency movement or scientific management, see Searle, 1971; M. Beer, *A History of British Socialism*, (London, 1929), Vol. 2, p. 276-82; Haber, 1964, p. 120; Hobsbawm, 1964, p. 359.

2. S. Webb, 1917a, p. 15.

3. *Beatrice Webb's Diaries, 1912-24*, ed. M. Cole, (London, 1952) p. 234.

4. For Lenin's views on syndicalism, see Marx, Engels, Lenin, *Anarchism and Anarcho-Syndicalism*, (Moscow, 1972) p. 185-339. George Bernard Shaw thought that Lenin and Stalin were Webbites because they opposed syndicalism and the Webbs acknowledged the affinity between Fabianism and Communism in this regard. See *Beatrice Webb's Diaries, 1924-32*, ed. M. Cole, (London, 1956) p. 278, 298.

5. Lenin, 1961, Vol. 5, p. 375, 384-5, 422, 426, 437. See also Lenin's favourable comments, in *What is to be Done?*, regarding the Webbs' views on "primitive democracy" within the trade union movement.

6. E. Bernstein, *Evolutionary Socialism*, (London, 1909), p. 119. The centrality of this idea in the Webbs' thought, which we shall explore in this chapter, is noted in M.A. Hamilton, *Sidney and Beatrice Webb*, (London, 1933) p. 63 and M. Cole, ed., *The Webbs and Their Work*, (London, 1949) p. 24.

7. Andrew, 1970, p. 241-56.

8. *Critique of the Gotha Programme*, in Karl Marx and Frederick Engels, *Selected Works*, in one volume (Moscow, 1968) p. 324.

9. Marx, 1973, p. 155-6.

10. *Diaries, 1912-24*, p. 3-5; *Diaries, 1924-32*, p. 92-5, 300-2; S. and B. Webb, *The History of Trade Unionism*, (London, 1920) p. 649-76; *Problems of Modern Industry*, (London, 1898) p. 196, 243-5, 269-76; *What Syndicalism Means*, (London, 1912) passim; *A Constitution for the Socialist Commonwealth of Great Britain*, (London, 1920a) p. 48-9, 152-6; *Soviet Communism: A New Civilization*, (London, 1947) p. 499-500, 562.

11. Hamilton, 1933, p. 11; *Diaries, 1912-24*, p. 5, 15, 183; A.M. McBriar, *Fabian Socialism and English Politics, 1884-1918*, (Cambridge, 1962) p. 114-5; W. Kendall, *The Revolutionary Movement in Britain, 1900-21*, (London, 1969) ch. 1; Pribicevic, 1959, p. 2.

12. G.D.H. Cole, *Labour in the Coal Mining Industry*, (Oxford, 1922) p. 91.

13. Hamilton, 1933, p. 217.

14. Compare Lenin's *State and Revolution*, written before the October revolution, with *Left-Wing Childishness and the Petty Bourgeois Mentality* or *Left-Wing Communism: An Infantile Disorder*, written after the revolution, On the post-revolutionary suppresion of syndicalism, see R.V. Daniels, *The Conscience of the Revolution*, (New York, 1967) p. 107-47 and I. Deutscher, *Soviet Trade Unions*, (London, 1950) p. 1-45.

15. *Diaries, 1924-32*, p. 95.

16. Ibid., p. 92.

17. *Diaries, 1912-24*, p. 109.

18. Ibid., p. 183.

19. M. Cole, 1949, p. 224.

20. Ibid., p. 244.

21. *Diaries, 1924-32*, p. 298. Mrs. Webb admitted that for this reason, she and her husband were favourably disposed to the Soviet Union before they visited Russia and added that "there is no d----d nonsense about Guild Socialism". Such strong language, lacking the refincment of Mrs. Webb's normal form of expression, attcsts to the feeling with which she opposed "workers control".

22. S. and B. Webb, 1947, p. 562.

23. Tom Mann, *Memoirs*, (London, 1967) p. 270.

24. G.D.H. Cole, *Self-Government in Industry*, (London, 1920) p. 210.

25. S. and B. Webb, 1912, p. 138-9. The Webbs believed that the essence of syndicalism is that "the manual working wage-earners should rely exclusively on themselves and their own organizations to work out their own salvation", thereby attempting to dispense with the services of the middle class and intellectuals. (p. 141).

26. Ibid., p. 148; 1898, p. 243-5; 1920a, p. 48-9.

27. S. and B. Webb, 1898, p. 272-5; 1912, p. 150.

28. S, and B Webb, 1898, p. 273.

29. See the Webbs' account (1947, p. 499) of the failure of the workers' councils in post-revolutionary Russia: c.f., 1912, p. 138-9, 151. *Industrial Democracy*, (London, 1897) p. 818.

30. S. and B. Webb, 1947, p. 500.

31. S and B. Webb, 1897, p. 818.

32. T. Mann, *The Miner's Next Step*, (London, 1912, p. 30) cited in S. and B. Webb, 1912, p. 143.

33. McBriar, (1962, p. 118) writes: "There was more of Guild Socialism in the phraseology of the *Constitution for the Socialist Commonwealth* that in its practical recommendations."

34. S. and B. Webb, 1920a, p. 160.

35. Ibid., p. 152-3; 1912, p. 151; 1897, p. 597, 809-10.

36. S. and B. Webb, 1920a, p. 300-1.

37. S. and Webb, 1947, p. 933-6.

38. Deutscher, 1950, p. 87-128; M. Dobb, *Soviet Planning In Peace and War*, (London, 1942) p. 70-98; L. Shapiro, *The Communist Party of the Soviet Union*, (London, 1964), ch. 21, 25. Shapiro (p. 460) states that, in 1934, wage differences in industry were in a proportion of 29 to 1 and that average real wages in 1937-8 were one-half of the 1928 level.

39. S. and B. Webb, 1920, p. 25-6.

40. Ibid., p. 46.

41. S. and B. Webb, 1897, p. 526-7, 561, 824.

42. Ibid., p. 451, 809-10.

43. Ibid., p. 476, 561.

44. Ibid., p. 597, 809-10.

45. Ibid., p. 571.

46. Ibid., p. 703.

47. Ibid., p. 819.

48. S. and B. Webb, 1920a, p. 180-1; c.f., 1912, p. 151; 1897, p. 818-24.
49. B. Webb, *Our Partnership*, (London, 1948) p. 120.
50. See the unpublished dissertation of D.J. O'Hagan, *Liberalism and Socialism: Some Aspects of the Social Thought of Sydney and Beatrice Webb*, (University of Toronto, 1976) ch. 6.
51. M. Cole, 1949, p. 295-6.
52. Ibid., p. 287.
53. *Diaries, 1924-32*, p. 298-9.
54. M. Cole, 1949, p. 292.
55. Hamilton, 1933, p. 296.
56. M. Cole, 1949, p. 226.
57. Ibid.
58. *Diaries, 1924-32*, p. 309.
59. B. Webb, 1948, p. 366. The religious character of Mrs. Webb's thought is discussed in S. Letwin, *The Pursuit of Certainty*, (Cambridge, 1965).
60. *Diaries, 1912-24*, p. 50.
61. B. Webb, 1948, p. 209-10.
62. Ibid.
63. S. and B. Webb, 1897, p. 426.
64. Ibid.
65. S. and B. Webb, 1920, p. 467-8.
66. Ibid., p. 467.
67. *Diaries, 1912-24*, p. 15.
68. Ibid.
69. See the conclusion to Carlyle's Inaugural Address at Edinburgh University in *Scottish and Other Miscellanies*, (London, 1928) p. 171; c.f., p. 188, 191, 206-9; *Sartor Resartus*, (London, 1934) p. 70-2, 87; *Corn-Law Rhymes* in *English and Other Critical Essays*, (London, 1925) p. 144, 161.
70. Carlyle (1925, p. 310) asserted: "For idleness does, in all cases, inevitably *rot*, and become putrescent; — and I say deliberately, the very Devil is in it."
71. Carlyle, 1928, p. 206, 209.
72. Carlyle, 1934, p. 71, 87, 93.
73. Carlyle, 1928, p. 171, 299-339; 1925, 309-20.
74. Beatrice Webb refers to her "chronic melancholy — perhaps *indifference* to life is the better phrase..." *Diaries, 1924-32*, p. 107.
75. S. and B. Webb, 1947, p. 733; c.f., 1920a, p. 219.
76. Child and MacMillan, 1973, p. 116; Yanovitch, 1963, p. 22-3; Dumazedier, 1974, p. 72.

Chapter 7

1. Clawson and Knetsch, 1974, p. 87; Dumazedier, 1974, p. 33.
2. Szalai, 1966, p. 23-4; F. Govaerts, 'The Family and Leisure-Masculine and Feminine Roles', in United Nations Office, *The Leisure of Workers in Modern Industrial Countries*, (Geneva, 1968) p. 33-66; Govaerts, 1969, p. 85-6; Andreae, 1970, p. 125; Wilensky, 1961, p. 54; Dumazedier, 1967, p. 92; Roberts, 1970, p. 44-7; Sillitoe, 1969, p. 46-7; P. Fougeyrollas, 'La famille, communauté de loisir', *Esprit*, (Juin 1959) 27:1074.
3. Szalai, 1966, p. 23-4; Govaerts, 1968, p. 48-9; G. Lippold, 'A Contribution to the Temporal Aspects of the Socialist Way of Life', *Society and Leisure*, (1974) 6:2:49-60; Dumazedier, 1967, p. 92-5; Anderson, 1961, p. 107; Linhart and Viteckova, 1975, p. 142; Wilensky, 1967, p. 21-2; Yanowitch, 1963, p. 22, 26; R. and R.N. Rapoport, *Leisure and the Family Life Cycle*, (London, 1975), p. 13.
4. Henle, 1966, p. 721.
5. Ibid., p. 723.
6. Wilensky, 1967, p. 22.
7. D. Wakefield, 'Labor Shudders at Leisure', in W. Fogel and A. Kleingartner, eds., *Contemporary Leisure Issues*, (Belmont, Calif, 1966), p. 178; Moore and Hedges, 1971, p. 7-11; H.V. Hayghe, 'Work Experience of the Population in 1969', *Monthly Labor Review*, (Jan. 1971) 94:1:46-7; J.M. Howells and P. Brosnan, 'The Ability to Predict Workers' Preferences', *Human Relations*, (July 1972) 25:3:267-70.
8. Noe, 1971, p. 220.
9. Rudas, 1971, p. 103.

10. Yanowitch, 1963, p. 22-3, 32; Dumazedier, 1972, p. 72-3; Filipcova and Jestrab, 1969, p. 32; Linhart and Viteckova, 1975, p. 147.

11. Touraine, 1974, p. 101-15; Riessman, 1954, p. 76-84; J. Curtis, 'Voluntary Association Joining: A Cross-National Comparative Note', *American Sociological Review*, (Oct. 1971) 36:5:874; M.N. Donald and R.J. Havighurst, 'The Meaning of Leisure', *Social Forces*, (May 1959) 37:4:358-60; Dumazedier and Latouche, 1962, p. 23-4; R.J. Havighurst and K. Feigenbaum, 'Leisure and Life Style', *American Journal of Sociology*, (Jan. 1959) 64:4:404; Kaplan, 1960, p. 182-3; Mayntz, 1960, p. 572-3; Sillitoe, 1969, p. 63; Wilensky, 1961, p. 219-22; Willmott, 1971, p. 580-1.

12. Riessman, 1954, p. 82; Clarke, 1956, p. 308.

13. Wilensky, 1964, p. 187-8.

14. Dumazedier, 1967, p. 208-14; Dumazedier and Latouche, 1962, p. 23-4.

15. Roberts, 1970, p. 27-9; Parker, 1975, p. 26; Parker, 1971, p. 60.

16. Willmott, 1971, p. 583.

17. A. Schlesinger, 'Implications for Government', in Kaplan and Bosserman, 1971, p. 76.

18. Meisner, 1971, p. 260.

19. Torbert, 1974, p. 133-5; Kohn, 1969, p. 190; Riessman, 1954, p. 208; Rudas, 1971, p. 103; Filipcova and Jestrab, 1969, p. 32; Linhart and Viteckova, 1975, p. 147.

20. Dumazedier and Latouche, 1962, p. 27.

21. Kornhauser, 1965, p. 76.

22. *Work in America*, 1973, p. 83.

23. R.O. Clarke, D.J. Fatchett and B.C. Roberts, *Workers' Participation in Management in Britain*, (London, 1972), p. 17; Dumazedier, 1973, p. 247; 1974, p. 45-54; Friedmann, 1964, p. 276.

24. J. Habermas, *Theory and Practice*, (London, 1974), p. 195; Habermas, 1976, p. 37, 84.

25. Dumazedier, 1967, p. 31.

26. J. Dumazedier, 'Leisure in Post-Industrial Societies', in Kaplan and Bosserman, 1971, p. 199-200.

27. Eliot, 1948, p. 19-27, 38-44, 86; S. DeGrazia, 'Politics and the Contemporary Life', *American Political Science Review*, (June 1960) 54.2:447-56; Pieper, 1952, p. 40-5.

28. Dumazedier, 1967, p. 23-4.

29. Dumazedier and Latouche, 1962, p. 26.

30. M.H. and E.S. Neumeyer, *Leisure and Recreation*, (New York, 1958), p. 25.

31. Friedmann, 1960, p. 521; *The Anatomy of Work*, (Glencoe, Ill., 1964), p. 159; Dumazedier, 1974, ch. 5.

32. J.C. Charlesworth, 'A Comprehensive Plan for the Wise Use of Leisure', in Charlesworth, 1964, p. 41.

33. W.C. Sutherland, 'A Philosophy of Leisure', *The Annals of the American Academy of Political and Social Science*, (Sep. 1957) 313:1.

34. Ibid., p. 3.

35. N. Samuel, 'Planning for Leisure, in United Nations Office, 1968, p. 67.

36. D. Riesman, N. Glazer and R. Denney, *The Lonely Crowd*, (New Haven, 1961), XIV-XV; c.f. Riesman, 1964, p. 164, 249.

37. R. Aron, 'On Leisure in Industrial Societies', in J. Brooke, ed., *The One and the Many*, (New York, 1962), p. 157-72.

38. Friedmann, 1964, preface.

39. Dumazedier, 1967, p. 83.

40. Dumazedier and Latouche, 1962, p. 27.

41. Marcuse, 1961, p. 178; c.f. p. 142; 1964, p. 16, 37.

42. Marcuse, 1964, p. 251.

43. Ibid., p. 40-4, 251-2; 1961, p. 205; 1969, p. 70.

44. Marcuse, 1961, ch. 7-10; 1969, p. 21-2.

45. G.C. Winston, 'An International Comparison of Income and Hours of Work', *The Review of Economics and Statistics*, (Feb. 1966) 48:1:30-8; I. Savicky, *International Selective Bibliography on Leisure*, (Prague, 1974), p. 3-5.

46. Burck, 1970, p. 87-8; Becker, 1965, p. 507, 513.

47. K. Mannheim, *Freedom, Power and Democratic Planning*, (London, 1951), p. 269.

48. Ibid., p. 273.

49. Marcuse, 1961, p. 172-9, 199-202; 1969, p. 21-2.

50. J. Perron and G. Ouellet, "Recherche sur la personne efficace: quelques relations entre les valeurs de travail et de loisir', *Conseiller Canadien*, (Oct. 1969) 3:4:41-7.

197

51. S. Cotgrove and S. Parket, 'Work and Non-Work', *New Society*, (11 July 1963) 41:2:18-9; J.E. Gerstl, 'Leisure, Taste and Occupational Milieu', *Social Problems*, (Summer 1961) 9:1:56-68; Noe, 1971, p. 220-49; L.H. Orzack, 'Work as a "Central Life Interest" of Professionals', in E.O. Smigel, *Work and Leisure*, (New Haven, 1963), p. 73-84; S.R. Parker, 'Work and Non-Work in Three Occupations', *The Sociological Review*, (March 1965) 13:1:65-75; S.R. Parker, 'Theory and Practice of the Work-Leisure Relationship', *Society and Leisure*, (Dec. 1969) 2:29-49; Riesman, 1964, p. 143-57; G. Salaman, 'Two Occupational Communities: Examples of a Remarkable Convergence of Work and Non-Work', *The Sociological Review*, (Aug. 1971) 19:3:389-407.

52. Parker, 1965, p. 74.

53. Cotgrove and Parker, 1963, p. 18.

54. H. Durant, *The Problem of Leisure*, (London, 1938), p. 94-5.

55. Parker, 1971, p. 111-24.

56. Hammond, 1933, p. 17.

57. Wilensky, 1964, p. 188.

58. Dumazedier, 1967, p. 73.

59. Dumazedier, 1971, p. 201.

60. Dumazedier and Latouche, 1962, p. 23-4.

61. Dumazedier, 1967, p. 210.

62. Ibid., p. 213.

63. Ibid., p. 212.

64. Ibid., p. 213; 1971, p. 201; 'General Adult Education-Permanent Education', *Society and Leisure*, (1971), p. 3, 5-20.

65. Dumazedier, 1967, p. 204.

66. Ibid., p. 205.

67. I. Berg, *Education and Jobs: The Great Training Robbery*, (New York, 1970), p. 82-3.

68. Ibid., p. 17; Sheppard and Herrick, 1972, p. 17; Braverman, 1975, p. 441; Kornhauser, 1965, p. 263.

69. Berg, 1970, p. 88.

70. Braverman, 1975, p. 442-3.

71. H. Entwhistle, *Education, Work and Leisure*, (London, 1970), p. 3.

72. Schlesinger, 1971, p. 77. Wakefield (1966, p. 178) reports that 67% of Americans did not read a book in 1965.

73. Dumazedier, 1967, p. 193.

74. *Toronto Star*, June 29, 1979, p. D1.

75. P. Jephcott, *Time of One's Own*, (Edinburgh, 1967), p. 162.

76. J. Curran and J. Tunstall, 'Mass Media and Leisure', in Smith, Parker and Smith, 1973, p. 204.

77. A. Toffler, *The Culture Consumers*, (New York, 1964), p. 16.

78. Ibid., p. 33; Dumazedier and Latouche, 1962, p. 24; Dumazedier, 1967, p. 208-14; Roberts, 1970, p. 28; Wilensky, 1964, p. 188.

79. Dumazedier, 1971, p. 219.

80. Ibid.

81. Dumazedier and Latouche, 1962, p. 26-7.

82. Prudenski, 1962, p. 99-100; Afanasyev, 1971, p. 103-13; Ignatiev and Osipov, 1959, p. 1062; V.A. Artemov, 'Socio-Economic Planning and the Problem of Leisure', *Society and Leisure*, (1975) 7:3:15.

83. Neumeyer and Neumeyer, 1958, p. 24.

Chapter 8

1. W. Gallacher and J.R. Cameron, *Direct Action*, (Glasgow, 1919). p. 5-6; cited in J. Hinton, *The First Shop Stewards' Movement*. (London, 1973). p. 99.

2. A.J. Gregor, *Italian Fascism and Developmental Dictatorship*, (Princeton, N.J., 1979), ch. 1-3; Joll, *The Anarchists*, (London, 1964), ch. 8. Spanish syndicalism is an exception to the general decline of syndicalism in the 1920's; it was defeated fighting both communism and fascism in the late 1930's.

3. G. Woodcock, 'Syndicalism Defined', in *The Anarchist Reader*. ed. G. Woodcock, (London, 1977), p. 208.

4. *Errico Malatesta: His Life and Ideas*, ed. V. Richards, (London, 1965), p. 122.

5. Ibid., p. 114, 123; c.f., E. Malatesta, 'Syndicalism: An Anarchist Critique', in Woodcock, p. 220-5.

6. M. Bookchin, *The Spanish Anarchists: The Heroic Years 1868-1936*, (New York, 1978), p. 132-5.

7. J.A. Estey, 'Syndicalism Not a Form of Anarchism', in *Patterns of Anarchy*, ed. L.I. Krimerman and L. Perry, (New York, 1960), p. 45.

8. The placard "We want bread and roses too" was borne by a striker in the textile strike at Lawrence, Mass. in 1912.

9. M. Dubovsky, *We Shall Be All*, (Chicago, 1969), p. 9, 148; P. Stearns, *Revolutionary Syndicalism and French Labor*, (New Brunswick, N.J., 1971), p. 10-12.

10. B. Holton, *British Syndicalism 1900-14*, (London, 1976), p. 18-31; S. Dolgoff, ed., *The Anarchists Collectives: Workers' Self-Management in the Spanish Revolution 1936-39*, (Montreal, 1974), ch. 6-7.

11. Dubovsky, p. 151.

12. For accounts of this repression, see J.S. Gambs, *The Decline of the I.W.W.* (New York, 1966), ch. 1; L. DeCaux, *The Living Spirit of the Wobblies*, (New York, 1978), ch. 14-5; E.L. Dowell, *A History of Criminal Syndicalist Legislation in the United States*, (Baltimore, 1939).

13. Hinton, ch. 11; V.R. Lorwin, *The French Labor Movement*, (Cambridge, Mass., 1966), p. 57.

14. *The Industrial Syndicalist*, (articles from the journal from 1910 to 1912 collected and introduced by G. Brown), (Nottingham, 1974), p. 221.

15. Lorwin, p. 53; Pribicevic, p. 12-14; Holton, p. 86-7, 139.

16. *The Industrial Syndicalist*, p. 148, 360, 380-1.

17. T. Mann, *Memoirs*, (London, 1967), p. 270.

18. *The Industrial Syndicalist*, p. 347-8.

19. R.V. Daniels, *The Conscience of the Revolution*, (Cambridge, Mass., 1960), p. 107.

20. V.I. Lenin, *Collected Works*, vol. 26, p. 105.

21. Ibid., vol. 27, p. 248-77.

22. Ibid., vol. 31, p. 107.

23. Ibid., vol. 30, p. 444-5.

24. Ibid., vol. 32, p. 50.

25. Ibid., c.f. p. 249-60.

26. Ibid., vol. 33, p. 189.

27. Ibid., vol. 27, p. 268-9; repeated in vol. 30, p. 475-6.

28. Ibid., vol. 27, p. 359.

29. Ibid.

30. Dolgoff, 1974, ch 6-7; Joll, 1964, p. 250-8, D. Guérin, *Anarchism*, (New York, 1970), p. 130-6; R. Rocker, *Anarcho-Syndicalism*, (London, 1938), ch. 4; C. Ward, *Anarchy in Action*, (London, 1973), ch. 2; F. Borkenau, 'The Spanish Cockpit' in M.S. Shatz (ed.) *The Essential Works of Anarchism* (New York, 1971), p. 492-508; V. Richards, *Lessons of the Spanish Revolution* (London, 1972), ch. 10.

31. Richards, 1972, p. 105-6.

32. Shatz, 1971, p. 507.

33. Richards, 1972, p. 110.

34. Ibid., p. 107.

35. To be sure, all existing functions of central, regional and municipal governments are unlikely to be farmed out to co-operatives of clerical, transport, educational, medical, sanitation, postal and other workers, although many governmental services could function as "productive" enterprises do.

36. Dolgoff, 1974, ch. 5-8.

37. Ibid., p. 67.

38. Ibid.

39. F.E. Emery and E. Thorsrud, *Form and Content in Industrial Democracy*, (London, 1969), p. 86, 107-8; R.O. Clarke, D.J. Fatchett and B.C. Roberts, *Workers' Participation in Management in Britain*, (London, 1972), p. 113, 169-73; G.D.H. Cole, *The Case for Industrial Partnership*, (London, 1957), p. 20; M. Bucklow, 'A New Role for the Work Group', *Administrative Science Quarterly*, (July, 1966) 11:1:76; M. Derber, 'Worker Participation in Israeli Management', *Industrial Relations*, (October, 1963) 3:1:71.

40. H.A. Clegg, *A New Approach to Industrial Democracy*, (Oxford, 1960), p. 50-7, 93; Clarke, Fatchett and Roberts, 1972, p. 20, 113, 148-9; Derber, 1963, p. 62-5; Emery and Thorsrud, 1969, p. 42-52.

41. Govaerts, 1969, p. 111.

42. To be sure, these political imperatives are to be understood in the context of international power relations as well as in the context of the internal patterns of authority in industrial organization.

43. "Job enlargement" is sometimes distinguished from "job enrichment" in that the former involves a combination of proletarian operations into a less limited job whereas the latter involves wage-earners taking on some of the functions which were previously the preserve of management. "Job enlargement" then refers to a horizontal integration of labour; "job enrichment" aims to reintegrate

the vertical division of labour. However, in our discussion, "job enlargement" will be used as a general term encompassing "job enrichment" and any developments opposed to the thrust of scientific management. *Work in America* (1973, 188-201) provided a number of case studies in which enlarged jobs have had a positive effect on morale and productivity. Also see Bucklow, 1966, p. 59-78; Daniel and McIntosh, 1972; N.C. Morse and E. Reimer, 'The Experimental Change of a Major Organizational Variable', *Journal of Abnormal and Social Psychology*, (January, 1956) 52:1:120-9; J. Kolaja, *Workers' Councils: The Yugoslav Experience*, (London, 1965): C.P. Hill, *Toward a New Philosophy of Management*, (London, 1971), p. 29-34. P. Blumberg, in *Industrial Democracy*, (London, 1968, p. 123) writes, supporting his statement with a survey of literature different from that provided above: "There is hardly a study in the entire literature which fails to demonstrate that satisfaction in work is enhanced or that other generally acknowledged beneficial consequences accrue from a genuine increase in workers' decision-making power. Such consistency of findings, I submit, is rare in social research." However a number of obstacles to job enlargement may also be found in industrial relations literature. They are: the tension between the demand for workers' control of production and standardized conditions set by central planning boards or negotiated with national unions, between the autonomy of the work-place and the authority of management, union leaders and civil servants; the indifference of workers, particularly the unskilled, to participate in management, relative to their desire for income or for benefits external to the nature of the work; the conflict between the demand for universal participation in management by means of rotating workers' delegates and for managerial or administrative competence; the greater unwillingness of workers to perform the more boring aspects of jobs once the job has been enlarged to include more challenging work; the opposition of workers to technological progress or organizational efficiencies that influence their employment; the lack of knowledge by workers of the markets for their produce, the lack of solidarity necessary for collective autonomy and self-management. Interesting studies of the obstacles to job enlargement and industrial democracy can be found in Clarke, Fatchett and Roberts, 1972; I. Clegg, *Workers' Self-Management in Algeria*, (London, 1971); Emery and Thorsrud, 1969; A. Sturmthal, *Workers' Councils*, (Cambridge, 1964).

44. Drucker, 1961, p. 271-2.

45. Braverman, 1975, p. 35; c.f. J. Gooding, 'The Fraying White Collar', *Fortune*, (December 1970), 241, no. 1447, p. 79.

46. Bucklow, 1966, p. 72; Clarke, Fatchett and Roberts, 1972, p. 171-3; H.A. Clegg, 1960, p. 121-4; Hill, 1971, p. 29-32.

47. A Gorz, 'Workers' Control is More than Just That' in G. Hunnius, ed., *Participatory Democracy in Canada*, (Montreal, 1971), p. 24.

48. W.E. Moore, *Man, Time and Society*, New York, 1963, p. 38.

Chapter 9

1. Berg, 1970, p. 108; Carter, 1970, p. 53; S.C. Florman, 'The Job-Enrichment Mistake', *Harper's*, (May 1976) 252:1512:20; C.W. Hobart, 'Recreation in Alberta: Current Practices and Prospects', in S.M.A. Hameed and D. Cullen, *Work and Leisure in Canada*, (Calgary, 1971) p. 79; Kornhauser, 1965, p. 9; P. Lafitte, *Social Structure and Personality in the Factory*, (London, 1958) p. 42, 49; L.H. Lofquist and R.V. Davis, *Adjustment to Work*, (New York, 1969) p. 11; Morse and Weiss, 1955, p. 192; N.C. Morse, *Satisfactions in the White Collar Job*, (Ann Arbor, 1953) p. 8-10; Salaman, 1971, p. 401-2; Sheppard and Herrick, 1972, p. 4-5; V.H. Vroom, *Work and Motivation*, (New York, 1964) p. 131; *Work in America*, 1973, p. 52; S. Wyatt and R. Marriot, *A Study of Attitudes to Factory Work*, (London, 1956) p. 5. The degree of satisfaction with work almost invariably is a direct correlation with the degree of skill, variety and responsibility of work. A majority of those doing repetitive unskilled work express job dissatisfaction in C.W. Mills, *White Collar*, (New York, 1956) p. 229; Kornhauser, 1965, p. 85; M. Kranzberg and J. Gies, *By the Sweat of Thy Brow*, (New York, 1975) p. 192-3.

2. R. Blauner, 'Work Satisfaction in Modern Society', in Fogel and Kleingartner, 1966, p. 146; R. Dubin, 'Industrial Workers' Worlds: A Study of the "Central Life Interests" of Industrial Workers', in Smigel, 1963, p. 64, 68; Florman, 1976, p. 20; Lafitte, 1958, p. 180; Orzack, 1963, p. 75; *Work in America, 1973*, p. 15, 83; Wyatt and Marriott, 1956, p. 12-14, 54.

3. Gerstl, 1961, p. 58; Hobart, 1971, p. 79; Orzack, 1963, p. 75; Salaman, 1971, p. 340-402; *Work in America*, 1973, p. 16.

4. Dubin, 1963, p. 64, 68; Dumazedier, 1967, p. 87; 1962, p. 364; 1974, p. 33; W.A. Faunce, 'Automation and Leisure', in Smigel, 1963, p. 89; Lafitte, 1958, p. 180; Orzack, 1963, p. 75; Parker, 1971, p. 70; 1965, p. 72; Willmott, 1971, p. 578; Samuel, 1968, p. 69; S. Cotgrove, 'The Relations of Work and Non-Work Among Technicians', *The Sociological Review*, (July 1965) 13:2:125.

5. Dumazedier, 1967, p. 87; 1962, p. 364; Hobart, 1971, p. 79; Kornhauser, 1965, p. 202, 249; Lafitte, 1958, p. 172; Parker, 1971, p. 70; 1965, p. 72; Willmott, 1971, p. 583; Cotgrove, 1965, p. 125.

6. Samuel, 1968, p. 69; Faunce, 1963, p. 92; Dumazedier, 1967, p. 42; T.A. Margerson, 'Hopes and Fears for the Age of Leisure', *The Political Quarterly*, (January 1967) 38:1:80.

7. H. Swados, 'Less Work—Less Leisure', in Larrabee and Meyersohn, 1958, p. 357; DeGrazia, 1962, p. 140; Wakefield, 1966, p. 178; Riesman, 1964, p. 165.

8. Dumazedier's estimate (1973, p. 231-6; 1974, p. 36) that 25% of workers in capitalist and socialist countries engage in moonlighting accords with the empirical research of others if it includes working overtime or on holidays, as well as those holding a second part-time or full-time job. See Linhart and Viteckova, 1975, p. 133-5; A. Blenkinsop, 'Some Problems of Leisure', *The Journal of the Royal Society of Arts*, (June 1971) 119:5179:453-4; DeGrazia, 1962, p. 69-71; Carter, 1970, p. 61, 65; Henle, 1966, p. 721-2; H.L. Wilensky, 'The Moonlighter: A Product of Relative Deprivation', *Industrial Relations*, (October 1963) 3:1:108-9, 115; Clawson and Knetsch, 1974, p. 83; Moore and Hedges, 1971, p. 7; Roberts, 1970, p. 21. Carter's estimate that 30% of Americans worked overtime in the 1960's and Blenkinsop's estimate that 33% of the British worked overtime in the 1960's are roughly 10% higher than average. DeGrazia (1962, p. 69, 442-3) and Dumazedier (1962, p. 342) estimate that 6 hours for moonlighting and overtime should be added on to the standard working week to obtain average working time of labourers while Parker, (1975, p. 24) estimates that 5 hours should be added on to the average British work week to include overtime.

9. Dumazedier, 1967, p. 87; 1962, p. 364; Fourgeyrollas, 1959, p. 1084; Parker, 1971, p. 70; 1965, p. 72; Cotgrove, 1965, p. 125; E. St. John Catchpool, 'Leisure in an Affluent Society', *The Journal of the Royal Society of the Arts*, (March 1965) 113:5104:239; Govaerts, 1969, p. 196; L.E. Larson, 'The Family and Leisure in Post-Industrial Society', in Hameed and Cullen, 1971, p. 137; Kornhauser, 1965, p. 249; Rapoport and Rapoport, 1975, p. 16; P. Willmott, (1971, p. 583) questions the assumption that people are either 'work-centered', 'family-centered', or 'leisure-centered'. Some, Willmott believes, have no deep involvement in work, family or leisure whereas others, who are 'involved' in their work, may have this 'involvement' spill over into their leisure and home life; c.f., Torbert, 1974, p. 134-5.

10. Andreae, 1970, p. 125; Szalai, 1966, p. 24; Govaerts, 1969, p. 85-6; 1968, p. 48-9; Dumazedier, 1967, p. 92; Wilensky, 1961, p. 54; Fougeyrollas, 1959, p. 1074.

11. Andreae, 1970, p. 125; Roberts, 1970, p. 41, Szalai, 1966, p. 25; Rapoport and Rapoport, 1975, p. 182.

12. Some studies of the significance workers attach to their work are: F. Herzberg, B. Mausner and B.B. Snyderman, *The Motivation to Work*, (New York, 1959); Lofquist and Davis, 1969, p. 6 10; E.L. Lyman, 'Occupational Differences in the Value Attached to Work', *American Journal of Sociology*, (September 1955) 6:2:138-44; Morse and Weiss, 1955, p. 191-8; R.W. Weiss and R.L. Kahn, 'Definitions of Work and Occupation', *Social Problems*, (Fall 1960) 8:2:142-58; D.C. Thorns, 'Work and Its Definition', *The Sociological Review*, (November 1971) 19:4.543-55. For psychoanalytic views of the "real" meaning of work, see I. Hendrick, 'Work and the Pleasure Principle', *Psychoanalytic Quarterly*, (1943) 12:3:311-29 and H. Feldman, 'The Illusions of Work', *Psychoanalytic Review*, (July 1955) 42:3:262-70. The former is as prosaic as industrial psychology or sociology. For example, Hendrick writes (p. 323): "When a housewife takes pleasure in cleaning up, she is normally not merely finding a substitute for a tabooed pleasure in dirt; nor is she merely preparing a clean genital substitute (her house) for exhibition to her guests that evening; nor simply protecting herself from the reproaches of her finger-snooping mother-substitute lady-friends." Feldman's more amusing piece at least does not deprive houswives of the pleasure of indulging in these Freudian illusions. D. Riesman (1954, p. 310-33) demonstrates that Freud's theory of work does not explain his and others' commitment to work. However, E. Erikson, in *Insight and Responsibility*, (New York, 1964), ch. 1, argues that Freud had a broader understanding of work than as a repressive necessity (the doctrine of Marcuse against which I have been arguing above.)

13. Morse and Weiss, 1955, p. 100; Morse, 1953, p. 10; Carter, 1950, p. 53.

14. W.H. Auden, 'Culture and Leisure', *Ekistics*, (November 1967) 24:144:419.

15. W. Wordsworth, *The Prelude*, (London, 1950), bk. V., lines 370-88.

Index

RADICAL PRIORITIES

by Noam Chomsky
edited by C.P. Otero

more books from BLACK ROSE BOOKS write for a free catalogue

In a new collection of the political writings of Noam Chomsky, Carlos-Peregrin Otero brings together some of the most outstanding reflections of the famous linguist. A broad range of subjects are covered with a view to alerting people about the problems humanity is facing, and possible solutions we can undertake.

Besides an introduction by C.P. Otero there are twelve chapters which include: The New Cold War; The Carter Administration: Myth and Reality; The secret terrorist organisations of the U.S. Government; Watergate: small potatoes; The Vietnam war—a monstrosity; The Student Revolt; The politization of the university; Political prospects; Some tasks for the left; The new radicalism; The relevance of anarcho-syndicalism; Industrial self-management.

Prof. Carlos-Peregrin Otero teaches linguistics at the University of California in Los Angeles.

Paperback ISBN:0-919619-50-3 $ 9.95
Hardcover ISBN:0-919619-51-1 $19.95
Publication Date—June 1981
Contains: Canadian Shared Cataloguing in Publication Data
BLACK ROSE BOOKS No. K70

CANADA AND THE LIMITS OF LIBERALISM

by Deborah Harrison

Even now 'Canadian sociology' comprises a small network. A critical evaluation of the 'founder of Canadian sociology' S.D. Clark is thus long overdue. Clark is important because he is the only important sociologist who studied under Harold Innis, and whose intellectual roots can be traced to the interdiscilinary tradition which was ascendant at the University of Toronto during the thirties and is now being revived.

Deborah Harrison offers a radical critique of Clark's attempt to produce simultaneously a nationalist style of scholarship in the tradition of Innis and a liberal-continentalist one. The author shows the connections between Clark's liberalism and his positivistic or 'value-free' social science. The book is of particular value for use in any Canadian Society course which has a theoretical, political and historical focus. Dr. Deborah Harrison is an assistant professor of sociology at Brock University.

Paperback ISBN:0-919619-21-0 $ 9.95
Hardcover ISBN:0-919619-22-8 $19.95
Publication Date —June 1981
Contains: Canadian Shared Cataloguing in Publication Data
BLACK ROSE BOOKS No. K67

BAKUNIN ON ANARCHISM

edited by Sam Dolgoff

A new and revised selection of writings, nearly all published for the first time in English, by one of the leading thinkers of anarchism and one of the most important practicioners of social revolution.

A titan among the social philosophers of the age that produce Proudhon, Marx, Blanqui, and Kropotkin, Michael Bakunin was involved in the Dresden uprising in 1848, which led to his imprisonment first in Germany, then in Russia, and his exile in Siberia, whence he escaped to Europe in 1861. Until his death in 1876, he lived and worked in London, Naples, Paris, Prague, Berlin and Geneva in opposition to the communist-statist Marx and the populist-liberal Herzen. Bukunin's voluminous writings are brought together in this collection for the general reader and student, having been edited, translated and introduced by Sam Dolgoff.

"...with the publication of Sam Dolgoff's lengthy and careful selection, the vitality of Bakunin's message is evident once again..."

Labour History

"(This book) is the most complete — and interestingly varied — anthology I've seen of this neglected writer. It confirms my suspicion that Bakunin is the most underrated of the classical 19th century theoreticians, definitely including Marx."

Dwight Macdonald

"... by far the best available in English. Bakunin's insights into power and authority, tyranny, the conditions of freedom, the new classes of spe~ialists and technocrats, social tyranny, and many other matters of immediate concern are refreshing, original, and often still unsurpassed in clarity and vision. This selection provides access of the thinking of one of the most remarkable figures of modern history. I read it with great pleasure and profit."

Noam Chomsky

Paperback ISBN: 0-919619-05-9   **$ 8.95**
Hardcover ISBN: 0-919619-06-7   **$18.95**
Contains: Canadian Shared Cataloguing in Publication Data
BLACK ROSE BOOKS No. J56

Printed by
the workers of
Les Éditions Marquis, Montmagny, Québec
for
Black Rose Books Ltd.